T0327338

Cyberwars in the Middle East

War Culture

Edited by Daniel Leonard Bernardi

Books in this series address the myriad ways in which warfare informs diverse cultural practices, as well as the way cultural practices—from cinema to social media—inform the practice of warfare. They illuminate the insights and limitations of critical theories that describe, explain, and politicize the phenomena of war culture. Traversing both national and intellectual borders, authors from a wide range of fields and disciplines collectively examine the articulation of war, its everyday practices, and its impact on individuals and societies throughout modern history.

Cyberwars in the Middle East

AHMED AL-RAWI

Rutgers University Press

New Brunswick, Camden, and Newark, New Jersey, and London

Library of Congress Cataloging-in-Publication Data
Names: Al-Rawi, Ahmed K., author.
Title: Cyberwars in the Middle East / Ahmed Al-Rawi.
Description: New Brunswick, New Jersey: Rutgers University Press, 2021. |
    Series: War culture | Includes bibliographical references and index.
Identifiers: LCCN 2020052863 | ISBN 9781978810105 (paperback) |
    ISBN 9781978810112 (cloth) | ISBN 9781978810129 (epub) | ISBN 9781978810136 (mobi) |
    ISBN 9781978810143 (pdf)
Subjects: LCSH: Information warfare—Middle East. | Cyberspace—Political aspects—
    Middle East. | Hacking—Middle East.
Classification: LCC U163 .A37 2021 | DDC 355.4—dc23
LC record available at https://lccn.loc.gov/2020052863

A British Cataloging-in-Publication record for this book is available from the British Library.

Copyright © 2021 by Ahmed Al-Rawi
All rights reserved

No part of this book may be reproduced or utilized in any form or by any means, electronic or
mechanical, or by any information storage and retrieval system, without written permission
from the publisher. Please contact Rutgers University Press, 106 Somerset Street, New
Brunswick, NJ 08901. The only exception to this prohibition is "fair use" as defined by U.S.
copyright law.

♾ The paper used in this publication meets the requirements of the American National
Standard for Information Sciences—Permanence of Paper for Printed Library Materials,
ANSI Z39.48-1992.

www.rutgersuniversitypress.org

Manufactured in the United States of America

To the memory of my best friend, Bahir Bahjat

Contents

Contents

Preface and Acknowledgments

This book is dedicated to my best friend, Bahir Bahjat, who was killed on July 23, 2006, in a terrorist suicide bombing targeting a courthouse in Kirkuk, Iraq. Bahir never finished high school, but he had one of the finest minds I have ever known. He never believed in traditional schooling, since he had started learning Russian, Chinese, Turkish as well as programming and numerous other technical skills on his own long before there were online tutorials, developing a sort of hacker's mentality. He is greatly missed!

This study is the result of over a decade of research on cyberoperations in the Middle East, an area of study that is without doubt under-researched. This book offers several case studies on cyberwars and international, regional, and internal politics. Due to the general clandestine nature of hacking and other cyberoperations, I decided to discard incorporating interviews with Arab hackers for several reasons. First, it is very difficult to ascertain the real individuals behind political hacking groups, and there is always some tension or fear that the hackers' true identities could be disclosed in the process of identifying and interviewing them. This could in fact endanger the well-being and safety of individuals in their struggle for social reform and democratic rule. Further, many hacking groups in the region are cybermercenaries. They are supportive of and/or directly and indirectly supported by certain authoritarian Arab governments, so interviewing those individuals would not serve the purpose of this book because their responses could be expected to reflect the views of their respective governments.

Special thanks go to Nicole Solano, the executive editor at Rutgers University, for her support and faith in this project from the very first time she heard about it. I would also like to thank the anonymous reviewers for their valuable comments and insight that greatly helped me in revising the manuscript and refining its theoretical arguments.

Finally, I would like to thank Mr. Abdelrahman Fakida, a graduate student at the School of Communication at Simon Fraser University, for his assistance in collecting some details about a few hacking groups in the Arab world. I would also like to thank Mr. Derrick O'Keefe for his support in copyediting this manuscript.

Cyberwars in the
Middle East

Introduction

● ●

This book contains six main chapters divided along different geographical scopes. The first chapter attempts to situate hacking and other cyberoperations within a theoretical framework whose details are provided below. Starting from the international scope of cyberoperations in chapter 2, chapters 3 and 4 offer case studies from the United States and Russia to better explain this scope. These two chapters highlight some of the online efforts employed to influence audiences in the Arab world using a variety of disruptive communication means. Chapter 5 turns into the regional dimension with a focus on offline and online rivalries and diplomatic tensions in the MENA region, while chapter 6 deals with the national scope by discussing a number of Arab cyber armies and the efforts of local Arab hackers in disrupting online politics in their respective countries. Overall, the book provides empirical findings on several case studies using mixed methodological approaches, and the sources in this book are drawn from academic references, social media, newly declassified documents, the WikiLeaks archive, news reports, and many other sources.

I argue in this book that hacking and other forms of cyberoperations are considered forms of online political disruption whose influence flows vertically in two directions (top-bottom or bottom-up) or horizontally. These disruptive cyber activities are performed along three political dimensions: international, regional, and local. Politically motivated hacking and cyberoperations are an aggressive and militant form of public communication employed by tech-savvy individuals, regardless of their affiliations, in order to influence politics and policies. Kenneth Waltz's theory of structural realism provides a relevant framework for understanding why nation-states employ cyber tools against each other. On the one hand, nation-states and their affiliated groups like cyber-warriors employ hacking as offensive and defensive tools in connection to the cyber activity or inactivity of other nation-states. This is regarded as a horizontal flow of political disruption. Some nation-states, including the United Arab Emirates (UAE), Saudi Arabia, and Bahrain, use hacking and surveillance tactics as a vertical flow (top-bottom) form of online political disruption by targeting their own citizens because of their oppositional or activist political views. On the other hand, hackers who are often politically independent practice a form of bottom-top political disruption to address issues related to the internal politics of their respective nation-states, as has been seen with a number of Iraqi, Saudi, and Algerian hackers. In some instances, other hackers target ordinary citizens to express opposition to their political or ideological views in what is regarded as a horizontal form of online political disruption. In this respect, offensive and defensive cyberoperations are signs of hierarchical power and forms of militaristic public communication. By employing technologically advanced methods, hackers can boast of their online achievements in politically disrupting their targets. These types of online disruptions are not an end but a means used when needed because they provide an extension to the state's geostrategic objectives. In other words, online political disruption is a manifestation of power whose goal is to directly or indirectly affect policies of other nation-states.

In addition to the theoretical engagement of expanding on the concepts of online political disruption, the book argues that offline political tensions that are often international, regional (sectarian), or local in nature play a vital role in accentuating the hacking attempts that frequently originate from and occur in the Middle East. This is partly borrowed from and Kenneth Waltz's structural realism theory (2010) which situates international relations within the changing dynamics of power structures. Here, power is a means whose end is unknown, and it has four main objectives: sustaining the independence of the state, providing a wider range of activities, offering broader security, and consolidating power. I borrow this theory because online political disruption is similar, for it is based on using advanced technology that is embedded in power and when used its future outcome is often unknown.

Here, cyberattacks and hacking attempts are used for espionage, tarnishing the image of and/or undermining the authority and credibility of governments, changing their policies, or causing economic damage. This book deals with different hacktivist and hacking groups active in the region, examining and considering how they are sometimes linked to or clash with global hacktivist groups like Anonymous, as has been the case with the Egyptian Cyber Army. From a critical point of view, nation-states and their affiliated cyberwarriors as well as terrorist hacking groups can be placed within the category of hegemonic powers, while independent hackers and sometimes global hacktivist groups are situated within the category of counterpowers.

In this book, I expand on the notion of cyberconflict and cyberwar to include different cyberoperations like state-sponsored astroturfing activities, cyber armies, digital surveillance, spying tools, and the coordinated spamming and doxing operations that often happen on social media to attack political opponents. This is because cyberwar is not only practiced today with the use of hacking but is evident in other contexts like the use of sockpuppets, bots, and trolls. This book maps some of these emerging digital phenomena in the Middle East region. Its goal, however, is not to archive and document all the hacking attempts and cyberoperations happening in or targeting the Middle East because this is an impossible task. Instead, the book aims at highlighting the major types, patterns, and trends in online political disruptions.

1

Toward a Theoretical Framework of Cyberwars

•••••••••••••••••••••

This chapter provides a theoretical framework on the concepts of online political disruption, hacktivism, cyberwars, and information warfare. It then delves into the cyberwars and hacking in the Middle East, which directly and indirectly affect geopolitical developments in the region. The Middle East region, I argue, has like many other regions been witnessing an ongoing cyberconflict waged among different factions separated along regional, political, and sectarian divisions. Some hacking attempts in the region against government-run websites are supported, indirectly encouraged, or at least tolerated by some governments in order to serve their interests and achieve political goals.

Throughout this book, I approach hacking as a form of online political disruption whose influence flows vertically (top-down or bottom-up) and/or horizontally, and as a means of militant public communication that serves different goals depending on the nature of the hack. *Online political disruption* is a term largely drawn from the concept of cultural jamming, which was introduced in the public sphere by "the 'audio-Dadaism' band Negativeland on a cassette recording called JamCon84 released in 1985 and reissued on CD in 1994" (Cammaerts 2007a, 71). Its means is cultural appropriation in a way that subverts the original hegemonic meaning in order to create confusion, interference, and disruption. In other words, jamming is a metaphor for technological disruption that often influences diplomatic relations and politics. Mark Dery (1993) describes culture jammers as practitioners of a form of poetic terrorism, "[introducing] noise into the signal as it passes from transmitter to receiver, encouraging idiosyncratic, unintended interpretations. Intruding on the intruders, they invest ads, newscasts, and other media artifacts with subversive meanings." Culture jamming has primarily been applied to analysis of resistance against exploitative capitalist practices with the use of mass media (Handelman 1999), while political jamming is more focused on the cultural politics of such resistance (Jameson 1992, 409) in order to influence politics or create political awareness or change (Cammaerts 2007b). The latter term is regarded as "a form of culture jamming that targets not only big corporations but the political in the bad sense." Rooted in the language of radio and TV jamming, it is intended to deal with "the messiness of reality, subverting meanings by combining mockery, satire and parody" (Cammaerts 2007b, 214).

In this regard, alternative and radical media outlets as well as social movements are often linked to the practice of cultural and political jamming in order to resist mainstream hegemonic ideologies, media, and power (Bailey, Cammaerts, and Carpentier 2007; Balnaves, Donald, and Shoesmith 2008, 167, 298; Fontenelle and Pozzebon 2017). For example, Laura Iannelli (2016) in *Hybrid Politics: Media and Participation* discusses how political jamming has been used by social activists in order to "influence media and political agendas, and to engage online and offline publics" (99). Cammaerts (2007a) cautions that the practice of political jamming does not necessarily provide counterhegemonic narratives, since "some political actors . . . just use jamming as a 'hip' political communication strategy, thereby reducing it to a marketing technique—unjamming the jam so to speak" (88). In other words, political jamming is not only a communication strategy deployed by subaltern groups but also by the powerful and "the dominant" (Payne 2012, 65).

Similarly, I argue that hacking is a form of political disruption in cyberspace. I call this activity *online political disruption*—terminology and conceptualization that can be situated as part of Manuel Castells's concept of communication power and counterpower in the sense that there are different types of communication flows that shape our networked society (2007 and 2013). In the model that I introduce here, communication powers are represented by nation-states and their cyberwarriors as well as terrorist hacking groups, while counterpowers are represented by independent hackers and sometimes global hacktivist groups. In this regard, nation-states as well as their affiliated hacking groups employ hacking as offensive and defensive tools in relation to the cyber activity or inactivity of other nation-states. This is regarded as a horizontal flow of online political disruption. Sometimes, nation-states use hacking and surveillance as a vertical flow (top-down) form of online political disruption by targeting their own citizens for their political views. On the other hand, regular hackers who are often politically independent practice a form of bottom-up political disruption to address the internal politics of their respective nations, and they are often aided by global hacktivist groups such as Anonymous. In

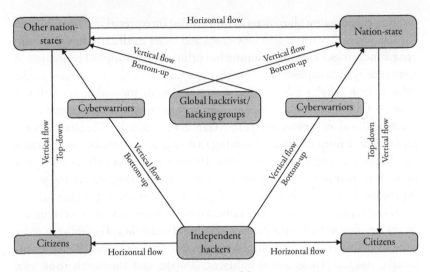

FIG. 1.1 Hacking as online political disruption model.

some cases, the same hackers target ordinary citizens to express opposition to their political or ideological views, which is regarded as a horizontal form of online political disruption (see Figure 1.1). In the Middle East context, these hacking activities are performed along three dimensions: local, regional, and international. In most cases, though, there is overlap along these geographical dimensions due to the affordances of the Internet, which has made it easier to reach different targets. This overlap is discussed in detail in the chapters that deal with electronic flies and armies.

In this regard, Kenneth Waltz's theory of structural realism is relevant as it envisions international relations and nation-state policies as mostly structured on power. Waltz (2010) argues that power is different from control because it is a "means, and the outcome of its use is necessarily uncertain" (192), stressing that using power is "to apply one's capabilities in an attempt to change someone else's behavior in certain ways" (191). Understood this way, power has four functions: (1) maintaining the state's independence, (2) allowing broader ranges of actions, (3) providing more safety and security, (4) and giving the more powerful a larger stake in the political system (194–195). In this book, I argue that offensive and defensive cyberoperations are manifestations of power whose offline and online outcomes are often unknown. These cyber powers are routinely exercised to serve the above functions. Hacking and other cyberoperations are, after all, a form of militaristic public communication that is built on the power of technology and its potential reach. In terms of regional and international politics, this theory is applicable because nation-states use their cyberoperations, when needed, as power tools that provide an extension to their international relations strategies. I emphasize here the phrase "when needed" because applying these cyberoperations toward friendly powers risks counter-effects, so they are only used when there is a need to show power and possibly influence the policies of the other nation-state(s). In the following section, a general account is offered on the meanings of hacktivism and hacking.

Hacktivism and Hacking

Hacktivism and *hacking* are terms that are often used interchangeably, but there are differences between the two. Hacktivism is believed to have "roots in the cyber-libertarian aspects of the internet" which originally "began as a movement for the freedom of information" (Siapera 2012, 89; see also Sauter 2014). Dorothy Denning (2001) describes hacktivism as the "marriage of hacking and activism," and the latter is related to using the "Internet as a medium that supports a group's cause or agenda." In other words, it refers to "operations that use hacking techniques against a target's Internet site with the intent of disrupting normal operations but not causing serious damage. Examples are web sit-ins and virtual blockades, automated email bombs, web hacks, computer break-ins, and computer viruses and worms" (Denning 2001, 241). There is an ethical dimension in hacktivism. In his book *Hackers: Heroes of the Computer Revolution* (1984), Steven Levy illustrated six main ethical principles that guide hackers' work, including that access to computers should be "unlimited and total" and that computers "can change your life for the better" (40). However, many official bodies find it difficult to distinguish between hacktivism and cybercriminality or cyberterrorism. The U.S. government, for example, regards Anonymous as an illegal online organization, classifying them as a group of "not-for-profit" cybercriminals (Snow 2011) despite the fact they are considered a hacktivist group by many others. One of the earliest hacktivist groups of note was known as the Cult of the Dead Cow (cDc); in fact, they coined the term hacktivism. Based in Texas, cDc first emerged in 1984 and was focused on privacy protection and antisurveillance issues. Later on, they were known for launching a campaign called Goolag against Google's decision to censor the Internet in China (Siapera 2012, 91).

Turning now to the etymology of the word *hack* or *hacker*, the term was originally used by MIT students in the 1950s to refer to "a clever, benign, and ethical prank or practical joke, which is both challenging for the perpetrators and amusing to the MIT community" (McQuade 2009, 87). In 1983, *Time* magazine defined hackers as meaning "computer fanatics" (Hirst, Harrison, and Mazepa 2014, 191), and some of the earliest "fanatics" acted as "phone phreaks" in the 1970s because they attempted to use computer technology to make free telephone calls (Coleman 2012). Indeed, hackers are often described as freaks or fanatics of some sort because "the pursuit of getting into established computer systems, breaking codes, and getting at the contents can become increasingly obsessive" and "relentless" (Hirst, Harrison, and Mazepa 2014, 192). The concept and word *hacker* emerged as an amalgam of two terms: *hobbyists* who have general curiosity about how things work and *safecrackers* who take it one step beyond the curiosity level to become someone "who discovers or breaks the established (or secret) code to get into the contents of a safe" (Hirst, Harrison, and Mazepa 2014, 192). Today, hacking is regarded as an attempt to obtain "unauthorized access into information systems including computer networks. Breaking into a computer system or exceeding network permissions are considered forms of computer trespassing" (McQuade 2009, 87). For most government agencies, hackers are regarded as criminals. The hackers themselves tend to view themselves as explorers (Hirst, Harrison, and Mazepa 2014, 191).

Most importantly, hacking is also associated with information warfare, which attempts to use information technology tools to attack enemy websites, including unauthorized intrusion into computer systems, distributed denial-of-service (DDoS), and domain name system (DNS) attacks by utilizing similar cyber tools that are used by hacktivists but for different purposes (Siapera 2012, 112). It is estimated today that cyber offensive operations are valued at about $12 billion, and some of these cyber techniques are regarded as "effective weapons in cyber-war" and might "herald hostility and forthcoming war" or "represents the escalation and/or spillover of conflicts into cyberspace" such as the case of the 2008 armed confrontation between Russia and Georgia which began with DDoS attacks by Russian nationalists against Georgia (Mazzetti, Goldman, Bergman, and Perlroth 2019, 112–113). The motive behind hacking, it is important to note, is one of the defining features by which hackers are categorized. Some hackers have financial motives. If they are involved in such illicit activities, they are regarded as cybercriminals provided that they do not have any political motives. It is estimated, for example, that the losses from online fraud cost the United States around $2.4 billion a year (Campbell, Martin, and Fabos 2014, 69), while the twelve costliest computer viruses "amounted to over $100 billion in financial losses." In this context, the two costliest viruses were MyDoom (2004) at $38.5 billion and SoBig (2003) at $37.1 billion (Lee 2013, 101). Other categories of hackers, however, have political, ethical, crypto-anarchist (Bartlett, 2017), or even entertainment motives (Sankin and Turton 2015). Political hacking, I argue, needs to be understood in a broader sense because it should not be limited to the conventional meaning of the word. In other words, the term needs to be applied to bypassing traditional methods of practice or gaming an online system to achieve certain political goals. For example, political hacking can be applied to the way online search algorithms are adjusted by users to send a political message. To take just two example, this type of political hacking has been illustrated by Indian activists expressing anger against attacks on Kashmir by associating the Pakistani flag with toilet paper (BBC News 2019a, 2019b) and by the linking of President Donald Trump with the word "idiot" on Google image searches (BBC News 2019b).

Hacking and Information Wars

In May 1993, the U.S. Joint Chiefs of Staff explained in their "Memorandum of Policy No. 30" that the traditional meaning of warfare had changed: "As 'first wave' wars were fought for land and 'second wave' wars were fought for control over productive capacity, the emerging 'third wave' wars will be fought for control of knowledge. And, since 'combat form' in any society follows the 'wealth-creation form' of that society, wars of the future will be increasingly 'information wars'" (as cited in Stein 1998, 154). Philip Taylor (2002) elaborates on this notion of third wave warfare, stating that the virtual or cyber "battle space" has blurred the lines between the battlefronts at home and abroad. This is because "instantaneous communication technologies are . . . obliterating previous distinctions between tactical and strategic information, and between military and civilian perceptions of what is happening there" (147). Cyberwars are waged as an alternative to real physical military confrontations, and they can be categorized as soft offensive operations even though they can still cause significant damage. A report by the National Security Agency (NSA) described the impact of cyberwars: "Cyberattacks offer a means for potential adversaries to overcome overwhelming U.S. advantages in conventional military power and to do so in ways that are instantaneous and exceedingly hard to trace. Such attacks may not cause the mass casualties of a nuclear strike, but they could paralyze U.S. society all the same" (National Security Agency 2012, 3).

Despite its widespread use, the term *cyberwar* remains vague and imprecise (Stein 1998, 154). Many seemingly friendly countries with strong to moderate trade and diplomatic relations like China and the United States, or China and Canada, are often implicated in hacking activities that target government and state-funded research agencies (Freeze 2017). The Five Eyes countries (U.S., U.K., Canada, Australia, and New Zealand) have been actively involved in hacking and harvesting data from many countries around the world (King 2013). Evidence released by WikiLeaks, furthermore, showed that the CIA is able to hack TV sets and phones throughout the world (Pagliery 2017). In fact, declassified NSA documents show that the U.S. government planned to target adversaries' computers as far back as 1997. This was known as a Computer Network Attack (CNA), which referred to "'operations to disrupt, deny, degrade or destroy' information in target computers or networks, 'or the computers and networks themselves'" (Richelson 2013, para. 4).

Indeed, the U.S. government is an active maker and user of software bugs that are often called "zero day" vulnerabilities which form part of its cyber arsenal (Gilbert 2017). According to revelations by former NSA contractor

Edward Snowden, the U.S. government allocated a $652 million budget for conducting 231 offensive cyberoperations worldwide back in 2011 (Gellman and Nakashima 2013). Teams from the FBI, CIA, and the Cyber Command, which coordinates U.S. military cyberoperations, worked with the Remote Operations Center (ROC) to plan, administer, and supervise the work of cyber-warriors whose job was to "infiltrate and disrupt foreign computer networks" in countries like Iran, North Korea, China, and Russia (Gellman and Nakashima 2013). Other tasks included "locating suspected terrorists 'in Afghanistan, Pakistan, Yemen, Iraq, Somalia, and other extremist safe havens'" (Gellman and Nakashima 2013). Snowden's revelations proved numerous other attempts to hack websites and computer networks in Europe and the Middle East including Al Jazeera TV channel's internal communications during George W. Bush's second term (Aljazeera, 2013b). Furthermore, leaked cables revealed the U.S. government had been preoccupied with the growing cyber technolo-gies and capabilities of some countries like China because Japan, a close U.S. ally, was far behind in the cyberwar race (WikiLeaks 2009b). The U.S. gov-ernment has also had discussions and some level of cooperation on cybersecu-rity with the Indian government (WikiLeaks 2004). All of these interstate partnerships and rivalries in cyberoperations are related to governments' con-cerns and their need to obtain information that has security, economic, and political significance as well as to protect vital technology-related sectors from potential cyberattacks, which seem to be a regular occurrence. A few days after the Sony Pictures hack by North Korea in November 2014, the U.S. gov-ernment allegedly shut down the Internet across North Korea for about ten hours (Walker 2014; M. Fisher 2015).

The Canadian government, similarly, has invested in developing the cyber offensive capabilities of its cyber arm, the Communications Security Estab-lishment (CSE), in order to counter the efforts of "terrorist organizations, state-sponsored hackers, and foreign governments (Ling 2017). This cyber development is a response to the increasing number of state-sponsored cyber-attacks against Canada; CSE reportedly identified "4,571 'compromises' of federal systems because of cyberattacks in the first nine months of 2016" (Deeby 2017). The Russian government is also known to have developed advanced cyber offensive and defensive tools (Valeriano and Maness 2015, 25), and it is estimated that the Russian cyber army that aids the Russian military's efforts consists of 1,000 members with an annual budget of $300 million (RT Arabic 2017). The Kremlin-linked Internet Research Agency was allegedly involved in hacking emails and creating fake Facebook pages in order to influ-ence the 2016 U.S. elections (Kosoff 2017). Other countries that are known to have advanced offensive and defensive cyber technologies include the United Kingdom, Iran, North Korea, Estonia, South Korea, Israel, Germany, and China (Valeriano and Maness 2015, 25). It is estimated that over sixty countries worldwide are actively developing cyberweapons (Valentino-DeVries and Yadron 2015). Interestingly, a study that examined hacking incidents over eleven years (2001–2011) found that there were III cyberattacks involving rival states, many of them involving neighboring countries, suggesting that "cyber conflicts are not disconnected from the typical international conflicts over space and place" (Valeriano and Maness 2015, 8–9). It's no wonder, then, that so many governments believe obtaining sensitive online information from other countries and countering cyberattacks are of vital importance to their national security.

Cyberwarfare, as a matter of fact, is conceived of as part of, and an extension from, classical warfare, involving various activities such as physical destruction, electronic espionage, and disruption. For example, prior to the U.S.-led invasion of Iraq in 2003, the U.S. Special Collection Service (SCS), which is a joint CIA-NSA agency (Bamford 2007, 405), installed sophisticated antennas in Iraq to intercept microwave communications and employed an Australian agent working for the UN agency UNSCOM in order to spy and collect valuable military information (Ritter and Hersh 2005). Additionally, before the beginning of the 2003 war, several hacking attempts were made from the United States against official Iraqi websites, defacing them and posting anti-Baathist messages (Al-Rawi 2012b, 24 and 51). The war on Iraq itself included a dimension of cyberwar, including the hacking of nearly 20,000 websites between mid-March and mid-April 2003, cyberoperations and hacking carried out either for or against the war (Rojas 2003). And in the aftermath of the 2003 war on Iraq, another cyberwar was initiated in the country to fight Iraqi insurgents. According to Bob Gourley, the chief technology officer for the U.S. Defense Intelligence Agency, technology experts conducted "reconnaissance on foreign countries without exchanging salvos of destructive computer commands" (Harris 2009). Iraqi insurgents themselves were believed to have hacked the U.S. Predator drone video feed in order to disclose the kind of footage it captured (Spillius 2009), while other sympathizers with the Iraqi insurgency stepped up their war against U.S. websites as a reaction to the U.S. invasion of Iraq. The leader of the Tarek Bia Ziad Group, who is believed to be a Libyan hacker, managed to design a virus that infected many computers in the United States and attributed his action to his support for the Iraqi insurgency (Heussner 2010). According to former secretary of state Hillary Clinton, the U.S. government also hacked into websites run by al-Qaeda's affiliates in Yemen and changed advertisements that bragged about killing Americans into pro-American advertisements (Hughes 2012).

Finally, many Arab armies created cyber or electronic warfare divisions whose tasks initially included jamming radio and radar signals and more recently have included hacking and surveillance. Examples include the case of Saudi Arabia, which established its cyberwarfare division on October 12, 1987

(RSLF n.d.), Jordan's Electronic Warfare Department, and the Egyptian Electronic Army. It is believed Saddam Hussein was working on developing Iraq Net in the mid-1990s as part of its cyber arsenal. Iraq Net "consists of a series of more than 100 Web sites located in domains throughout the world. Iraq Net, he said, is designed to overwhelm cyber-based infrastructures by distributed denial of service and other cyber attacks" (as cited in Stohl 2008). However, these attacks have never materialized. I interviewed an Iraqi hacker in 2002 who mentioned that Uday Saddam Hussein, the son of the Baathist leader who was responsible for administering many media divisions including the *Babel* newspaper, was planning on creating a cyber offensive unit in order to conduct cyberattacks against Western targets. The alleged plan, however, was never operationalized due to the preparations for war and other logistical constraints. More recently, the Egyptian Cyber Army (ECA) was established by young Egyptian hackers who were once affiliated with Anonymous and who support the country's armed forces; they are headed by a former police officer called Khalid Abu Bakr (hussein adriano 2014; Abdelhamid 2015). During the Arab Spring events, some of these self-proclaimed nationalist hackers felt that Anonymous sided with the protesters against Egyptian interests, so they created their own group in 2014, which had an official Twitter account (@egyptianarmy30). ECA became more clandestine as its online presence diminished, but we know it was actively involved in countering ISIS's radical messages (Franceschi-Bicchierai 2014) as well as hacking the websites, emails, and social media outlets of dissidents who oppose El-Sisi's rule, especially those run by members of the Muslim Brotherhood (hussein adriano n.d.).

Cyberwars and Political Conflicts

The term *cyberwar* was introduced by John Arquilla and David Ronfeldt (1993; Arquilla 1996), who differentiated between netwar and cyberwar based on the type of actors involved. "Cyberwar refers to knowledge-related conflict at the military level," while "netwar applies to societal struggles most often associated with low intensity conflict by non-state actors, such as terrorists, drug cartels, or black market proliferators of weapons of mass destruction." Dorothy Denning coined the term *information warfare* (1999), which is similar in meaning to other relevant terms such as "information war, information-based war, command and control warfare, information operations, C3I, electronic warfare, and, in Russian usage, sixth-generation warfare" (Stein 1998, 169). Political hacking has become integral to this new information warfare because it is one of the main means by which to wage cyberwar, which has been defined as "aggressive operations in cyberspace, against military targets, against a State or its society" (Ventre 2011, ix). Another definition describes cyberwar as involving "Internet-based attacks by one nation-state on another nation-state" (Jordan

2008, 78). Some definitions attempt to distinguish between cyberconflict and cyberwar. The former means "the use of computational technologies for malevolent and destructive purposes in order to impact, change, or modify diplomatic and military interactions among states," while the latter is understood to be more serious because it entails the "escalation of cyber conflict to include physical destruction and death" (Valeriano and Maness 2015, 3). There is overlap and ambiguity in this distinction, as Valeriano and Maness's definitions suggest. A further challenge is how to distinguish between cyberwar and cyberterrorism, since the latter is also defined as an act that causes "great harm," "severe economic damage" (Denning 2001), or "destruction" (Conway 2003). The distinction between cyberwars and cyberconflicts, ultimately, is not easy and clear to establish. A prudent approach takes into account the nature of the actors and their intentions when categorizing a cyber offensive act. This conceptual aspect of cyberwars will be further examined in chapter 4.

Many political hackers operating in these categories are sponsored, supported, or employed by states to achieve political goals (Hirst, Harrison, and Mazepa 2014). They may be known as cybermercenaries (Mazzetti, Goldman, Bergman, and Perlroth 2019) or as cyberwarriors, who are defined as people who "possess the characteristic of being sponsored by states and being subject to the oversight of their governments" (Baldi, Gelbstein, and Kurbalija 2003, 18). An Iranian hacking group known as APT33, for example, conducts routine electronic espionage operations and "reconnaissance for attack . . . with a sudden geopolitical shift, that behavior could change" (Greenberg 2017). In 2017, hackers sympathetic to the Turkish president Recep Tayyip Erdogan posted Twitter messages on the accounts of Amnesty International, UNICEF, and the BBC, calling Germany and the Netherlands Nazis for their critical stances against Turkey. The tweets were directly aligned with Erdogan's political stances toward these EU countries (Kareem 2017). In this context, George Lucas comments on the difficulty of categorizing state and nonstate hackers due to the secrecy surrounding their actions:

> States are increasingly engaging in this "soft" or "unarmed" conflict that differs from the kind of low-intensity conflict traditionally associated with espionage. As in the Sony-North Korea case, states are behaving more and more like individual hackers, carrying out crimes of petty vandalism, theft, disruption, destruction, and even cyberbullying to advance their national political interests. Nations are also increasingly behaving like nonstate vigilante groups, such as the former LulzSec and Anonymous; that is, they are randomly attacking the digital property, vital information, essential activities, or other valuable organizational resources of their adversaries, while also engaging in threats, extortions, and blackmail. (Lucas 2017, 9)

In other words, cyberwar does not follow the traditional definition of armed conflict or military aggression due to the unconventional methods that are employed. However, there are many similarities with the goals of offline operations, since "most cyber attacks, regardless of whether they are state-sponsored, try to gain something by espionage, sabotage, or subversion" (Springer 2017, 70). According to the *Tallinn Manual on the International Law Applicable to Cyber Warfare*, the main problem in understanding this concept lies in the fact that "there are no treaty provisions that directly deal with 'cyber warfare.' Similarly, because State cyber practice and publicly available expressions of *opinio juris* are sparse, it is sometimes difficult to definitely conclude that any cyber-specific customary international law norm exists" (Schmitt 2013, 5). In other words, cyberoperations seem to be an ongoing reality that occurs online between many countries, and they are sometimes used aggressively when there is an actual military or hostile operation. The *Tallinn Manual* concludes that the "law of armed conflict applies to cyber operations as it would to any other operations undertaken in the context of . . . both international and non-international armed conflicts (Rules 22 and 23)" (Schmitt 2013, 75). Indeed, these provisions correspond with international law, the Geneva Conventions, and international humanitarian law.

Worldwide, there have been numerous examples of political hacking attacks linked to offline military and political tensions and conflicts. The history of cyberattacks include the Serbian sympathizers who hacked about 100 online businesses in NATO nations as a result of the Bosnian conflict in late 1990; the online attacks that accompanied the actual military war between Georgia and Russia in 2008; the Sri Lankan cyberwar in May 2009, which coincided with that country's civil war; the denial-of-service attack (DoS) in 2009 by Russian hackers against Kyrgyzstan; and the Indian Cyber Army's attack on forty Pakistani websites, which saw the Pakistani hacking group called Predators PK retaliate by attacking India's Central Bureau of Investigation in 1998 (Benham et al. 2012, 85–94). Other significant cyberattacks include the Flame, Red October, and Titan Rain (U.S. vs. China).

We now turn to a discussion of two of the most significant examples of destructive cyberwar attacks. The first concerns the Siberian transcontinental pipeline that suffered the largest non-nuclear explosion in history in the summer of 1982 (Russell 2004; Markoff 2009). The CIA allegedly sabotaged the "software controlling the valves at both ends of sections of the pipelines" when these parts were still manufactured in Canada (Richards 2014, 36). The second example is related to Stuxnet, which was allegedly created by the U.S. and Israeli governments. Stuxnet 0.5 was originally deployed in 2005 to attack Iran's nuclear facilities (Arthur 2013), but it was further developed into the Stuxnet worm that actually destroyed the nuclear "centrifuges for enriching uranium at the highly secretive Natanz plant in Iran" in 2010 (Richards 2014, 37;

Nakashima and Warrick 2012; Valeriano and Maness 2012; *Guardian* 2013). This worm was part of Operation Olympic Games, secretly ordered by President Barack Obama (Sanger 2012), and it was regarded as a significant step forward in the development of information warfare tactics due to the highly sophisticated nature of the worm, which caused targeted physical damage (Grimes 2011).

The alleged U.S.-led cyberattacks in coordination with Israel against Iran did not stop with Stuxnet. Several other attempts were made, including the case of the miniFlame or Flame virus which has been described as a super-cyberweapon. The CEO of Kaspersky Lab, Eugene Kaspersky, has discussed the Flame virus, which targeted high ranking Iranian officials as well as Hezbollah operatives (Erdbrink 2012), stating: "The Flame malware looks to be another phase in this war, and it's important to understand that such cyber weapons can easily be used against any country. Unlike with conventional warfare, the more developed countries are actually the most vulnerable in this case" (Rapoza 2012). The aim of Flame, in this case, was to steal information from specific targets in Iran. This malware has the ability to "remotely take screenshots of infected computers, record audio conversations that took place in the same room as the computer, intercept keyboard inputs and wipe data on command" (Ferran 2012). The Flame, interestingly, has also been found in Bahrain, Saudi Arabia, Qatar, and the UAE, countries that are supposed to be close allies with the United States (Flangan 2012).

Cyberwar with Iran has not been one-sided. As a reaction to ongoing cyberattacks and political tensions, Iranian hackers have targeted the Facebook and Twitter accounts of U.S. State Department officials, and the emails of British MPs and Iranian dissidents living in the diaspora in order to steal vital information on their networks (Sanger and Perlrot 2015). The cyberconflicts in the Middle East, a region ripe with geopolitical tensions, have wide-ranging implications for governments and policy makers.

Cyberwarfare, Surveillance, and Politics in the Middle East

Due to technological developments in many facets of life, governments around the world, including those in the Middle East, have become increasingly reliant on online services. This kind of progress has come with a price. Many governments "have adopted laws that purport to combat cyber crimes and terrorism. However, these laws also serve as conduit to curb citizens' rights and freedom" (Khan 2012, 19). This reality has made many countries in the Middle East act like surveillance states (Weller 2012). OpenNet Initiative has observed that the MENA region (Middle East and North Africa) is regarded as one of the most heavily censored regions in the world, with cyber laws that are often ambivalent in nature. The UAE, for instance, criminalizes hacking even though the government itself is often implicated in hacking activities. Many other Arab countries, such as Jordan, Iraq, and Saudi Arabia, have cyber laws that nominally penalize hacking but often target political dissent more widely.

It is estimated that billions of dollars are spent to protect the online infrastructure of many Middle Eastern countries, spending that is increasingly needed due to the online threats faced by these countries. The Algerian government, for example, introduced a cybercrime bill in May 2008 after reports found government websites received about 4,000 hacking attempts per month (International Telecommunication Union 2012). Jordan, for its part, claimed that it countered 70 million cyberattacks in 2016 alone (HuffPost Arabi 2017j). In November 2017, the Saudi National Cyber Security Center (NCSC) announced that the kingdom faced a fierce cyber espionage campaign by a hacking group called MuddyWater, which also affected five other countries in the Middle East (*Gulf News* 2017b).

On September 15, 2014, WikiLeaks started releasing a series of spy files, a trove of hacked documents and emails from the German FinFisher (formerly known as Gamma Group International) and the Italian HackingTeam (Spy Files 2014). An examination of these files shows that almost all Arab states, with only a few exceptions like Yemen, have purchased services from these hacking companies. For instance, the Bahraini National Security Agency (NSA) and Defense Forces (BDF) were interested in HackingTeam's services. The Iraqi counterterrorism unit, as well as the defense and interior ministries, also reportedly sought information from HackingTeam, especially in relation to the Remote Control System (RCS) Galileo tool, which provides a backdoor to monitor desktop computers, work computers, and phones.[1] Other regional security bodies that reportedly needed RCS include the Jordanian General Security Directorate as well as the Armed Forces—Electronic Warfare Department, the Royal Omani Police, the Emirati Armed Forces, and the Kuwaiti Ministry of Interior. In the case of Saudi Arabia, contacts were made between HackingTeam and the Ministries of Defense and Aviation, the Center for Media Monitoring and Analysis at the Saudi royal court in the king's office, and the Ministry of Interior—Saudi Interpol. In some cases, several private intermediaries were involved, including Aecom Security System and Ezah Company for Technologies. In the case of Iraq, a scientific company called Al-Qiffaf contacted HackingTeam on behalf of the Iraqi government and asked for methods to hack Iraqi citizens. The following is excerpted from an email sent to HackingTeam by Al-Qiffaf on December 24, 2014:

> our VIP costumer [*sic*] in government sector asking [for] training for 10 person
> for how to be government hacker and the training most [*sic*] be including:
> 1. Wifi hackers, 2. Network hackers, 3. Mobile hackers, 4. Mobile apps. Like
> (viber, whatsup [*sic*], tango and another apps.) hackers, 5. Email hackers,

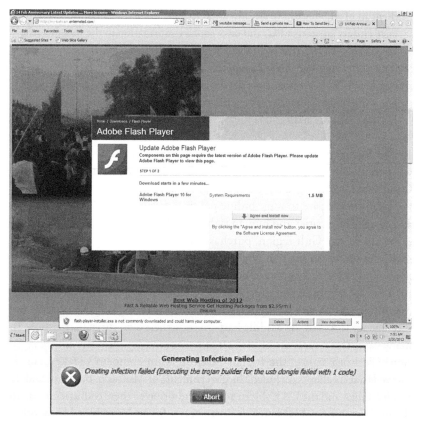

FIG. 1.2 A leaked screenshot image sent to FinFisher from Bahraini authorities. The image in the screenshot shows that the targeted website belongs to Bahraini Shiite activists. The malware can be installed by disguising itself as an Adobe Flash Player update. Also, the tab in the bookmarks bar shows the name "14 February Anniversary," which is a reference to the Bahraini popular protest.

6. Website hackers, 7. Facebook, twitter, instegram [*sic*] hackers. (WikiLeaks 2015)

As for FinFisher, the leaked documents show Bahrain was charged €1,126,800 for 380 targets (WikiLeaks 2014b). In the emails sent to FinFisher, there were often complaints that some of the spying tools targeting activists were not working properly (see figure 1.2). For example:

Dears, Please note that we are facing a critical issue in the system, where we are not benefiting any more from this system. . . . . referring to the last Tracking ID: AAFC76C1, we are explaining here more about the same issue in which to make the picture more clear: since we have 30 target licenses, we are now using them all in which we have already 30 targets. we would like to inform you that once i infect any target PC, and once i got a confirmation in the system as the target is ONLINE, that means we caught the fish. But, unfortunately, that if the target went OFFLINE, he will stay OFFLINE in the system, even if he uses his PC or Laptop. even we have a confirmation that the target uses his PC, but unfortunately that the system didnt show the second and next use of his PC. (WikiLeaks, n.d.)

The documents reveal that an officer from the Qatari State Security Bureau was periodically in contact with FinFisher in order to request training, and the Qatari state was charged a total of €1,945,140 for 890 targets.

Given their desire to wage online political disruption activities to subvert and spy on state critics and human rights activists, several Arab governments, especially in the Gulf region, purchased expensive hacking tools and hired services from companies like NSO Group, Cellebrite in Israel, FinFisher in Germany, and HackingTeam in Italy. As explained, this activity, in which powerful states are spying on their own citizens, is regarded as a form of vertical online disruption. Some U.S. companies are actively training official security and intelligence forces in the Middle East "to code their own surveillance tools. In many cases these tools are able to circumvent security measures like encryption" (Perlroth 2016). The Italian HackingTeam company's leaked emails showed that its clients included the governments of Morocco, Bahrain, Sudan, Saudi Arabia, and the UAE (Hern 2015). In addition to these countries, Human Rights Watch found evidence of "intrusion software" purchased from other sources by states like Oman and Qatar (Human Rights Watch 2016). The Bahraini government, for its part, bought "FinSpy, a commercial trojan from the FinFisher suite of surveillance tools sold by Gamma Group International" in order to target dissidents inside and outside the kingdom (Boire 2012). The British firm BAE Systems sold a mass surveillance software called Evident in order to spy on pro-democracy activists. BAE's clients included Saudi Arabia, the UAE, Qatar, Oman, Morocco and Algeria (Middle East Eye 2017). Ironically, these Western-made spying tools are provided to autocratic states that primarily use them to silence pro-democracy activists at the time when many Western governments are urging these very autocratic states to implement democratic reforms.

Although no Arab country can compete with Israel and Iran in terms of their cyber offensive capabilities, there is no doubt that the UAE and Saudi Arabia are ahead of many other countries in the region in terms of their offensive cyber capabilities (Perlroth 2016). The UAE's interest in cyberwarfare capabilities can be attributed to its concern for protecting its national security as well as quelling local political opposition. One of the first surveillance controversies was related to the use of BlackBerry devices in the UAE back in 2010, as the Emirates pressured Research in Motion, the maker of the mobile device, to hand over the encryption software in order "to monitor e-mails and messages." The UAE also asked to "maintain servers within the country so that, when it identifies someone who is acting suspiciously, it can find out what else he or she has been up to." Saudi Arabia has also demanded similar measures in the kingdom (Gapper 2010). As part of its cyber offensive strategies, the UAE has hired the services of DarkMatter to monitor Emirati citizens and foreigners visiting and/or working in the country. Faisal Al Bennai, the CEO of Dark-Matter, used to be the vice president of the country's National Electronic Security Authority (NESA), which is responsible for providing sensitive intelligence to the state. DarkMatter and NESA are currently working together closely on cyber espionage. DarkMatter has employed "an army of cyberwarriors from abroad to conduct mass surveillance aimed at the country's own citizens" (McLaughlin 2016). The company is interested in "exploiting hardware probes installed across major cities for surveillance, hunting down never-before-seen vulnerabilities in software, and building stealth malware implants to track, locate, and hack basically any person at any time in the UAE." (McLaughlin 2016). Another Emirati company focused on surveillance and hacking is the Royal Group, which is "a conglomerate run by a member of the Al Nahyan family, one of the six ruling families of the Emirates." The spyware used by the Royal Group was sold by FinFisher and HackingTeam, and invoices from 2015 showed that the UAE paid HackingTeam alone more than $634,500 to use the spyware on 1,100 people (Perlroth 2016). Finally, the UAE government provided the Egyptian leader El-Sisi with a French-made spying tool in order to monitor Egyptian citizens. (The UAE opposes the Muslim Brotherhood, who are regarded as a security threat in the Emirates.) The espionage tool is estimated to be worth about 10 million euros (HuffPost Arabi 2017i). The surveillance and spying technologies used and developed by the UAE have assisted in effectively targeting opposition figures. Well-known Emirati human rights advocate Ahmed Mansoor, for example, has repeatedly been targeted with cyberattacks to steal information from his electronic devices and silence him. "On August 10 and 11, 2016, Mansoor received SMS text messages on his iPhone promising 'new secrets' about detainees tortured in UAE jails if he clicked on an included link." Mansoor did not click, and a digital forensic examination later showed that he was targeted with "an exploit infrastructure connected to NSO Group, an Israel-based 'cyber war' company that sells *Pegasus*, a government-exclusive 'lawful intercept' spyware product" (Menn 2016). The virus would have turned his device into a spying tool recording everything. The hacking attempts against Mansoor did not stop with this incident. He was later targeted with spyware sold by FinFisher and HackingTeam. As a result, he was "jailed and fired from his job, along with having his passport confiscated, his car stolen, his email hacked, his location tracked and his bank account robbed of $140,000. He has also been beaten, twice, in the same week" (Perlroth 2016). Other UAE human rights activists were targeted by emails sent from a fake organization called the Right to Fight, asking them to click on links related to human rights issues (Perlroth 2016). Other countries, such as Qatar, appear to seek hackers for hire, cybermercenaries, who freelance "for all sorts of different clients . . . adapting their skills as needed" (Kirkpatrick and Frenkel 2017). This phenomenon is not limited to the Middle East; it is believed an FBI informant once instructed some U.S. hackers, including Jeremy Hammond, to attack certain targets in countries that were supposed to be allies with the United States, including Turkey, Iraq, and Brazil (Cameron 2013). As we will examine more in chapter 2, emails of targeted Arab diplomats, obtained using phishing techniques to lure their victims into clicking on links, were leaked by a group of hackers sympathetic to Qatar (Kirkpatrick and Frenkel 2017).

In conclusion, this chapter has provided an overview and summary evaluation of the politics of hacking, online political disruption, and cyberwars, with emphasis on the Middle East. Hacking is a form of aggressive and militaristic public communication, because hackers practice online political disruption and are sometimes sponsored, supported, or employed by states to achieve political goals (Hirst, Harrison, and Mazepa 2014). These cyberoperations are manifestations of power, serving several functions including showing the technological superiority of some nation-states in an effort to influence or pressure their opponents and influence policies (Waltz 2010). The definition of cyberconflict in this book diverges from the traditional definition of armed conflict or military aggression because of the unconventional methods that are employed. The motivations for cyberoperations, however, are similar to those driving traditional military and diplomatic conflicts. Evidence shows that many neighboring rival states engage in frequent hostile cyber activities due to disagreements or clashes over their geopolitical or economic interests.

The majority of Arab countries have purchased, used, or employed cyber offensive measures, surveillance tools, and spying techniques in order to hack their opponents as well as monitor and target dissidents and human rights activists. These hacking and surveillance acts are regarded as vertical online political disruption activities meant to compromise, undermine, weaken, and pressure oppositional groups and dissidents. Some Arab countries created offensive cyber divisions to gather intelligence and hack their enemies—mostly their neighbors—as part of their horizontal political disruption operations. The UAE, in particular, seems to be more advanced than the others in this area due to the fact that many Western hackers were hired to provide intelligence for the Emirates, but different neighboring states that have some opposed stances on political issues have actively used hacking methods to undermine each other.

The ongoing cyberwar in the Middle East closely corresponds with geopolitical developments in the region, and it "has the potential to escalate" (Valeriano and Maness 2015, 96) in the future. To gain a deeper understanding of the cyberspace dimension of this powder keg, the next chapter will examine some of the region's cyberoperations in more detail, including providing an analytical account of the Qatari hacking incident.

2

Cyberwars and International Politics

● ●

This chapter dives deeper into cyberoperations and hacking as forms of horizontal political disruption because they often involve nation-states' attempts to influence each other as well as international audiences in a vertical manner. Waltz's theory of structural realism in international relations (2000) emphasizes issues of hierarchy and anarchy as characteristic forces in the political structure, highlighting the ways in which the powers of nation-states are not only limited to their military capabilities but can extend to other realms like cyberspace. One of these new realms, I argue, is the development of online offensive and defensive capabilities, which can be analyzed in terms of Waltz's argument on balancing the structures of power. This chapter also includes a brief discussion on cyberterrorism, the use of political hacking to wage cyberwars that complement offline terrorist objectives.

For many years, various cyberoperations and hacking have been directed at the Middle East region with the involvement of international actors including, among others, the United States, China, Russia, and the U.K. Bradshaw and Howard (2017) conducted a cross-national comparative study of what they called "global cyber troops" in twenty-eight countries around the world. They found that these social media activities reached different audiences around the world, indicating the international reach of these cyberoperations. All told, there have been thousands of cyberoperations that can be situated within this kind of international online disruption activity, and it would be impossible to list them. However, a few examples can help show the major patterns in these cyberoperations and illustrate the importance of power as emphasized by Waltz's structural realism.

Data clandestinely harvested from various sources, and strategically used to undermine the political objectives and influence the policies of foreign powers, represents an important new power on the global stage. Similar to the Cold War era and its Star Wars weapons race, what we are witnessing today is another type of race, one focused on obtaining and developing cyber weapons. One significant difference here is that most of these activities are done in clandestine ways to avoid detection and responsibility. Some Russian hackers, to take one example, often pretend to operate as if they are in fact an Iranian hacking group (Corera 2019), while the CIA routinely conceals its activities and leaves traces to give the impression that its operations are conducted by Russian hackers (Pagliery 2017). There are many other examples of this kind of astroturfing hacking activities, some of which are examined later in this book (see for example chapter 5). At other times, cyber weapons are traded, leaked, and exchanged for political favors, as we saw with the NSA's cyber weapons leaked by Chinese hackers in 2016 (Brewster 2019) or with the mobile phones spying software that the U.S. government gave to Iraq's prime minister and intelligence body but was handed over to the Iranian government after the U.S. withdrawal from the country (Arango et al. 2019).

When it comes to offensive cyberoperations with an international scope, the U.S.-Israeli–made Stuxnet virus targeting Iranian nuclear facilities, discussed in chapter 1, is one relevant example. Israel is on its way to being one of the world's top cyber superpowers (Awad 2018), while the United States has been the top country in the field for many years. In fact, the United States has frequently attacked Iran's cyber infrastructure in recent years, such as the cyberattack against Iran's paramilitary arm allegedly responsible for plotting operations against oil tankers (Barnes 2019) as well as against the country's rockets and missiles' electronic system (Associated Press 2019).

Iran has responded in kind with hundreds of cyberattacks against different Western targets, including Iranian dissidents abroad, attacking the Sands Casino in Las Vegas, whose owner had previously called for detonating a nuclear weapon in the Iranian desert, hacking the British MP's emails in 2017 as well as the social media accounts of U.S. State Department officials. These offensive cyberoperations were conducted with the help of its numerous hacking groups like APT35 (Newscaster), OilRig, Charming Kitten, the Mabna Institute, and the Advanced Persistent Threat 33 (Sanger and Perlroth 2015; MacAskill 2017; Greenberg 2017; BBC 2018b; FireEye Intelligence 2018a; Corera 2019; Mitre 2019). These state-sponsored Iranian attacks were not limited to hacking; they also extend to other activities like using fake social media accounts to disseminate news that fits with Iran's political agenda. For example, Facebook removed hundreds of Facebook public pages and accounts in 2018 and 2019 because of violations of the platforms' policies on coordinated inauthentic behavior. These astroturfing cyberoperations used compromised or fake accounts and focused on promoting the Iranian government and spreading disinformation to the United States, U.K., Latin America, the Middle East, and French-speaking users living in North Africa, often using fake media organizations like "Liberty Front Press" and "Instituto Manquehue" (FireEye Intelligence 2018b). The favorable topics that Iranian trolls focused on included Donald Trump in the United States as well as regional issues like Yemen because of the Shiite Houthi rebels, Israel, and support for Palestine (Facebook Newsroom 2018a; Gleicher 2019). These offensive cyberoperations, importantly, are often a reaction to offline political tensions and an expression of perceived political grievances. For instance, when the United States killed Iranian general Qassim Suleimani in early January 2020 in Iraq, Iranian hacking operations against U.S. websites tripled in just a few days, with some successful attempts including the hacking of the website of the Federal Depository Library Program (Fung 2020; Agence France Presse 2020).

Other countries in the Middle East region are aggressively using cyber weapons to monitor their dissidents who live abroad. This includes Saudi Arabia (Kirchgaessner and Hopkins 2019) as well as the UAE, which has recently developed a mobile telecommunication app that is used as a spying weapon (Mazzetti, Perlroth, and Bergman 2019). Further afield, the Chinese government was allegedly responsible for hacking the computer servers of the Organization of African Union in Addis Ababa, Ethiopia, and transferring all the data to a Shanghai-based station (Tilouine and Kadiri 2018).

There are also numerous international nonstate players who are involved in online political disruption, including the hacktivist group Anonymous. As was touched on in chapter 1, there are many members of this hacking group from the Middle East who play various roles in influencing its diverse activities and messages. For example, the author downloaded the tweets from the group's Twitter account on February 15, 2015, using Crimson Hexagon and found several tweets related to issues of social justice and political inequality in the Middle East. One tweet expressed shock that while people widely shared the sentiment #JeSuisCharlie in relation to the Charlie Hebdo terrorist attack, "there's a decades-deep pile of dead Arab kids that no one ever raises a whisper about." Other messages were critical of human rights violations in Saudi Arabia and other authoritarian states, as well as Israeli policies toward Palestinians using hashtags like #ApartheidIsrael and #GazaUnderAttack. Anonymous, in fact, launched the online campaign #OpIsrael in 2013 to raise awareness about the plight of Palestinian civilians living under Israeli occupation.[1] This initiative prompted the creation of an annual event called "Hack Israel Day." Anonymous was also actively involved in supporting pro-democracy activists during the Arab Spring events, spreading hashtags like #OpTunisia (Coleman 2014) and hacking ISIS-affiliated websites and social media accounts (Brown and Markovitz 2015) as part of its online political disruption activities.

As for the religious dimension of international hacking, there are actually dozens of Islamic-affiliated hacking groups, including Islam4ever, Islam swords team, Islam hack team, iSlam AttaCk, and many others. Certain controversial global issues can heighten the hacking attempts against Western websites, especially when it comes to issues related to Islam such as Muhammad cartoons and incidents of burning the Quran which encouraged cyberattacks and motivated some to take up cyber jihad (Al-Rawi 2017b; 2016, p. 28). One group of hackers, Izz ad-Din al-Qassam Cyber Fighters used major DDoS attacks against American banks like Wells Fargo, PNC Bank, JPMorgan Chase, and Bank of America in September 2012 in what was called Operation Ababel, following the release of the anti-Islam *Innocence of Muslims* film (Shachtman 2012). The hackers, who appeared to be independent, used botnets involving thousands of compromised servers and a computer tool called "itsoknoproblembro" ("it's OK, no problem, bro") to overburden the networks with about 70 gigabits of data per second (Goodman 2012; Klobucher 2013). Since these hackers were targeting powerful political and financial institutions, their acts can be regarded as a form of bottom-up online political disruption.

In some cases, these kinds of actions have created a vicious cycle of hacking and counterhacking attempts. For instance, an unknown group calling itself "Islam Fucker" defaced several websites, posting the following message: "We believe IRAN must be wipe [*sic*] off the map of the world" accompanied by an image that reads: "Fuck Islam" with President George W. Bush flipping the bird. In this and other cases, we see how offline political events can lead to online operations and counteroperations on different fronts. In the following section, we turn to the phenomenon of cyberterrorism and efforts to counter it online.

Cyberterrorism

Cyberterrorism is a form of political online disruption that aims to complement offline terrorist objectives. Terrorist groups practice horizontal and vertical cyber activities, targeting governments and citizens alike. The first person to coin the term *cyberterrorism* was Barry Collin around 1987 in reference to the intersection of offline and virtual terrorism (Collin 1997). James Lewis later described cyberterrorism as "the use of computer network tools to shut down critical national infrastructures (such as energy, transportation, government operations) or to coerce or intimidate a government or civilian population" (CSIS 2002). Dorothy Denning, similarly, defines cyberterrorism as "the convergence of cyberspace and terrorism," often involving "politically motivated hacking operations intended to cause grave harm such as loss of life or severe economic damage" (Denning 2001, 241). Denning offered a deadly example of cyberterrorism, "penetrating an air traffic control system and causing two planes to collide." Weimann confirms that the line between the concepts of cyber-terrorism and hacktivism is blurry, since it is difficult to define the actions of hacktivists attacking "national infrastructure, such as electric power networks and emergency services" (Weimann 2005, 137). Weimann does acknowledge that cyberterrorism is done if some nation-states are involved in hacking acts (Weimann 2005, 141). William Tafoya (2011) offers a problematic, limited con-ceptualization of the term, asserting that cyberterrorism exclusively targets civilians. This definition, however, risks equating cybercriminals with cyber-terrorists while ignoring state-sponsored cyber acts that can cause physical damage and possible loss of civilian lives. This definition of cyberterrorism, ulti-mately, only serves to help sustain the dominant hegemony of the political elite (Vegh 2002), and it can have dire consequences when attempting to assess political hacking done with the aim of creating a more transparent government. Most authoritarian countries in the Middle East, for instance, automatically criminalize political hacking by classifying it as a form of cyberterrorism in order to silence political dissent and send a loud message to other would-be hackers that they cannot take this route in opposing the state and its legitimacy. There have been severe punishments against cyberterrorists in the Middle East. In 2017, the Iraqi government executed an Iraqi hacker for allegedly being a member of ISIS's Cyber Caliphate Army. Also, Junaid Hussain, a British ISIS recruit, was killed in a U.S.-targeted air strike in August 2015 in Syria after click-ing on malware. Before his death, Hussain's phones were hacked by the British intelligence agency GCHQ, which was able to track his movements (Dearden 2015; Murphy 2015). In Israel, a Palestinian hacker called Majid Auydha was imprisoned by the Israeli government and accused of terrorism for collaborat-ing with the Islamic Jihad Movement (SWI 2017). Auydha hacked the Israeli drone system used to monitor the Palestinian territories.

When we examine hacking groups affiliated with terrorist organizations in the Middle East, we find that their activities are not only done through vari-ous offensive cyberoperations and hacking attempts but also through "the sub-version of popular memes to propagate pro-terrorist messages" (Huey 2015; aee also Alperen and Russo 2017). The targets often include national, regional, and international websites, with terrorist groups and their sympathizers often using satire to look "cool" and practice political disruption "to appeal to younger audiences raised within cultures that treat forms of dark, political humour as hip, trendy and counter-culture. Disseminated through online milieus to indi-viduals already potentially interested in receiving such messages, political vio-lence becomes 'jihadi cool'" (Huey 2015, 2 and 14). Al-Qaeda, whose hacking groups include Al-Qaeda Electronic Army and the affiliated Tunisian Cyber Army, used to periodically ridicule the U.S. State Department's online campaigns against the terrorist group in its cyber jihad operations (Berton and Pawlak 2015).

After al-Qaeda, the Islamic State in Iraq and Syria (ISIS) took cyberoperations to a new level in its "Jihad 3.0" efforts and through the use of different state-of-the-art media productions and techniques (Al-Rawi, 2018, 745). Initially under the banner of United Cyber Caliphate, ISIS ran about five hacking groups, such as the Cyber Caliphate Army and the Hackers' Union of the Caliphate (Al-Rawi and Groshek 2018) which succeeded in hacking many Western websites and social media accounts (BBC News 2015; Steinblatt 2015; HuffPost Arabi 2016b; Alkhouri, Kassirer, and Nixon 2016). The online political disruption efforts of these terrorist hacking groups not only focused on defacing websites but also on spamming people or organizations on mobile apps and social media, such as in the case of blocking "Raqqa is slaughtered in Silence" on Telegram (Shiloach 2016). In another example, ISIS followers hacked the Ohio governor's website and hundreds of U.S. school websites using the nickname "Team System DZ." The message they posted read: "You will be held accountable Trump, you and all your people for every drop of blood flowing in Muslim countries" (Silverman 2014).

On the other side of the cyber barricades, Emily Stacey writes about the concept of political disruption in the context of the efforts to counter terrorists' narratives and ideologies (Stacey 2017, 75). The activities of the 83-country Global Coalition (https://theglobalcoalition.org/en/) are relevant here since their mission is to fight ISIS in different spheres, especially on social media. The Global Coalition itself, in addition to a number of other U.S.-led anti-terrorist campaigns, has been trolled by ISIS with the use of spamming, hashtags, and parodies like #CalamityWillBefallUS, "Run, Do Not Walk to U.S. Terrorist State" (Miller and Higham 2015). Alberto Fernandez notes how ISIS ironically used "the Terms of Service of an American social media company to silence the U.S. government messaging" (Fernandez 2015, 494) in relation to its efforts to shut down the Digital Outreach Team's (DOT) Twitter account.

U.S.-U.K. Cyberoperations in the Middle East

The British government, like the United States, has increasingly been focused on countering extremism. For example, the British Army's 77th Brigade, formed in 2015 and comprising 1,500 members, is responsible for its psychological warfare unit and disinformation campaigns on social media. Incidentally, one of the unit's reserve members was hired by Twitter as a senior officer (Gilbert 2019). Furthermore, the U.K. Home Office established the Research, Information and Communication Unit (RICU), and the government developed a Counter-Terrorism Strategy (CONTEST) to counter al-Qaeda's ideology (Schmid 2014). The U.K. government was also involved in funding some local NGOs, like the Islamic anti-terrorism foundation Quilliam, to fight radicalization (Russell 2013). There are indications the British government works to boost moderate Muslim leaders such as the Egyptian preacher Amr Khalid, and "there is also evidence of British government moral and/or financial support to selected Arabic-language media," allegedly including Al-Hiwar TV, whose headquarters is located in London (Sakr 2008, 293–294). The British government is also part of the previously mentioned Global Coalition in its fight against ISIS. Together with the UAE and the United States, the U.K. is involved in "exposing IS' true nature" (McInnis 2016) via the Coalition's Counter-Messaging Working Group. The work of this group is "supported by the Coalition Communications Cell, based in the U.K.'s Foreign and Commonwealth Office in London" (Global Coalition 2016).

The United States has probably been the most active country in terms of its cyberoperations in the Middle East, due to its geostrategic political interests in the region. Prior to the 9/11 attacks in 2001 the U.S. Department of Defense (DOD) only targeted Americans, with the exception of psychological operations during times of war. But after the start of the War on Terror, the DOD started targeting foreign noncombatant nationals, even though it "overlap[ped] with the work of the public diplomacy civilians at the State Department" (Rugh 2014, 4). The Pentagon, in fact, "spends about $150 million each year to influence public opinion and win 'hearts and minds'" (Miller and Higham 2015), and it spent hundreds of millions to fund PR companies in Iraq in order to plant and publish newspaper stories and air TV commercials that were favorable toward the United States (Democracy Now 2006; Cary 2010), including support for anti-terror campaigns like "Terrorism Has No Religion" (Proctor 2012). In 2009 alone, the Pentagon hired 27,000 people for "recruitment, advertising and public relations" with tasks related to "winning hearts and minds at home and abroad"; the total budget for this operation was $4.7 billion (Shachtman 2009).[2] One of the Pentagon's early online initiatives was called Operation Earnest Voice. First developed in Iraq with the help of the Ntrepid web-security company, it was later used in other countries including Afghanistan and Pakistan. Using "sockpuppet" software or fake identities (Fielding and Cobain 2011), the objective of the program was to spam al-Qaeda followers and sympathizers with the use of fifty operators and "online persona management." Originally developed as a psychological warfare program that cost about $200 million (Holtmann 2013, 142; Soules 2015, 73; Bennett 2013, 47; Gray and Gordo 2014, 255), it was highly problematic because it is hard to pretend to spread democracy and transparency while using "a deliberate attempt to conceal and deceive." As it happens, it's hard to use "non-democratic methods of communications and propaganda without being tarred with the same brush as governments who control the media and information for their own political ends" (Rawnsley 2011, 28–29). The U.S. Center for Strategic Counterterrorism

Communications (CSCC), which is part of the State Department, had a $5 million budget to target ISIS followers on Twitter with campaigns like "Think Again Turn Away" (@ThinkAgain_DOS on Twitter) (Silverman 2014). Together with the UAE, the U.S. government was also involved in running the Sawab Center (@sawabcenter on Twitter) in order to counter ISIS's ideology. The center launched several campaigns on its Twitter and Instagram pages, including one called "#MercyToTheWorlds" which aimed to refute ISIS's claim that the terrorist group followed the Prophet Muhammad's teachings.

Following the National Security Agency (NSA) leaks by Edward Snowden in 2013, Reporters without Borders classified the U.S. and U.K. governments as "Enemies of the Internet" in 2014 in relation to issues of state surveillance. Specifically, they held both the U.K.'s Government Communications Headquarters (GCHQ) and the NSA responsible for spying on millions of people and hacking "into the very heart of the Internet using programmes such as the NSA's Quantam Insert and GCHQ's Tempora" (Reporters without Borders 2014, 3). The massive and coordinated hacking operations of the Five Eyes surveillance alliance (the U.S., U.K., Australia, Canada, and New Zealand) exposed the double standards followed by some of these great powers who periodically urge third-world countries to become more transparent and democratic even while they continuously conduct myriad clandestine and antidemocratic practices.

In pursuit of their major objectives, some divisions in GCHQ such as the Human Science Operations Cell (HSOC) and the Joint Threat Research Intelligence Group (JTRIG) offered training courses for their employees and allies to become "cyber magicians" using Online Covert Action (OCA) techniques, which utilize psychological experiments borrowed from different research disciplines like sociology, cyber-psychology, cultural studies, and media to influence specific targets. Geert Hofstede's theory of cultural dimensions was employed to interpret the general frameworks of national cultures; the OCA techniques also involved different types of information operations as well as the use of online HUMINT (human intelligence) gathering by agents (GCHQ 2014). Examples of these practices were found in Snowden's leaked documents (Snowden 2014), which revealed the spying agencies created numerous hacking programs like MYSTIC, PRISM, XKeyScore, and Optic Nerve as well as scores of other tools on how to set honey traps, carry out hacks, and disrupt online communication, including hacking a country's telephone system, spying on computers, servers, webcams, WiFi networks and mobile GSM locations. Other cyberoperations techniques include online spamming, "pushing stories," call bombing, denial of service, astroturfing, collecting emails from Yahoo and Gmail, monitoring a whole country or a city's Internet traffic, spying on online gaming networks like the World of Warcraft, as well as collecting data from

Facebook, Twitter, YouTube, LinkedIn, Messenger, and other social media (GCHQ 2000; Gellman and Soltani 2014). These agencies, additionally, created a virus in 2012 called Ambassadors Reception which was able to "encrypt itself, delete all emails, encrypt all files, make [the] screen shake." GCHQ itself was responsible for an online attack against the hacking group Anonymous in September 2011 (NBC News 2014). Though online political disruption is often used by Anonymous against state actors, we see that countermeasures have also been used in the form of state-manufactured cyber weapons to disrupt the activities of this hacktivist group.

As for the U.S. State Department, it has also been very active in terms of its cyberoperations in the Middle East, which are carefully designed to serve the country's strategic interests. In addition to the Digital Outreach Team, which is discussed in more detail in the following chapter, there are a few other initiatives run by the State Department, including the 2002 "Shared Values" campaign which "profiled Muslims living contentedly in the United States, including a baker in Ohio and a fire department medic in Brooklyn." The campaign, which ended in failure, cost $15 million and was dubbed a "Happy Muslim" initiative (Miller and Higham 2015). In addition, the U.S. State Department Alliance of Youth Movements initiative was involved in the Arab Spring in Egypt (Bratich 2011) by supporting the Egyptian April 16 Youth Movement as far back as 2008 in what Linda Herrera calls "cyberdissident diplomacy" (2014). Oliver Boyd-Barrett notes that the Egyptian youth group met in 2009 with CANVAS, whose partners include the Albert Einstein Institution and Freedom House (2014, 82). These cyber democracy promotional programs have not been confined to the Middle East. They extend to other regions, as seen in efforts to support the Orange Revolution in Ukraine in the 1990s, the Rose Revolution in Georgia, and the funding of the Otpor program in Serbia in 2000 (Boyd-Barrett 2014, 82).

Other U.S. agencies such as USAID, the National Democratic Institute for International Affairs, the National Endowment for Democracy, the International Republican Institute, Freedom House, and George Soros's Open Society Institute have also been involved in online initiatives in the Middle East and worldwide to promote U.S. interests and agendas (Boyd-Barrett 2014, 82). For example, in 2010 during Barack Obama's presidency, the U.S. government launched a $1.6 million social media initiative called ZunZuneo, dubbed "Cuban Twitter," to undermine the communist government in Cuba (Arce 2014). To achieve its astroturfing objective, USAID created front companies in Spain and the Cayman Islands to conceal the sources of money and used fake ad banners to give the impression ZunZuneo was a commercial enterprise. The objective was to encourage and organize "smart mobs" and trigger a so-called Cuban Spring. Before shutting down in September 2012, ZunZuneo had created a strong online community, reaching 40,000 subscribers who had been

encouraged to use text messages (Arce 2014). There are also many cyberoperations by the CIA in the Middle East, but due to their highly clandestine nature
it is not possible to fully estimate or understand their magnitude. Snowden's
leaks showed that the CIA "spent more than $250 million to monitor social
media" outlets (Miller and Higham 2015), while WikiLeaks revealed in 2017
that the spying agency managed to create online tools to hack smart phones
and television webcams for the purpose of eavesdropping on people around the
world (Pagliery 2017).

The DOD's Strategic Programs Operations Center

As for the U.S. Department of Defense (DOD), it ran several initiatives, including one that began in June 2005 when the Joint Psychological Operations
Support Element was established and awarded a $300 million contract to
SYColeman, Lincoln Group, and SAIC to develop propaganda campaigns for
the U.S. government (Cary 2010, 7). The Lincoln Group, which was one of the
PR companies contracted by the Pentagon to assist in its Iraqi media operations,
stated that the goal was "to counter the misinformation that is put out by our
adversaries. . . . Trying to get out accurate information is an important part of
what the U.S. needs to do to show our side of the story" (White 2005). These
objectives are similar to what DOT aims to achieve, and there is obviously some
overlap between the two agencies. The Lincoln Group, which received about
$10 million a month to run its Iraqi online media campaigns (Democracy Now
2006), created several front groups, such as Iraqex, to conceal its identity. In
one of its advertised job postings, it mentioned the need to hire employees "to
mount an aggressive advertising and public relations campaign that will accu-
rately inform the Iraqi people of the coalition's goals and gain their support"
(White 2005).

In recently declassified official documents exclusively used in this book,[3] the
U.S. Department of Defense (DOD)'s Strategic Programs Operations Center
(SPOC) internally released its final report to detail its operations in Iraq
between October 1, 2005, and November 30, 2011, only a few days prior to the
official U.S. withdrawal from Iraq. Its program is regarded as "the largest mass
media campaign ever launched by the United States Government in support
of U.S. strategic objectives" (SPOC 2011) and was conducted with the assistance
of the British PR company Bell Pottinger, which was awarded a $540 million
contract on September 27, 2005 (Smith, Black, and Thomas 2016).

Instead of its old term *psychological operation*, or PSYOP, the DOD started
using a new and milder term, *military information support operations* (MISO),
which they described as designed to "convey selected information and indicators
to foreign audiences to influence their emotions, motives, objective reasoning,
and ultimately the behavior of foreign governments, organizations, groups, and

individuals" (SPOC 2011). This change in terminology can be likened to Western governments' use of the term *public diplomacy* as opposed to talking openly about propaganda.

For the DOD, effective strategic communication appears more subtle than old-fashioned propaganda, and is achieved by creating a façade and "shaping an environment in which people and groups can think and feel their way to new attitudes, behaviors and actions," instead of it being a "question of 'us' messaging to 'them.'" In other words, it is not about "winning an argument, but [about] shaping a narrative" (SPOC 2011). In order to effectively achieve these objectives, online activities are deemed to be best deployed anonymously since astroturfing efforts are believed to be highly effective. SPOC's final report boasts about how all of its efforts were done without any "breach" and "zero attribution to the U.S. Government. To this day, SPOC's brands remain some of the most popular in the country with little or no questioning of their provenance or attribution, an important factor in the campaign's success" (SPOC 2011). These astroturfed online U.S. propaganda efforts are a significant part of the political disruption phenomenon, especially in relation to social media use. DOD's online operations followed what is described as the digital drawdown process. This important concept is described as follows:

> Facebook and YouTube were deemed low threat environments where a positive use of this battle-space could reinforce existing messaging. Similarly, the un-attributable nature of the operation precluded producers from assisting crews directly in order to improve their performances—there was no contact between them for OPSEC reasons. A phased digital drawdown plan was coordinated to ensure that all of the MISO products were deleted in accord with the SPOC drawdown plan. Each product was deleted to remove all possible instances as a means of protecting attribution. This process was strictly adhered to so any digital information compromise was minimized. By deleting the component parts of each platform followed by the platform account itself, in that specified order, provides the greatest safety against any residue digital footprint being left behind. (SPOC 2011)

As we can see, the DOD invests meticulous efforts into concealing its cyber activities in order to avoid any attribution. The reasons for these techniques of concealment are partially elaborated on in the following chapter on the "Future of Iraq" program. For the DOD, concealment of the true source of its cyber-operations is a key part of a coordinated information campaign:

> Campaigns should take full advantage of the unattributed space and align attributed and unattributed messaging. Messaging into a hostile environment is challenging enough; doubly so when the "messenger" is inherently distrusted

and the perceived imposition of a foreign agenda prompts cynicism within the TA [target audience] at best, and more likely total rejection of the message. To circumvent this problem, IOTF [Information Operations Task Force]/SPOC took full advantage of the "unattributed space" to remove the automatic prism of anti-U.S./Western sentiment. However, as target audiences exist in a single, integrated communications environment, both attributed and unattributed communications efforts must be aligned to ensure coordination of effort. (SPOC 2011)

These kind of astroturfing activities were not only confined to social media. The video game Labaik Ya Iraq (Iraq, We Answer Your Call) misled many famous Iraqi gamers, who believed it was actually designed and produced by Iraqis themselves (Parkin 2013).

The DOD's final report, interestingly, directly states that its approach is not about disseminating the truth: "Facts, though important, are less important than stories. . . . we use compelling, credible stories which speak to the TA through the prism of their own experience and aspirations, and which tap into the underlying narrative of their history, identity and value systems, in order to 're-tell' those stories in ways that support USG strategic objectives" (SPOC 2011). In other words, the DOD's online policy is to spread any type of information, even if it is fake, in order to achieve its strategic goals. The Bureau of Investigative Journalism released a news report in 2016 on Bell Pottinger's activities in Iraq, which included creating "short TV segments made in the style of Arabic news networks and fake insurgent videos which could be used to track the people who watched them" (Bureau of Investigative Journalism 2016). Martin Wells, one of the company's employees, described how the task was carried out:

The team was given precise instructions and was told: "We need to make this style of video and we've got to use al-Qaeda's footage. We need it to be 10 minutes long and it needs to be in this file format and we need to encode it in this manner." The video files needed to be played on RealPlayer, which connected to the Internet to operate and were embedded with a code. It meant that when the file was played, the IP address of the user's computer was relayed back to a secure military site. Wells said the video files would be transferred to CDs and U.S. marines would drop them "in the chaos" when they raided targets. They could then be used to track potential al-Qaeda supporters (Smith, Black, and Thomas 2016).

Overall, despite all their efforts, the DOD's different contractors such as Bell Pottinger, SYColeman, the Lincoln Group, and SAIC, as well as their local and regional front organizations, were for the most part not successful in concealing the identity of the U.S. government sponsors. This was because the Iraqi public was largely aware that such anti-terrorist and pro-democracy campaigns were carried out by the U.S. government as "part of America's huge psychologi-cal warfare campaign to influence Iraqis' behavior and attitudes" (Londoño 2009). Indeed, the campaigns' primarily objectives were to serve U.S. interests and create a façade that positive improvements had occurred in Iraq.

In the following chapters, I will present case studies on online political dis-ruption and international politics, offering detailed insight into the U.S. gov-ernment's Digital Outreach Team and their "Terrorism Has No Religion" campaign as well as the "Future of Iraq" online initiative. Then we will pro-ceed to examine Russian trolls' treatment of Islam and their targeting of audiences in the Middle East and North America. These are key examples of U.S. and Russian online political disruption activities aimed at countering the messages of their opponents and promoting their respective policies and inter-ests in the Middle East region and beyond.

3

U.S. Cyberoperations in the Middle East

● ● ● ● ● ● ● ● ● ● ● ● ● ● ● ● ● ● ● ●

This chapter focuses on two cases regarding the U.S. government's cyberoperations in the Middle East by examining in some detail the U.S. Department of State's Digital Outreach Team (DOT) initiative as well as the "Future of Iraq" and "Terrorism Has No Religion" campaigns as a form of vertical online political disruption. The identities of the first initiative are publicly disclosed, unlike the second program whose funders have remained anonymous in the hope that it garners more credibility.[1]

There is no doubt that the United States is the most active country in the world in terms of its cyber activities in the Middle East, due to its interests and previous political engagement. On May 1, 1953, President Eisenhower issued Executive Orders 10476 and 10477, and authorized the director of the United States Information Agency to perform the following tasks, which are still for the most part being followed by different U.S. administrations:

> explaining and advocating U.S. policies in terms that are credible and mean-
> ingful in foreign cultures; providing information about the official policies of
> the United States, and about the people, values, and institutions which
> influence those policies; bringing the benefits of international engagement to
> American citizens and institutions by helping them build strong long-term
> relationships with their counterparts overseas; and advising the President and
> U.S. government policy-makers on the ways in which foreign attitudes will

> have a direct bearing on the effectiveness of U.S. policies. (United States
> Information Agency 1998, 5)

These goals still seem to be complementary to other projects in which the U.S. government is involved, such as its anti-terror activities and other psychological operations. For example, the National Strategy for Counterterrorism's stated focus is on promoting declared U.S. core values abroad, including respect for human rights, privacy rights, civil liberties, and civil rights, encouraging responsive governance, balancing security and transparency, and upholding the rule of law (National Strategy for Counterterrorism 2011). Similarly, the recommendations given to the U.S. president by the Review Group on Intelligence and Communications Technologies for Global Communications Technology include similar U.S. core values like promoting prosperity through trade, security, and openness. including Internet freedom (White House 2013, 11). The promotion of these state core U.S. values should align well with their geostrategic interests in the region, although some of the above declared goals are contradictory to the realities on the ground when we consider the avid U.S. support for authoritarian regimes in the region such as Saudi Arabia, the UAE, and Bahrain, not to mention other revelations made public by the NSA leaks (Turner 2003; Pressman 2009; Chomsky, Achcar, and Shalom 2015).

After 9/11, U.S. cyber efforts greatly intensified. The Bush administration founded the Office of Global Communications (Rugh 2006) in order to "win the hearts and minds" of people in the Middle East and among Muslim populations more broadly (Ezell 2012). One of the new projects to emerge was the Shared Values Initiative, which was directed by the advertising firm Charlotte Beers. The campaign was coordinated with the Council of American Muslims for Understanding (CAMU), and it highlighted various aspects of Arab Americans' lives with a focus on values like the American Dream, equality, and tolerance. CAMU, however, was in fact merely a front group created by funding from the U.S. State Department (Rampton 2007), and the astroturfing campaign ended in failure and was quickly abandoned (Alsultany 2007). Numerous other communication efforts followed, including the establishment of Radio Sawa (2002) and the Al Hurra TV channel (2004) that airs in Arabic and aims to cover the whole Arab world (Kruckeberg and Vujnovic 2005; El-Nawawy 2006). Other Arabic websites were also established, such as the Bureau of International Information Programs IIP Digital (2016).[2]

As can be seen, the common thread in these communication efforts is the promotion of U.S. policies in the Arab region, countering the U.S. government's critics and opponents through a form of online political disruption. The perceived communist threat had been the main preoccupation of these efforts (Al-Rawi 2012a), but that shifted after the fall of the Soviet Union and even more so after the 9/11 attack, as the focus turned to countering and attacking Islamic jihadi groups and extremism. Jian Wang (2007) describes the various U.S. communication efforts in the region as "principally an ad hoc instrument of American foreign policy to meet wartime exigencies and has been underscored by the promotion of American values of democracy and freedom" (21). Mohan Dutta-Bergman (2006) studied many documents, press releases, and publications related to U.S. communication initiatives in the Middle East and found five major recurring themes: "U.S. interests in the Middle East, influencing the other, hidden agendas, propaganda–rural population dynamic, and propaganda–national elite dynamic." Many of these themes continue to guide current efforts, though it's worth noting that the word *propaganda* is never used by U.S. officials. (Pamment 2012); reaching out to the masses is often done in subtler, innovative ways (Rugh 2014). In the following section, a more in-depth discussion of the Digital Outreach Team (DOT) is presented.

Digital Outreach Team (DOT) and Online Political Disruption

DOT was established in November 2006 as part of the U.S. Department of State's efforts to counter extremists online in what has been dubbed "the war of narratives" (Cottee 2015). The initiative was initially headed by Richard LeBaron, a U.S. diplomat who once served as the U.S. ambassador to Kuwait. Based on what we know from two WikiLeaks cables dating back to December 2006, DOT requested information feedback and assistance from some U.S. embassies in the Middle East. For example, the U.S. embassy in Turkey sent a cable in response to a request for identifying Arabic and English extremists websites in order to fight radicalism. The cable, however, stated that "there are very few websites in Turkey that fit the criteria outlined . . . by the Digital Outreach Team" (WikiLeaks 2006b). In the sultanate of Oman, the U.S. embassy sent a list of "popular web destinations for Omani surfers, preceded by some background that . . . will be of use to IIP's new Digital Outreach Team" (WikiLeaks 2006c). On its Facebook page (https://www.facebook.com/DigitalOutreach Team), which was created on March 19, 2009, DOT's mission is described as follows:

> [DOT] is the link between the U.S. Department of State and the Arab masses via the Internet. It consists of members of the U.S. Department of State who are active on several forums and political debates available online in Arabic, Somali, and Urdu languages. The team was established . . . to present and clarify U.S. foreign policies as well as present and explain several social and cultural aspects of the U.S. society in a way that is easy to understand. The DOT team is committed and devoted to encouraging and enhancing civilized debates between the USA and the international community.

This mission statement text on Facebook, however, was different from the one posted on DOT's YouTube channel, which stated: "DOT ... aims at educating and enlightening people about the dangers of violent extremist groups like Al Qaeda and ISIS and exposing their false stories. These groups maliciously try to exploit religion and legitimate political grievances to cover their goals for destruction, death, and spreading hate" (DOT n.d.). Despite the somewhat inconsistent messaging across social media platforms, it's clear DOT aims to better explain U.S. policies in the region and to counter extremists, especially those who express animosity against the United States.

In 2011, the Center for Strategic Counterterrorism Communications (CSCC), which was headed by U.S. diplomat Alberto Fernandez, took over DOT with a budget of about $5 million a year and fifty staff members (Schmitt 2015). According to the Department of State, CSCC's mandate was to be "guided by National Strategy for Counterterrorism and operates under the policy direction of the White House and interagency leadership. The Coordinator reports to the Under Secretary of State for Public Diplomacy and works closely with the Coordinator for Counterterrorism, other State bureaus, and many government agencies" (U.S. Department of State 2011). Fernandez changed DOT's mission from primarily disseminating positive news about the United States to a focus on spreading negative information about al-Qaeda (Dewey 2013). By 2012, DOT "had 7,000 online engagements" with the public (Dewey 2013), increasing in 2015 to "50,000 ... in four languages—Arabic, Urdu, Somali, and English" (Cottee 2015). One of the most popular videos posted by DOT Arabic was entitled "What you don't know about 9/11 attacks," garnering 368,888 views. The video was posted in 2007 and was meant to counter conspiracy ideas about 9/11 (DOT 2007).

As noted, DOT turned its attention to targeting al-Qaeda leaders. After the killing of Osama bin Laden, his deputy Al Zawahiri became DOT's new focus and the team released several videos ridiculing him (Dewey 2013). When the Al Nusra group in Syria and ISIS emerged, DOT once more shifted its attention and made these groups the new preferred targets. DOT effectively functioned "like a war room in a political campaign—shake things up, attack ads, opposition research" (Miller and Higham 2015). Fernandez believed that an effective way of countering ISIS's messages was to mock the terrorist's organization's members. In describing the DOT's strategy under his watch, he also made an analogy to a political campaign: "It's not about Louis Armstrong and isn't jazz great and America loves Muslims. It's not about quoting the secretary of state, because that's boring, that's lame. Our focus is not on the positive message. What we do is counter-messaging. We're the guys in the political campaign that [do] negative advertising. We're in people's faces" (Cottee 2015). Some of DOT's communications revolved around showcasing ISIS's "hypocrisy" and emphasizing "accounts of its defectors, and document its losses on the battlefield—without recirculating its gruesome images or matching its snide tone" (Miller and Higham 2015). Another approach involved comparing ISIS to Nazis and mocking them, as was seen with the "ISIS bucket challenge" (Revise 2014). Fernandez thinks that DOT has "to answer the adversary" (Brown 2014). The adversary answers back, however. In response to DOT, ISIS members created their own Twitter account (@Al-Bttar) to counter DOT's messages. The terrorist group remains far more popular than DOT online; in a rather scathing comparison, one observer contrasted ISIS's "shock and gore" social media presence to the DOT's strategy of "mock and bore" (Cottee 2015), since the latter's approach did not seem to be working as well. In mid-2015, another change occurred to DOT, as the Information Coordination Cell (ICC) led by Rashad Hussain, Obama's former U.S. envoy to the Organisation of Islamic Cooperation, became responsible for coordinating DOT's messaging and communications. This move came after complaints that DOT had become inefficient and ineffective (Schmitt 2015). Fernandez has acknowledged the difficulties, bemoaning that the United States does not "have a counter-narrative [to ISIS]. What we have is half a message: 'Don't do this.' But we lack the 'do this instead.' That's not very exciting. The positive narrative is always more powerful" (Cottee 2015).

The new agency, ICC, consists of about thirty CIA and Pentagon experts and analysts, and aims "to enlist U.S. embassies, military leaders and regional allies in a global messaging campaign to discredit groups such as the Islamic State" (Miller and Higham 2015). According to Richard Stengel, the new DOT strategy is focused on spreading messages exponentially by leveraging "a network of networks" (Schmitt 2015). Stengel, who served as President Obama's Under Secretary for Public Diplomacy and Public Affairs until 2016, after having served as *Time* magazine's managing editor for seven years. Stengel believed that DOT should use an integrative online approach, linking different U.S. agencies and embassies to its network: "It would use more than 350 State Department Twitter accounts, combining embassies, consulates, media hubs, bureaus and individuals, as well as similar accounts operated by the Pentagon, the Homeland Security Department and foreign allies" (Schmitt 2015). Intended to create a wide network in which pro-U.S. and anti-ISIS messages can go viral by targeting a variety of audiences around the globe, this new approach seems to be effective.

Some of DOT's members, it is important to note, were active on various other platforms and websites, openly disclosing their identities in order to engage the Arab public in a discussion on U.S. foreign policy issues. Malek Fares, for example, has a page on the ask.fm website (http://ask.fm/MalekFares) on which he responded to thirty-nine questions on various matters, especially those related to extremism. In one of these responses, Fares defends the U.S. stance and charges Bashar Assad's regime in Syria with being responsible for the emergence of ISIS and other militant groups. Walid Jawad was another DOT member who often published articles defending U.S. policies in the Saudi-owned *Asharq Al Awsat* newspaper. Jawad, however, also published other articles, including on the website of the Saudi-run Al Arabiya TV channel, in which he did not disclose his position with DOT (Al Arabiya 2008).

As noted, DOT started with mocking al-Qaeda online as part of LeBaron's strategy. Many of these early videos can be found on DOT's YouTube channel, while shorter versions such as GIFs are uploaded on Vine (https://vine.co /u/1025483311101165568), where there are twenty-two GIFs with ninety-five followers. The videos (loops) have been viewed 1,504,077 times. In general, the GIFs can be regarded as rather immature in their attacks against al-Qaeda and ISIS's leaders. For example, in 2014 DOT posted a Vine video with an Arabic statement referring to the group's leader: "Al Baghdadi is braying from his hole, while ISIS is ending" (Vine 2014). In both conception and execution, many of these GIFs are quite simplistic, and they do not leave a positive impression about the professionalism of the Department of State's digital team. One former CIA agent and counterterrorism expert describes DOT members as sometimes "acting like a social-media punk," lamenting these attempts for "backfiring" (Miller and Higham 2015).

One of the few empirical studies on DOT was conducted by Khatib, Dutton, and Thelwall (2012). The study analyzes thirty discussion threads on nineteen websites discussing Obama's famous 2009 speech in Cairo. The Arab audience mostly discussed the following topics, in relation to DOT's engagement: 26.1 percent U.S. imperialism, 21.7 percent Palestinian suffering, 21.7 percent U.S. downfall, 19.6 percent U.S. support for Israel, 15.2 percent Iraqi suffering. The tone of comments on DOT's posts was predominantly negative, as 50 percent consisted of ridicule and 19.6 percent contained condescending views (Khatib, Dutton, and Thelwall 2012). As for the DOT posts, they revolved around nine key themes, including "challenging perceptions of U.S. foreign policy towards the Middle East" and refuting the notion the United States was at war with the Muslim world. Responses to the DOT posts were also categorized into nine themes, including "posting photos of Usama bin Ladin and other al-Qa'ida figures" or "refuting views on American foreign policy by citing Palestine and Iraq as examples" (Khatib, Dutton, and Thelwall 2012). The majority of audience responses were negative, illustrating the way DOT and its messaging were generally viewed poorly by the Arab public.

In terms of DOT's social media presence, we find that the agency is active on multiple platforms, but that does not mean it is popular. Its Facebook page had 404,182 likes as of August 30, 2016. Based on the figures collected from SocialBakers, we find that the highest number of Facebook followers is from Iraq, followed by Egypt, Morocco, Sudan, and Libya (table 3.1).

Table 3.1
The Geographical Location of DOT's Facebook Page

Countries	Local Fans	Percentage of Fan Base
1. Iraq	81,480	0.502
2. Egypt	16,465	0.101
3. Morocco	9,772	0.06
4. Sudan	5,108	0.031
5. Libya	4,366	0.027
6. USA	4,204	0.026
7. Turkey	4,044	0.025
8. Syria	3,721	0.023
9. Jordan	3,634	0.022
10. Tunisia	3,573	0.022

NOTE: Data retrieved via SocialBakers.

As for DOT's YouTube channel (https://www.youtube.com/channel /UCDtf1c8SvUTENjwtls8_IqA), it was created on November 6, 2007. As of 2016, it had 492 videos, 5,300 subscribers, and 5,262,638 views. This was up from June 10, 2015, when the channel 361 videos, 4,178 subscribers and 4,202,910 views, and from December 8, 2013, when it had 220 uploaded videos, about 1,000 subscribers, and over 2.5 million views. These figures indicate a very slow but steady increase in audience engagement, but again, like its overall social media reach, DOT's YouTube presence was not significant when compared to viral campaigns and other more popular channels on YouTube.

When it comes to Twitter, DOT used to run three official accounts with new content on an almost daily basis (Yon 2016). One of these accounts (@dsdotar) recently got deleted. The other Twitter accounts included @DigitalOutreach, which was created on February 20, 2009. It is the oldest and mostly contains text rather than images or videos like the two other ones. As of November 22, 2019, the account had tweeted 8,961 times and had 16,605 followers. The second account is @DOTArabic, which was created on November 20, 2013, and had 137,505 followers and 25,382 tweets as of November 2019. The final, and most active, of the three accounts was @Dsdotar, which was created in November 2012 and deleted in late 2018. Based on data retrieved from the Wayback Machine, the last capture was on December 2, 2018, at which time the account had tweeted 98,004 times and had 10,320 followers with only forty-five likes. This account was often used "to engage jihadist accounts in Arabic," and it was often assessed as ineffective in countering ISIS's messages and garnering enough followers (Fisher 2015, 13–14; Bouzis 2015, 889). The reason for the massive number of tweets, in comparison to the other two DOT accounts, is that almost every tweet was repeatedly sent about four or five times, a practice that is characteristic of spamming in bot accounts (Al-Rawi, Groshek, and Zhang 2019). This now-deleted Twitter account did not start out as a bot in 2012 and 2013, but it seems the pressure to catch up with ISIS's messaging on Twitter, especially in 2016, led the employees to use bots (see figure 3.1). This supposition was corroborated by Alberto Fernandez, who in 2014 boasted about this account's achievements, stating it had "generated almost 45,000 tweets, often jumping on ISIS hashtags to spoil their day" (Fernandez 2015, 495).

Analysis of the Digital Outreach Twitter account found that for the period from December 19, 2013, to March 16, 2015, the highest percentage of audiences was from Saudi Arabia, followed by the United States, Iraq, Turkey, and the U.K. This reveals that the majority of the account's followers were actually living in the diaspora (see table 3.2). Of the 991 tweets that were sent during the above period, they were retweeted 375 times and received only 268 replies. This clearly shows DOT's weak engagement with Arab online audiences.

In order to better understand DOT's messaging, three social media platforms were examined. First, a content analysis of one of DOT's Twitter accounts, @DigitalOutreach, was conducted, extracting 1,346 tweets and retweets from the period of December 19, 2013, to March 17, 2015 using Crimson Hexagon's online platform. In order to get insight on the way audiences reacted to DOT's tweets, only the 425 replies and mentions were coded. After removing forty irrelevant posts, the results revealed the posts were mostly negative (75.3 percent, n = 290), while far fewer ones were positive (22 percent, n = 85) or neutral (2.5 percent, n = 10). For example, the Twitter user @raif_badawi questioned DOT's message on U.S. policy in the region, writing: "Have we forgotten Guantanamo or Abu Ghraib [prisons]? Have we forgotten how you enslaved a large segment of your society . . . the black people . . . and then you expect we don't know!" Another Twitter user, @Mujtahid_i, responded with irony to DOT's attack against ISIS, tweeting: "Though I hate Daesh [ISIS], my hatred of this team [DOT] will make me love Daesh." Finally, one Twitter user, @raedalhamed, asked DOT members: "Who told you we support these [suicide] bombings? Don't avoid answering my questions, were there bombings before you invaded Iraq?" These are just a few of dozens of other similar examples that clearly show that DOT's mission of changing people's "hearts and minds" is not simple, and the task of countering deep mistrust and misunderstanding is not an easy one.

As for DOT's YouTube channel, data was extracted in December 2013 using a webometric tool (Al-Rawi 2013 and 2015). The collected sample included 4,200 audience comments posted between January 30, 2008, and December 8, 2013. From this data, a random sample of 586 comments was selected. After removing the irrelevant comments (n = 145), the results showed that the comments were, similar to the results of DOT's Twitter, highly negative. In fact, a

@DSDOTAR فريق التواصل · 1 ٢٥o.
بالمناسبة، ماهو عدد أهل السنّة الذين قتلتهم الدواعش بالموصل لحدّ الآن؟   #إصدارات_الخلافة #اخبار_الخلافة #وكالة_اعماق #الدولة_الإسلامية

↩   ↻   ♥   •••

@DSDOTAR فريق التواصل · 1 ٢٥o.
بالمناسبة، ماهو عدد أهل السنّة الذين قتلتهم الدواعش بالموصل لحدّ الآن؟   #اخبار_الخلافة #وكالة_اعماق #إصدارات_الخلافة #الدولة_الإسلامية

↩   ↻   ♥   •••

@DSDOTAR فريق التواصل · 1 ٢٥o.
بالمناسبة، ماهو عدد أهل السنّة الذين قتلتهم الدواعش بالموصل لحدّ الآن؟   #وكالة_اعماق #إصدارات_الخلافة #الدولة_الإسلامية #اخبار_الخلافة

↩   ↻   ♥   •••

@DSDOTAR فريق التواصل · 1 ٢٥o.
بالمناسبة، ماهو عدد أهل السنّة الذين قتلتهم الدواعش بالموصل لحدّ الآن؟   #إصدارات_الخلافة #الدولة_الإسلامية #اخبار_الخلافة #وكالة_اعماق

↩   ↻   ♥   •••

@DSDOTAR فريق التواصل · 1 ٢٥o.
بالمناسبة، ماهو عدد أهل السنّة الذين قتلتهم الدواعش بالموصل لحدّ الآن؟ #الدولة_الإسلامية #اخبار_الخلافة #وكالة_اعماق #إصدارات_الخلافة

↩   ↻   ♥   •••

FIG. 3.1 A screenshot of sample repeated tweets from DOT's bot account, @dsdotar. Screenshots are taken from the Wayback Machine.

Table 3.2
The Geographical Locations of DOT Twitter Followers

1. Saudi Arabia	139
2. United States	60
3. Iraq	59
4. Turkey	27
5. United Kingdom	25
6. South Africa	8
7. United Arab Emirates	7
8. Egypt	5

NOTE: Data retrieved via Crimson Hexagon.

large majority, 70.9 percent, of comments were negative (n = 313), while 29 percent were positive (n = 128), in addition to a few neutral comments. In fact, many YouTubers expressed dissatisfaction with and mistrust toward DOT. For instance, "Lotfi Iskal" asked DOT about one of their videos: "Can you use the sound effect that you added to the video to make another clip that highlights your crimes against Iraqi civilians?" YouTuber "Ala Mohsen" wrote the following: "Look Americans, it's true we're against Al Qaeda, but editing a video to serve an agenda is not a good practice." A third YouTube user, "carl erlington," stated in a comment responding to one of DOT's anti-al-Qaeda videos: "This is a very cheap and bad propaganda."

In relation to DOT's Facebook page, the analysis focused on DOT's messages rather than on reactions posted by the audience. Data was retrieved on July 18, 2013, using another webometric tool called N-Capture (Al-Rawi 2014b). In total, there were 1,976 DOT posts, 6,974 comments by the audience, and 690 responses by DOT (see table 3.3). Eighteen themes were identified using inductive coding, a well-known approach in grounded theory (Corbin and Strauss 1990; Bryman and Burgess 1994). The most prominent posts, grouped by theme, were as follows: praising American people and/or society, 30.4 percent (n = 601); praising and/or defending U.S. foreign policy in the Middle East, 16.4 percent (n = 326); news on U.S. diplomacy engagement with the Middle East, 14 percent (n = 278); U.S. diplomacy and engagement with non-Arab countries, 13.9 percent (n = 276); and critical of al-Qaeda, 7.8 percent (n = 156). Very few of DOT's posts were critical of ISIS because it was not yet a well-known terrorist organization at the time the YouTube data was mined; instead, DOT's emphasis at this time was more focused on al-Qaeda, Bashar Assad (n = 63), Al Nusra Front (n = 23), Hezbollah (n = 5), and Iran (n = 6).

As part of its online political disruption activities, the U.S. Department of State sponsored other anti-terror campaigns. As discussed above, the Center

Table 3.3
DOT Posts on Its Facebook Page

Themes	Freq.
1. Critical of ISIS	13
2. Critical of al-Qaeda	156
3. Critical of Hezbollah	5
4. Critical of Al Nusra Front	23
5. Critical of Bashar Assad	63
6. Critical of Iran	6
7. Critical of Qaddafi	1
8. Critical of non-Islamic terrorism	2
9. Praising and/or defending U.S. foreign policy in Middle East (serving the interest of Arabs)	326
10. Praising Arab and Kurdish people and/or armies	41
11. Praising Islam	53
12. Praising American people and/or society	601
13. DOT promotion	11
14. News on U.S. diplomacy engagement with Middle East	278
15. U.S. diplomacy and engagement with non-Arab countries	276
16. General world events	110
17. Against sectarianism	9
18. Other	2

for Strategic Counterterrorism Communications (CSCC) was established in 2010 in order to enhance the U.S. government's objectives of countering online extremism, especially against al-Qaeda and later ISIS (Suebsaeng 2014). The Global Engagement Center, which works closely with DOT, has been active online on English language platforms. Its English-language video "Welcome to the 'Islamic State' land" became popular in 2014, garnering 897,138 views as of August 31, 2016 (Global Engagement Center 2014).[3] The Arabic version of the same video, however, which is posted by DOT, has not received the same audience attention. Some of the other anti-terrorist online campaigns that were sponsored or supported by the U.S. Department of State included "Think Again Turn Away" and "Sawab" (U.S. Department of State 2015b; Global Engagement Center 2016). The "Think Again Turn Away" campaign was canceled shortly after its launch and was replaced by a new tag line: "Terror Facts." The latter campaign is run by DOT under the supervision of CSCC and the newly formed Information Coordination Cell (Miller and Higham 2015). Rita Katz (2014) describes the "Think Again Turn Away" campaign as a failure because it is "not only ineffective, but also provides jihadists with a stage to voice their arguments."

As for the "Sawab" digital campaign, which targets ISIS and is based in the UAE, Richard Stengel argues it was created because the "coalition does not communicate well internally and externally" (U.S. Department of State 2015a, 1). Given earlier failures, Stengel describes the need to establish a coalition campaign with the following features:

> [It is a] full-time coalition communication hub. This unit of about 20 people (one each from 20 countries, or two each from 10, etc.) would live in the region and do daily and weekly messaging around coalition activities and counter-ISIL. It would produce a daily thematic guidance, similar to the world of the Center for Strategic Counterterrorism Communications/Information Coordination Cell (CSCC/ICC); it would communicate internally to all the partners and liaise with the coalition spokesperson that we hope to put in Baghdad. (U.S. Department of State 2015a, 2)

The second case study focuses on the U.S. government's online political disruption activities in the Middle East in the astroturfing online media campaigns called "Future of Iraq" and "Terrorism Has No Religion."

Astroturfing Campaigns and Online Political Disruption

In this section, we turn to a number of astroturfing online media campaigns which were sponsored by the U.S. government but which took extra measures to conceal the identity of their funders in order to avoid any of the negative association. In Iraq, the "Future of Iraq" (or "Iraq's Future") campaign had a mission to strengthen ties between the different Iraqi ethnic and minority groups, with a special focus on healing divisions between Sunnis and Shiites due to the tensions created after the 2003 war, which culminated in the 2006 civil war that followed the bombing of the Shiite holy shrine in Samara city. The organization's website, which is no longer functional, was created around 2004 and featured the slogan "Future Iraq Assembly One Nation, promising future." The organization produced dozens of video advertisements that called for unity. On its website, accessed through the Wayback Machine, the organization's stated objectives are: "(1) To convince all our fellow Iraqis that we have the will and the capability to progress; (2) To adopt a value system that has at its very heart openness and acceptance of the other; (3) To eradicate pessimism, fear, hesitation, and isolation from our fellow Iraqis' hearts and reinforce trust, initiative, and honest competition for the sake of a future Iraq that is worthy of the sacrifices we've made to regain our right to a decent living." The real impact of these advertisements, which used to be aired repeatedly on various Iraqi channels, remains unclear.

The videos posted by the "Future of Iraq" campaign were mostly well produced, which suggests a high budget and the kind of professional and specialized staff who are mostly lacking in Iraq. In fact, the videos, each of which cost about $1 million to produce, were made by the Los Angeles–based company 900 Frames in collaboration with Lebanon's EFXFilms (Johnson 2006). The real identity of the campaign's funders "decided to remain anonymous" since it could have been "regarded as propaganda in a region already plagued by anti-American sentiment" (Ali 2006). A study involving two focus groups from the Arab world found that the campaign was viewed with suspicion and was largely discredited as Western propaganda (Farwell 2010, 147).

The "Future of Iraq" campaign aired a famous advertisement on the dangers of civil war with the message "not to be a lesson for history" in which scenes of causalities from civil wars and the number of people killed and maimed are shown from various countries including Bosnia, Rwanda, and Lebanon (Future of Iraq 2007). Another advertisement shows an Iraqi man packing a suitcase to go to the hospital to meet his newborn baby as his wife is giving birth, while the other scene shows a terrorist preparing his booby-trapped car to explode it. The two men meet on the street, and we hear an explosion. The ad then concludes with the new father having survived and meeting his wife and their new baby at the hospital. The ad concludes with a message: "When divided, we'll be defeated; when united, we'll defeat it" (Future of Iraq 2009a). Another ad calling for voting during the governorates elections on January 31, 2009, shows U.S. soldiers departing Iraq while Iraqi kids watch them. With music in the background, the kids start playing football while a subtitle reads: "They leave and we stay" and "Freedom is a responsibility, so practice it with awareness" (Future of Iraq 2009b). The message communicated to the Iraqi public is that U.S. forces are leaving soon, so it is better to build the country rather than fight them. In brief, the ads produced for the "Future of Iraq" campaign were meant to increase awareness and convince the public about the importance of unity and peace.

Terror Has No Religion

In and around 2006, Iraq was running an anti-terrorist campaign called "Terror Has No Religion." The video and print advertisements produced for this campaign were aired and published on state-run and pro-Iraqi government media channels like the *Assabah* newspaper and Al-Iraqiya TV, as well as on social media like YouTube. According to the campaign's website, which is no longer functional, the campaign's mission was to combat extremism and terrorism:

> Our Mission is to expose the fallacy of the distorted and politicized Islamic teachings used by ungodly extremists to sanctify and justify terrorism.

It has become crucial to inform the Muslim and Arab people—particularly the Iraqi people—about the deceptions terrorists employ in distorting the peaceful teachings of Islam. These terrorists, who claim to follow the Islamic Faith, are in truth only drowning in an abyss of mistaken beliefs. (Terror Has No Religion 2006)

The main goal of the "Terror Has No Religion" campaign, it appears, was to highlight "extremist ideology that breeds terrorism." According to the campaign's sponsors, "We use Quranic Verses in their true Islamic meaning; free of the distortion committed by the misguided malicious terrorists" (Terror Has No Religion 2006). The motivation for this strategy was to show "the true image of Islam and combat extremist ideology," as well as to "reveal the true and ample doctrines of Islam and expose the contempt these terrorists hold for the spiritual essence of our religion. These terrorists and their ungodly way are the ones responsible for making Islam an easily marked target in the eyes of the world, as well as causing Muslims to be the subject of criticism before the world community" (Al-Rawi 2015, 185).

In the first advertisement released for this campaign, a suicide bomber explodes himself in a busy market. The explosion is rendered in elaborate detail and presented with carefully produced special effects (Terror Has No Religion 2007a). On the campaign's English-language website, the advertisement is described as follows: "Even the word 'War' does not justify attacking secure civilians and turning the streets into a heinous scene that is open for the slaughter of both innocent women and children. The ethics of war—any war— refute this mass elimination, and we have, in the form of the Prophet, a decent example to follow" (Terror Has No Religion 2006). The video, which appears to have been filmed in Morocco, contains graphic violent scenes; after the suicide bomber ignites his bomb in the market, dead bodies are scattered everywhere, including a little boy whose shoe is the only thing left of him in the market after the impact of the explosion. This advertisement seems to be mostly directed against Sunni Salafists who also fought the U.S.-led coalition forces. Another advertisement shows a mysterious and sinister man wearing a black cloak crossing the Iraqi border, suggesting that those carrying out suicide bombings and other terror attacks are not truly Iraqis. As the cloaked man crossed the border, the ad says: "Be alert, people of Iraq. Terrorists trespass our borders to sow the seeds of death in our land" (Terror Has No Religion 2006). The ad then shows the man walking around searching for a suitable target while being watched by other Iraqis with suspicion, indicating to viewers that the presence of any such suspicious people must be reported to the authorities. The man later ignites a bomb in the market, and the lethal consequences of his murderous act are highlighted (Terror Has No Religion 2007b).

Much like the main focus of the "Future of Iraq" campaign, "Terror Has No Religion" appealed for unity among Iraqis. One of the advertisements is entitled "Know Your Enemy" and is described as follows: "For every disease there's a cure. The disease spreading in Iraq plants the seeds of fear, hatred, dissension and terrorism among its people. The cure to this disease is the unity of citizens in the face of those who compromise security, values and life. Know your enemy is a call for a unified front in refusing the criminal practices that endanger Iraqis" (Terror Has No Religion 2006). The advertisement starts with images of children playing soccer and people seemingly living in peace, when suddenly a convoy of cars filled with armed men enters the neighborhood. Everyone starts fleeing as bearded men who look like Sunni insurgents start shooting randomly and beating people. Then an Iraqi man who has the appearance of a tribal sheikh stands alone to confront the armed men. This lone resister is soon joined by other religious clerics who, based on their costumes, appear to come from different sects. Next, a group of ordinary-looking Iraqis join them and hold hands to show unity while someone from the crowd lifts the Iraqi flag from the ground, stressing a unified nationalist spirit. When the armed men see the number of people gathered together, they start to retreat. The advertisement concludes with a series of simple messages such as "Know your enemy," "Terror has no religion," and "Terrorism has no country" (Terror Has No Religion 2007c).

The second advertisement also uses soccer as its theme, aiming to generate positive feelings and associations due to the game's popularity in Iraq and the fact that the Iraqi national football team won the AFC Asian Cup Championship in 2007. The description for the second advertisement reads as follows: "Terrorism feeds on the division of people, wanting to subjugate even the most basic of daily pleasures. The fight against terrorism is all the more potent when people come together in strength and when they refuse to allow sectarianism to divide their ranks" (Terror Has No Religion 2006). The advertisement starts with a subtitle, "In a dark day, terrorism wanted to defeat Iraq," while showing football players from Iraq's national team playing against terrorists wearing outfits similar to the ones worn by the Afghan Mujahideen and by Abu Musab Al-Zarqawi's outfit. In the match, the terrorists use explosive devices, machine guns, and hand grenades; in the end, these deadly weapons are all thrown aside by the soccer players who then win the match. The concluding message reads: "Terror has no country" (Terror Has No Religion 2007d). Yet another advertisement making use of the country's most popular sport features testimonies from famous Iraqi soccer players who recount how there were doubts about their performance during the Asia Cup tournaments, and how they managed to push past the adversity and win through perseverance and unity. The ad, making a clear analogy between teamwork in sports and national unity, hammers home its key message: "We came from all around Iraq united under one dream" (Terror Has No Religion 2007e).

Finally, the most controversial advertisement was related to the theme of kidnapping. On the English-language website, the advertisement is described as follows: "Terrorists are criminals who try to garner political gain by terrorizing people. They function devoid of morals or conscience. They nurture the illusion that they are fighting for a higher cause when in reality they use sectarianism to divide and conquer the Iraqi people" (Terror Has No Religion 2006). The advertisement again starts in a marketplace, showing ordinary Iraqis going about their business in peace when all of a sudden a car speeds into the market, a number of armed men jump out of the vehicle, start shooting randomly, and kidnap a few men. One of the kidnapped men, whose name is Tariq, is taken as a hostage and severely beaten with the butt of a machine gun. One of the masked men, whose face is concealed, starts shouting repeatedly, "Answer me! Are you Sunni or Shiite?" As the kidnapped man struggles to answer, flashback scenes show serene and peaceful images, a stark contrast to the explosion of violence just shown. In the end, Tariq responds, "I am Iraqi," after which he is summarily executed. The ad's final message reads: "Sedition is worse than murder" (Terror Has No Religion 2007f).

All of these advertisements incorporate either verses from the Quran or Prophet Mohammed's sayings urging Muslims to resort to peace and reject violence. The insertion of these Islamic texts is designed to bolster the favorability and credibility of the messages these advertisements are sending to the public. One of the problematic issues about the campaign as a whole, however, was its focus on the Sunni insurgents and terrorists rather than on Shiites in Iraq who were also involved in the insurgency. The reason for this imbalance is probably related to the fact that the majority of attacks against the U.S.-led coalition forces were organized and conducted by Sunni fighters (Baram 2005). This kind of bias plays into and enhances the stereotypes in Iraqi society against the Sunni as a whole, as we will elaborate on shortly.

Since "Terror Has No Religion" has neither an official Facebook page nor a YouTube channel, it is difficult to gauge the overall online reaction toward this campaign.[4] Several commentators, going by usernames such as "sikmadeforreal" and "Khaled891987" stated online that the ads are "definitely" "American production" (YouTube 2007; Iraqi Sumer 2009). Other comments also featured negative reactions to and critiques of the campaign. To take but one characteristic example, user "MoroccanAnwar" commented in English on one of the clips, saying: "fuck this propaganda shit weve [sic] had enough of it from the west. . . ." (YouTube 2008b). Since the campaign seems to target Sunnis more than Shiites, some YouTubers used the clips to bolster the idea that Sunnis are exclusively involved in terrorism. Two YouTubers, for example, uploaded a video from the "Terror Has No Religion" campaign. One of them tagged the video "killing + terrorism = Wahhabi Religion" with a homophobic reference; the clip generated 14,781 views and thirty-five comments (YouTube 2008a), while the other user who posted the video emphasized that terrorists are sectarian (YouTube 2011a). The two videos, both of which attack Wahabis and associate them with Iraqi Sunnis, generated a great deal of inflammatory discussions that are filled with hateful remarks against Sunnis and Shiites. In other words, some of the video clips enflamed sectarian tensions and had negative influences on peoples' perception of each other. After the conclusion of the "Terror Has No Religion" campaign in Iraq, which coincided with the U.S. troop withdrawal from the country in 2011, a new campaign emerged, this time mostly targeting people in Saudi Arabia.

Say No to Terror

The sponsors of the anti-terrorist campaign "Say No to Terror" remain unknown. The campaign produced about seventeen videos posted on YouTube and repeatedly aired on the Saudi-owned pan-Arab MBC and Al-Arabiya TV channels. As the U.S. Army withdrew from Iraq, it seems that interest shifted to Saudi Arabia, whose society is well known to breed many Salafists who adhere to a conservative version of Islam called Wahabism. Most of the Arab fighters who went to Afghanistan in the 1980s, for example, were from Saudi Arabia, as were most of the 9/11 hijackers (Hegghammer 2006). It is important to note that the United States and Saudi Arabia have had a very close relationship, based on mutual interests, for a very long time. First, the United States was directly involved in financing and helping the "Arab Afghans" who came mostly from Saudi Arabia to fight a jihadi war against the Russian invasion of Afghanistan in the 1980s (Scott 2007, 122). Second, the United States on the one hand provides intelligence and protection for Saudi Arabia against external threats such as the danger of Islamist terrorists and Iran. On the other hand, Saudi Arabia, which is the largest oil producer in OPEC, continues providing oil to the United States and other markets, which helps in stabilizing prices (Long 1985; Hart 1998; Pollack 2002). In light of this mutual interest in maintaining the status quo, it's understandable there would be a joint focus on the need to address religious extremism in Saudi Arabia.

With just two exceptions, the videos in this campaign are designed to target Saudi society. This campaign is clearly a continuation of "Terror Has No Religion" because both have the same style and are similar in terms of their anonymous sponsors, video production techniques, print format, religious citations, and key themes and objectives. One of the videos used in the Saudi-focused campaign contains the same messaging found in the previous Iraqi campaign, including phrases such as "Know your enemy" followed by messages like "There's no life where terrorism resides." In this advertisement, a convoy of cars filled with armed men enters a neighborhood and terrorizes it, a very similar example to one of the advertisements described above (Say No to Terror 2010a). Even the text font and editing style are similar. In comparison to the modest production efforts found in the Saudi-sponsored anti-terrorism campaign "Assakina" (2012), the ads in the "Say No to Terror" campaign are far superior in quality.

The campaign's website, which is no longer active, was hosted in Montenegro, likely to conceal its true sponsors due to the anti-American attitudes in Saudi Arabia and elsewhere. The Saudi public, like other Arab populations targeted in this campaign, would not accept messages directly sent by the United States, for several reasons. There is a general mistrust of foreign and Western interventions aimed at changing the hearts and minds of the locals as well as a general anti-American sentiment that is not only confined to Saudi Arabia but stretches to other parts of the Arab and Muslim, mostly due to U.S. foreign policy in the region (Baxter and Akbarzadeh 2012; Esposito and Mogahed 2007, 156).

There were a total of thirteen videos on the website, but three videos were highlighted: "The Remorseful Terrorist," "The Mother," and "The Terrorist Returnee." The first and third videos deal with the problem of Afghan Arab fighters who returned to their homeland in Saudi Arabia but are facing difficulties adapting to normal life after long years of jihad. Each highlighted campaign has at least one video and posters that include the following themes and slogans: "Awakened consciousness," "Open your eyes," "The cry," in which small children are used, "The Clowns," "I'm innocent from your crimes," "Charity," and "There is no life where terrorism resides." Finally, there is the campaign on E-jihad in which a young man is shown being radicalized and recruited to join a militant Islamic group (Say No to Terror 2010c). The main target groups of these advertisements seem to be potential terrorists, their family members, and their close networks like neighbors and friends.

The official Facebook page of "Say No to Terror," which was created in August 2009, has over 2.7 million followers, and its new Arabic name is "Muslims against injustice." In addition, there is also a Twitter page with over 16,000 followers and 1,215 tweets, as of December 2019 (Say No to Terror 2009). The campaign's last activity on these social media outlets appears to have been in November 2017. Interestingly, an initial study conducted by the author in 2012 shows that the campaign's Facebook page did not have any negative comments. This does not seem normal, as some YouTube commentators pointed out. A user called "mimed ilyes" wrote: "Those dogs, when I commented on their [Facebook] page that Al-Qaeda is affiliated to the CIA, they deleted my comment. This campaign is financed [and has an agenda]. America is the sponsor of terror in the world." Since commentary on its YouTube channel is not deactivated, others have been allowed to freely post their views.

On YouTube, the author mined the details on the videos and comments using a webometric tool (Thelwall 2009) on June 26, 2013. The YouTube channel, which was created in August 2010, has seventeen videos with a total duration of 792 seconds. These videos, as of June 26, 2013, have had over 281 comments and 1,348,791 views (Say No to Terror 2010b). Currently, there are thirty-four videos, with the last one uploaded in April 2015. Two particular video clips generated most of the comments. The first video is "The Terrorist Returnee," featuring a handicapped Iraqi man, which garnered 177 comments. This is followed by "The Deviated Terrorist," which racked up eighty comments discussing the video about a Saudi man who realizes that his captors from the Saudi government are as faithful as he is. The 281 comments were posted during the period from August 16, 2010, to June 14, 2013. Among the commentators, ninety-six self-identified their geographic location, and most of those (50 percent, n = 48) were from Saudi Arabia, 15 percent (n = 15) from Egypt, and 10 percent (n = 10) from the United States.

The analysis of these comments showed that 60 percent (n = 170) had a negative tone against the campaign, while 20 percent (n = 57) were positive, and 18 percent (n = 52) were either neutral or irrelevant. One significant feature that characterized the negative comments was anger, mistrust, and even threats posted against the campaign's sponsors. Instead of changing people's views, it seems that the advertisements mostly enhanced or solidified stereotypes about the U.S. government and its allies in the region. Tens of comments included phrases like "Terrorism, I'm Muslim and I'm with it," "Proud to be a terrorist," or "If Jihad is regarded as a form of terror, then I'm a terrorist." Interestingly, despite the carefully concealed identity of the campaign's sponsor, a number of commentators flatly stated that the advertisements were produced and sponsored by the United States. Some YouTubers posted anti-American and anti-Semitic views such as "These [videos] are made by dirty American-Jewish companies," or they are "CIA production," or "Damn to America in whatever it does to convince the world," or "America is the first terrorist." Several others expressed their suspicion about the videos, such as a person with the username "misryeen":

> Warning: The website, the video clips posted on YouTube and Vimeo and other social media outlets including this page do not contain any reference to the sponsors of this campaign or the side that promotes it. Further, there is no information that can be obtained from the Internet which makes the campaign suspicious having in mind the great efforts and size of propaganda which relies on sending negative but implicit messages on Islam.

In conclusion, the main aim of the campaigns "Terror Has No Religion" and "Say No to Terror" is to combat extremism terrorism. The campaigns are sponsored and run by the United States, in coordination with the Saudi and Iraqi governments. In order to raise awareness and attract attention, the advertisements contained shocking images and were professional and seemingly expensive productions. These advertisements were posted on different social media outlets and aired on some of the most popular TV channels in the Arab world, such as Al-Arabiya, MBC, and Abu Dhabi TV, indicating that the sponsors are keen to disseminate the messages to as many people as possible. The campaign has certainly succeeded in achieving a wide audience; however, this does not mean the campaign has been effective, for a number of reasons.

First, while wanting to conceal the identity of the real sponsors is understandable because of the unpopularity of U.S. policies in the region and a desire to avoid appearing to dictate to people what the United States wants them to think, hiding the campaign's real authors may have done more harm than good to its aims. Based on the comments posted below the campaign's YouTube videos, the U.S. role is very obvious to most of the public. And the failure to disclose, and attempt to conceal, the real sponsors seems to negatively affect the credibility of the messages sent because the public starts viewing the messages with suspicion.

Second, some of the messages are problematic, as they seem to dictate to the public basic facts about Islam; sometimes these messages are misunderstood, with people thinking that the campaign associates Islam with terrorism or encourages sectarianism in the society due to its focus on certain groups. Third, the format of the advertisements does not help as the very unsubtle, direct messages look like mere propaganda, making many people defensive especially if some messages challenge their cultural or religious values or are regarded as a foreign intrusion on their core beliefs.

Finally, there is a clear lack of interactivity between the campaign sponsors and public, as illustrated by the Facebook page that does not contain any negative comments. Raising awareness or reaching a wide audience does not necessarily guarantee compliance or effectiveness, since "people are willing to listen to that which collides with or is new to their worlds when those communicating at them change to communicating with them" (Dervin and Foreman-Wernet 2012, 153). Instead of having campaign sponsors communicating with the public, they are communicating at them, making the whole communication process monodirectional rather than multidirectional. Besides, the framing of would-be insurgents as evil terrorists does not leave a lot of space for people on the fence to change their minds, and ultimately obstructs the chance for reasonable and equal debate between the two sides.

The contradictory nature of much U.S. policy in the region also affects the effectiveness of these kinds of campaigns. U.S. cyberoperations in the Middle East are focused on promoting values like freedom and democracy in the region as well as attacking its political adversaries, yet the U.S. government has been actively protecting and defending authoritarian and sectarian regimes in the Gulf region and elsewhere. The main problem is related to actual U.S. policies on the ground that historically favor U.S. economic and political interests in the region while ignoring the concerns of the "Arab Street." Besides, the direct and rather blatant astroturfing advocacy approach followed by the U.S. government cannot be effective because Arab audiences largely view them as American propaganda even if covert operations are practiced. Kruckeberg and Vujnovic (2005) recommend that the U.S. government start viewing the different audiences it targets as active receivers, and begin to take an approach based on "a two-way symmetrical communication and community-building" (296) rather than old-fashioned one-way communication.

4

Russian Trolls, Islam, and the Middle East

•••••••••••••••••••••

This chapter focuses on the nature of disinformation disseminated by Russian trolls (RTs) on social media, examining the ways in which they have microtargeted their diverse audiences with an emphasis on the Middle East and discussion of the issues of Islam and immigration. The chapter looks at the Russian trolls' online political disruption, carried out via strategies such as the microtargeting of different groups. The results of analysis of three main datasets, taken from Facebook, Instagram, and Twitter, show stark differences in the English and Arabic messages. Despite the constant message variations in English, RTs more often connected Muslims and Islam to the Democrats, liberals, and social movements like Black Lives Matter. On the other hand, when conservative and Republican users are targeted, Islam is often treated highly negatively; when American Muslims are targeted, Islam is framed in a positive way. This chapter is situated within the broader discussion of online political disruption and international politics with a particular focus on what I call microtargeted disinformation, which has become an easily accessible political strategy due to the marketing features afforded by social media platforms.

This microtargeted disinformation activity, I argue, is done in a concealed manner and represents a form of vertical online political disruption because the goal is to divide and distract audiences and in some cases to mobilize them as well. Although the use of social media by the Russian trolls gives the impression that it is done in a bottom-up approach, the reality is that it is an international, top-down cyberoperation because the trolls are ultimately paid by the

Kremlin. The study uses three publicly available datasets to analyze the framing of RTs' social media messages and strategies. The theme of Islam has been chosen because it is the dominant religion in the Middle East, and because of the way it has been seen as a wedge issue in the West, often discussed in political debates on immigration and refugees during election campaigns.

Generally, social media sites as well as Google's search engine have facilitated the microtargeting of audiences using certain algorithms to target people with tailored ads based on their own preferences and backgrounds (Manjoo 2017; Hern 2017). Facebook, for example, has 98 data points on each user that assist advertisers in their microtargeting of customers (Dewey 2016). In terms of marketing and digital campaign activities during the 2016 U.S. election cycle, the big tech companies were actively involved in the political process in multiple ways and were even regarded as "active agents in political processes" (Kreiss and Mcgregor 2017). Facebook later announced that Russian operatives linked to the so-called Internet Research Agency (IRA) created thousands of fake accounts and spent $100,000 on ads that were meant to "spread controversial views on topics such as immigration and race and promoted 470 'inauthentic' pages and accounts" prior to and during the 2016 U.S. election (Levin 2017). It is estimated that the total reach of the 80,000 posts sponsored by this Russian agency was in the range of 126 million people on Facebook (Shapiro 2017), and, according to documents released by the U.S. House of Representatives in 2018, RTs purchased 3,519 Facebook ads to which over 11.4 million Americans were exposed. On Twitter, more than 36,000 Russian bot accounts disseminated news on the U.S. election, resulting in 288 million impressions (U.S. House of Representatives 2018a).

As a matter of fact, disinformation activities by RTs were not limited to the United States. For instance, RTs spread messages about the conflict in Syria, periodically linked the White Helmets (WH) with al-Qaeda and ISIS in order to undermine the Nobel Peace Prize–nominated group's efforts and justify the military attacks against them, no doubt in part because WH often documented human rights violations in Syria (Solon 2017). IRA operatives also pretended to be members of the Cyber Caliphate, ISIS's hacking group, targeting U.S. veterans' wives and threatening to kill them as well as hacking the website of the French TV station TV5 Monde. Their aim was to "keep tension at a boil and radical Islam in the headlines" (Associated Press 2018).[1]

As for their main areas of focus, RTs seem especially preoccupied with Muslims and Islam in addition to Black Americans, conservatives, LGBTQ people, Latinos, liberals, and Native Americans (Chan and Dale 2018). Islam, as mentioned, is a vital theme because it is regarded as a wedge issue in the West. According to a number of polls, Islam and Muslims are unfavorably viewed in the United States. The Pew Research Center, for instance, found Muslims are regarded the least favorably among all communities in America, polling worse than atheists, Mormons, and Hindus (2017). Islamophobia, the fear of Muslims, has been a well-documented trend in Western countries for many years, coming to the forefront especially after the events of 9/11 (Welch 2006; Kundnani 2014; Morgan 2016). Islam itself has been racialized in the West by many politicians, policy makers, and media outlets, which further assists in othering Muslims and enhancing Islamophobia (Elver 2012). In the following section, a theoretical discussion is provided on the meaning and spread of various types of disinformation and propaganda through microtargeting and other means.

Microtargeted Disinformation as Online Political Disruption

Since this chapter deals with the spread of disinformation, it is important to begin by making a distinction between two nefarious forms of communication: misinformation and disinformation. There is obvious overlap, similar definitions, and more than occasionally some confusion about their meanings (Ciampaglia 2017), since both types of disseminated information contain some falsehoods. There is, however, one key distinguishing feature (Born and Edgington 2017). With misinformation, those who disseminate it believe it to be true; therefore it is the "inadvertent sharing of false information" (Jackson 2017). Disinformation, in contrast, is known by the disseminator to be false from the beginning; in other words, there is a "deliberate intent to deceive or mislead" (European Commission 2018, 5), and it is often used for "propagandistic purposes" (Lewandowsky et al. 2013, 488). Finally, there is "fake news," a highly politicized and weaponized term of late, which can fall within either of the misinformation and disinformation categories depending on the user's knowledge and intention for spreading it. Unfortunately, social media users have a tendency to spread or share false news far more than true or factual information, probably because of the often-sensational nature of false information (Vosoughi, Roy, and Aral 2018).

Propaganda is another concept connected to disinformation that is important to define and categorize precisely. In general, there are three main types of propaganda: (1) *white*, which is "the open distribution of information regarded as truth," (2) *gray*, which is related to the dissemination of information of "doubtful quality, which systematically avoid identification of the source," and (3) *black*, which contains "lies whose source is concealed, with the aim of embarking upon deception" (Wilke 2008, 3). O'Donnell and Jowett (2012) describe gray propaganda as neither about stating facts nor lies, since "the accuracy of the information is uncertain" and the source is not clearly identified (20). In relation to this study, it is not possible to identify one type of propaganda and apply it to RTs' messages since they have used all three types in their framing of messages on social media. Propaganda, however, according to O'Donnell and Jowett, can also be conceived of and categorized in two other ways: agitative and integrative. Agitative propaganda refers to the intention of rousing "an audience to certain ends and usually resulting in significant change," while integrative propaganda attempts "to render an audience passive, accepting, and nonchallenging" (O'Donnell and Jowett 2012, 17). The RTs' efforts in this case study seem to be largely agitative, with the help of microtargeting and tailored framing of messages. More recently, a number of communication scholars have begun to refer to computer-mediated political persuasion as *computational propaganda*, a trendy term that became increasingly relevant after the 2016 U.S. elections (Howard and Kollanyi 2016; Woolley and Guilbeault 2017). There is no doubt that new computational techniques in propaganda make it easier to microtarget audiences in order to attempt to influence them.

Microtargeting is basically narrowcasting information rather than broadcasting it to wider audiences (Rackaway 2014, 10). It is not a new phenomenon in political communications, having been extensively used in different eras dating back to the nineteenth century. Since the 1960s, microtargeting has developed significantly as voters became the subject of routing targeting by mail based on the location of their residence and on how that might correspond with their previous voting choices (Burton, Miller, and Shea 2010, 125). Microtargeting, it is believed, is primarily used when there is a lack of data on specific voters' affiliations and ideologies (Hersh 2015, 107); it is a campaign tactic most often focusing on swing voters (Johnson 2016, 80). This political marketing technique is not an end in itself but rather a "way to make smarter direct-contact decisions" (Lundry 2012, 163). And it can be a risky strategy, especially if voters realize that contradictory and tailored messages are being sent to them (Fowler, Franz, and Ridout 2016, 143). Microtargeting is most effective when the tactic remains largely unknown to those receiving the political messages.

Microtargeting, there is no doubt, requires a lot of money, effort, and time. Campaign managers, consultants, and officers need to:

> comb public and private documents to create political profiles. They use voter registration files to get party affiliation and to determine whether the voter cast ballots in recent elections. Real estate documents—typically filed in city or county courthouses—show how much a person paid for a home and how much its property taxes may have risen. And private market research information, available for a fee from list brokers and other sources, details what magazines a person gets and what kind of car he or she drives. (Mark 2006, 231)

With the advent of new technologies, microtargeting has greatly evolved in recent years (Schneider 2007; Turow et al. 2012): "Changes in the information environment and lessons from commercial marketing, grassroots mobilization, and direct-mail fundraising have made contemporary microtargeting more precise, efficient, and individualized" (Hillygus and Shields 2008, 155). In the early 2000s, both Republicans and Democrats set up microtargeting platforms (Magleby and Patterson 2006, 180), but the Republicans were ahead of the game, testing their platform in 2003 in preparation for the 2004 U.S. election (Strauss 2012, 182). During the 2008 U.S. election, Barack Obama successfully used microtargeting by, for instance, sending emails asking young people to text "hope" to 62262 (Kenski, Hardy, and Jamieson 2010, 307).

In terms of microtargeting voters based on their religious beliefs, the 2004 U.S. election saw an enhanced use of this strategy (Campbell 2007; Kreiss and Welch 2015, 16), known as the politics of religion (Robbins and Magee 2008). Today, microtargeting has become part of data science as digital analysts and programmers are hired by campaign managers to understand the available demographics. Different methodologies are used, including "predictive modeling, data and text mining, discriminate analysis, discrete choice, neural networks, CHAID, genetic algorithms, and support vector machine analysis, along with regression and factor analysis" (Johnson 2016, 80).

In relation to Russia's IRA, it used highly Islamophobic and anti-Muslim messages in its English-language tweets targeting Australians, for example. The intention was to amplify social and religious divisions by othering Muslims and framing them as terrorists posing a threat to the security of Australia (Karp 2018). In addition, Russian trolls targeted Canadians with various negative messages about Muslims, mostly in relation to immigrants and the travel ban imposed by Donald Trump and the Quebec mosque shooting incident in January 2017 (Rocha and Yates 2019). As a form of online political disruption, the IRA's media campaigns can be understood, I argue, as an extension of Vladimir Putin's ethno-nationalistic policies (Tolz 2017) and media strategy, which tends to use the method of *agitainment*—a combination of agitation and entertainment defined as "ideologically inflected content that, through adapting global media formats to local needs, attempts to appeal to less engaged and even sceptical viewers" (Tolz and Teper 2018, 213). This media strategy emphasizes techniques of othering through division and rage, with foreigners (especially Muslims and immigrants) frequently demeaned and otherwise negatively presented (Tolz and Teper 2018, 217 and 219). This is not just a technique of the RTs. Official Russian channels like Russia and Channel 1 often look more like Western tabloid media outlets instead of neutral public service broadcasters (Tolz 2017, 745). The above discussion can be related back to Waltz's theory of structural realism, since official media outlets as well as social media channels are used as power tools whose ultimate objective is "to apply one's capabilities in an attempt to change someone else's behavior in certain ways" (Waltz 2010, 191). The tailored messages in these various media outlets are directed at different audiences in order to appeal to them and ultimately influence them.

In terms of the general methodological approach followed in this chapter, framing is used in an attempt identify the most recurrent words, phrases, associations or co-occurrences in the social media posts (Xenos 2008; Park et al. 2011, 293). Framing provides insight into the potential impact of messages on people's perception and political attitudes (Cacciatore et al. 2015; Druckman 2004; Hoewe and Bowe 2018). Robert Entman says that frames can be found through the identification of certain keywords, especially those with negative or positive connotations (Entman 1991, 7; Entman 2010), while Neuman et al. (1992) examine framing through identifying words that reference ideas that have implicit or explicit connotations. Since there are large datasets in this study, the computer software QDA Miner–WordStat was used to identify the most recurrent words and phrases, which assisted in providing a better understanding of the predominant frames (Entman 2010; Entman and Stonbely 2018). Other digital methods are used such as creating pivot tables with Excel for the most retweeted posts, offering more insight into the dominant frames. These retweets are longer phrases or sentences, and Entman mentions that the "text contains frames, which are manifested by the presence or absence of certain keywords, stock phrases, stereotyped images, sources of information, and sentences that provide thematically reinforcing clusters of facts or judgments" (Entman 1993, 52).

According to Miller and Riechert, computer programs conducting large-scale quantitative analyses "allow for an enormous array of precise comparisons and statistical tests relating to frame prominence and shifts in frame dominance" (2001, 119). Matthes and Kohring, additionally, stress that such methods can provide objective findings since "words that tend to occur together in texts are identified with the help of cluster algorithms. . . . Frames are not 'found' by the researcher but 'computed' by the computer program" (2008, 261). Indeed, this frame mapping approach "minimizes problems of research judgment" because there is "little argument against allowing frame terms to emerge in the source's own words" (Miller 1997, 376).

As noted earlier, the raw data for this chapter is derived from three public sources. The first dataset analyzes Twitter data provided by the social media platform. In total, 9,806,554 tweets sent by Russian trolls are examined (Twitter 2019). Only the 157,266 tweets that mention "Islam" and "Muslim" and their derivations like "Islamic," "Islamist," and so on are investigated in this study. The tweets were sent in the period from April 9, 2010, to November 2, 2018; in that time frame, March 22, 2016, had the highest number of tweets (n = 4,300) since it coincided with the terrorist attack at Brussel's Zaventem airport (see figure 4.1).

The second dataset is retrieved from Facebook, consisting of the top most-liked posts from five Facebook pages run by RTs as well as the most-liked posts on their Instagram accounts (Digi 2017a and 2017b). Finally, the third dataset consists of over 3,000 RTs' Facebook and Instagram paid ads and their meta-data, which was provided by the Permanent Select Committee on Intelligence

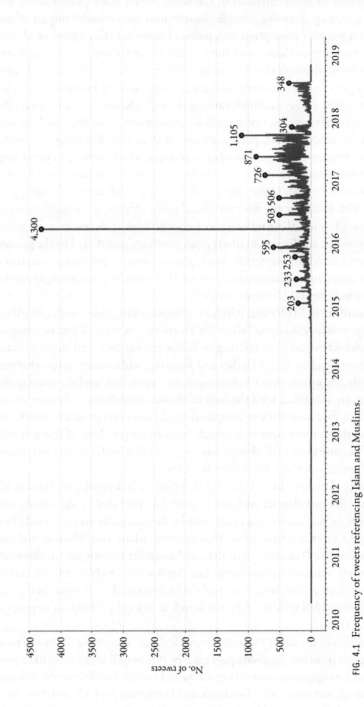

FIG. 4.1 Frequency of tweets referencing Islam and Muslims.

at the U.S. House of Representatives (U.S. House of Representatives 2018a, 2018b, and 2018c). The author then conducted an in-depth qualitative assessment to interpret and elaborate on the nature of the relevant top posts and images on Facebook and Instagram.

Figure 4.2 provides a visual illustration of the top 100 hashtags and their co-occurrences. Here, there are many words that contain negative or pejorative connotations, providing ample evidence on the nature of the framing being employed. Table 4.1 shows the top hashtags. Most of these are highly negative, including the top-ranked recurrent hashtag, #IslamIsTheProblem (n = 22,310), #Stopimportingislam (n = 15,261), #Bansharialaw (n = 14,801), and #BanIslam (n = 13,058). In order to microtarget audiences, some of these negative hashtags are often associated with other ones that are popular among very conservative Republican users in the United States, like #TCOT (Top conservative on Twitter) (n = 3,865) #Wakeupamerica (n = 3,597), #MAGA (Make America Great Again) (n = 1,663), and #Trump (n = 1,457). The following tweet provides an illustration of the way these messages are framed for microtargeting: "#Brussels We may not be at war with Islam, but it sure seems Islam is at war w/us! #TCOT #IslamKills."

This does not mean, however, that only negative frames are used. Other hashtags that express sympathy toward Islam are also found, like #Islamophobia (n = 630), which is used in different contexts to defend Muslims against alleged cases of discrimination and harassment. Again, audiences are microtargeted with the use of sympathetic and/or critical hashtags such as #StopIslamophobia, #racism, or #stupidwhitemen, or broader messages like "RT @JackTheFact29: #ThingsNotTaughtAtSchool Internet safety LGBT history Popular culture Mental health Sexism Anti-Semitism Islamophobia." Here and elsewhere, Muslims are framed as vulnerable, marginalized, or underrepresented communities and groups, as can also be seen in the following tweet: "My Cousin Is a Muslim: Black Families Against Islamophobia."

These positive associations can be found when investigating the Arabic-language tweets posted by Russian trolls. By including a more recent RT dataset provided by Twitter, I extracted a total of 37,537 tweets written in Arabic from a total of 9,806,554 tweets. Due no doubt to the geostrategic interests of Russia, we find that the majority of the tweets deal with the conflict in Syria. In fact, we know, based on the geographic location of users, that over 87 percent of them were located in different Syrian cities to give the false impression that they lived in this Arab country. Though the raw data is not available, in 2018 Facebook removed several public pages that were run by Russian military intelligence services to spread disinformation with a focus on Syria and Ukraine. These cyberoperations involved, for instance, supporting the Inside Syria Media Center, a propaganda media organization whose objective is to disseminate favorable news reports on Syria and Russia (Facebook Newsroom 2018b).

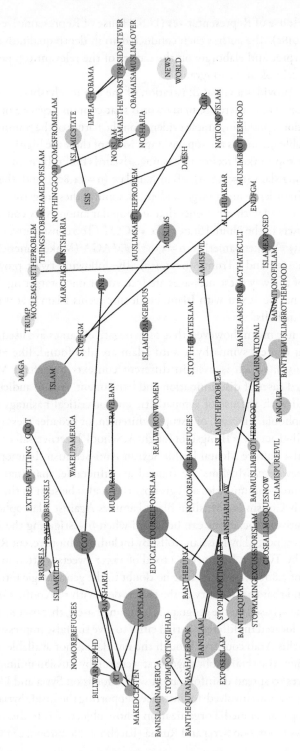

FIG. 4.2 The top 100 most recurrent hashtags visualization and their co-occurrences.

Table 4.1
Top Twenty Most-Used Hashtags

No.	Hashtag	Frequency
1.	#Islamistheproblem	22,310
2.	#Stopimportingislam	15,261
3.	#Bansharialaw	14,801
4.	#Banislam	13,058
5.	#Stopislam	11,481
6.	#Islam	11,275
7.	#Educateyourselfonislam	8,299
8.	#Banthequran	7,000
9.	#Stopmakingexcusesforislam	6,856
10.	#Bancairnational	5,812
11.	#Islamisevil	4,760
12.	#ISIS	4,746
13.	#Closeallmosquesnow	4,716
14.	#Bantheburka	4,463
15.	#News	4,051
16.	#Islamkills	4,045
17.	#TCOT	3,865
18.	#Banthequranasahatebook	3,622
19.	#Wakeupamerica	3,597
20.	#Banislaminamerica	3,309

In terms of references to Islam and refugees, we find that the tweets are overwhelmingly positive or neutral. The second-most retweeted post reads: "RT @a1one1a: Discover #Islam. More than 100 languages لغة ١٠٠ من أكثر "الإسلام اكتشف" #Instagram #iPhone #travel #life http://t.co/WcmXj." This is meant to show that the user is interested in promoting Islamic people and nations. Another tweet states, "Terrorism kills in the name of religion, but Islam has only been a religion of love and forgiveness, and countries should collaborate to eliminate [terrorism]," while a third tweet reads, "(Muslims are not terrorists) #ارهابيين_ليسوا_المسلمين https://t.co/Tsr8D6e9Lw." While offering kind words for Muslims and Islam, Russian trolls were critical of Saudi Arabia, Daesh (ISIS), and the Nusra Front due to the opposition of these groups to the Assad regime, which the Russian government vigorously protected and promoted through its conventional media outlets as well. Arabic-language messages disseminated by those Russian trolls are oftentimes retweets of news reports originally produced by the Russian channel RT Arabic.

Islam is generally described in negative terms in the English-language messages, including sometimes when the frame being used is seemingly positive. The hashtag #ReligionOfPeace (n = 589), for example, has almost exclusively been used in an ironic way to attack Islam and its practices, especially when there is a reference to terrorism. Take one Twitter user's message following the Brussels terrorist attacks: "Are we done with the #ReligionOfPeace bullshit yet? #IslamKills #islam #Brussels." Another RT on Twitter wrote: "Muslims believe that America is a muslim area and it's not #TCOT #BanIslam #ReligionOf-Peace." In some cases, the hashtag was insultingly altered to #ReligionOfPeace-myAss (n = 1,174) and #ReligionOfHate (n = 688).

In order to provide a closer look at what the data reveals, the most recurrent phrases (between two and seven words) are also examined. Once again the majority of phrases are negative in nature, meant to demean the religion of Islam and associate it with terrorism. One of the most recurrent phrases is "Islamic State" or ISIS (n = 4,986), while a combination of hashtags is used to spread tweets as broadly as possible to select audiences. Another recurrent phrase is "refugees are terrorists" (n = 279) and "refugees are ISIS" (n = 153), a highly negative frame that is most frequently associated with the word "Syrians." For instance, one user says: "Syrian refugees are terrorists. If not, then most likely you're retarded #IslamKills #StopIslam," while another one states: "#StopIslam If you don't think all Syrian refugees are terrorists you are part of the problem. #IslamKills." And, once again, we find that the phrase "Religion of Peace" (n = 671) is mostly used in an ironic way to negatively frame and demean Islam.

To further examine the discourses on immigrants by RTs, I extracted tweets referencing the following words: "immigration," "refugees," "immigrants," and "asylum seekers"; duplicates were removed. A total of 47,803 tweets were retrieved (see figure 4.3). The textual analysis shows that the RTs predominately represented immigrants in a highly negative manner, calling for banning them, restricting their access to Western countries, and mostly connecting them to Muslims and the threat of terrorism. The RTs primarily promoted "us versus them" narratives. These kind of othering strategies tacitly tap into the existing "affective network" (Siapera et al. 2018) of White, nationalistic, male-dominated, alt-right, and pro-Trump campaign actors. The RTs, I argue, have a vested interest in fueling uncertainty and a politics of division in the West through the constant "reproduction of othering" of refugees as a threat. This is a central feature of their online political disruption activity. Indeed, these online tactics are an extension of Vladimir Putin's political strategy and media policy inside Russia, which emphasizes ethno-nationalistic policies (Tolz 2017). Foreigners, especially Muslims and immigrants, are periodically attacked and framed negatively in Russian media (Tolz and Teper, 2018, 217 and 219). For instance, fake news was broadcast by the Russia One television channel about a Russian girl being raped by migrants. The false story was used as an excuse for organizing an anti-Islam rally in Germany by the Patriotic Europeans Against the Islamisation of the West (Pegida), who were collaborating with a Kremlin-supported Russian diasporic group (Dobrokhotov 2017). RTs also

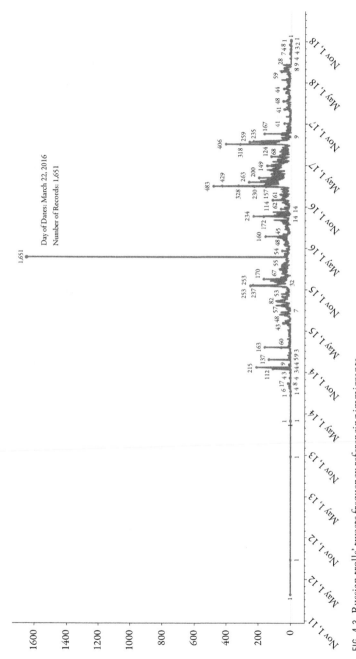

FIG. 4.3 Russian trolls' tweets frequency referencing immigrants.

supported far-right groups in Canada by disseminating fake news about Canadian Muslims in relation to the 2017 attack on a Quebec mosque (Al-Rawi and Jiwani 2019). Finally, by examining the top ten hashtags that reference the above four words (see figure 4.4), we once again find highly negative hashtags associated with them, similar to the results presented in table 4.1.

To sum up, the analysis of the Twitter data indicates that the predominant English-language messages from the RTs employ a negative framing of Islam, Muslims, and refugees, although there are a few messages, particularly those written in Arabic, that express sympathy or support for Islam. Arabic tweets do not contain negative references to Islam, Muslims, and refugees, but they convey political messages that are aligned with Russia's geopolitical interests in the Middle East region especially in relation to supporting Assad's regime in Syria.

The strategy followed by Russian trolls shows that audiences are microtargeted by hashtags associated with diverse ideological and ethnic groups, with specific messages tailored to fit their respective backgrounds and biases.

As for the Facebook data, all the top 500 posts from the United Muslims of America Facebook page (https://www.facebook.com/United-Muslims-of -America) showed deep sympathy toward and support for Islam against any negative accusations and associations. The page, which had a total of 71.4 million shares and 2.13 million interactions (Digi, 2017a), made use of the name of a similar U.S.-based Islamic organization to conceal the identity of its true sponsors and organizers (Collins, Poulsen, and Ackerman 2017), who bought about eighty-six ads that promoted the positive role and nature of Islam. The page was linked to the Instagram account @muslim_voice, and the two platforms were used to disseminate the same messages, some of which were written in Arabic in order to target different audiences including Arabs living in the diaspora.

The qualitative assessment of the most-liked Facebook messages show that they all framed Islam positively, often using Arabic to target diasporic communities. For instance, the most-liked post (n = 150,200) deals with a social experiment about a Muslim-looking man who is allegedly harassed in New York City (table 4.2). The post, which is made by a famous YouTuber, is intended to agitate users who are actively engaged with the issue of Islam. The second post is also taken from a popular Facebook user, and deals with accepting Muslim women's veils. Some of the top posts, however, also include controversial messages that are ambivalent in nature, such as the following one that received 35,275 likes: "Share if you believe Muslims have nothing to do with 9/11. Let's see how many people know the truth!" As noted, the page was created to sway the public and possibly agitate them, while the real identity of its organizers, who pretended to be Muslims running an Islamic association, was carefully concealed. The eighth most-liked post states the following: "SHARE IF YOU

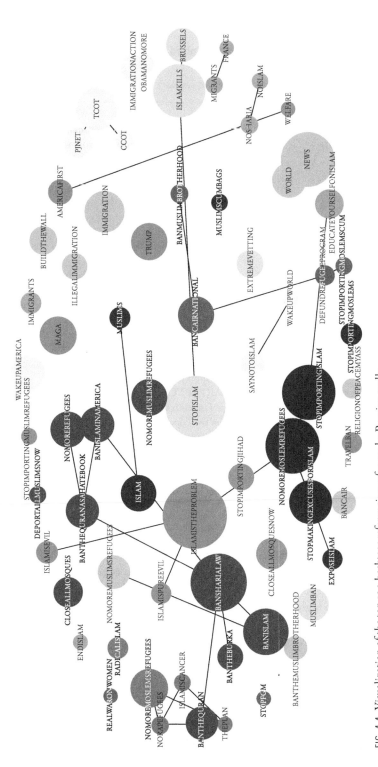

FIG. 4.4 Visualization of the top 100 hashtags referencing refugees by Russian trolls.

Table 4.2

The Top Ten Most-Liked Posts on the United Muslims of America Facebook Page

No.	Date	No. likes	Post
1.	12 June 2016	150,200	New York city Muslim Harassment Social Experiment!!! watch and subscribe on youtube
2.	7 Feb. 2016	133,500	I think God has ordered all mankind with modesty, so what is your problem with the Islamic veil (Hijab)????
3.	25 Aug. 2016	80,066	What Halal meat or Halal food means? You shouldn't be scared after watching this video;)
4.	29 June 2016	79,918	Because the media wants you to know ONLY when a tragedy happens in a non-Muslim country and calls it a 'terrorist attack' [on Istanbul Airport terrorist attack]
5.	11 Sept. 2016	35,275	Share if you believe Muslims have nothing to do with 9/11. Let's see how many people know the truth!
6.	7 Feb. 2017	22,340	But you won't see that on FoxNews, Share and tell everyone! [news on Muslim Americans opening a free health clinic in Florida]
7.	8 Feb. 2017	22,156	Praying JamaAa, #Manhattan #NewYork, MashaAlah! Share and show the world! [image of Muslims praying in groups]
8.	18 Oct. 2016	19,368	SHARE IF YOU RESPECT HER TOO.
9.	2 Aug. 2016	13,453	Pope Francis is telling some truth. Watch and share. [on the Pope defending Islam from terrorism accusations]
10.	3 Oct. 2016	13,011	ISIS ARE NOT MUSLIMS, AND MUSLIMS ARE NOT ISIS!

NOTE: The majority of the posts are accompanied by links and images. Explanations are added in brackets.

RESPECT HER TOO" (n = 19,368), and it deals with an American Muslim woman wearing the U.S. flag as her head veil, which is meant to frame Islam positively by associating it with U.S. nationalism and social integration.

Aside from highlighting the positive aspects of Islam, the page is critical of Donald Trump and repeatedly praises Hillary Clinton by encouraging Muslims to vote for her. This is similar to the findings on the Twitter data, in which there is a frequent association between Muslims and liberals as well as Democrats. One of the popular posts, from January 26, 2016, reads: "Hillary Clinton Slams Donald Trump's Anti-Muslim Rhetoric as 'Shameful, Offensive, Dangerous' (SHARE)" (likes = 4,351), while one posted on April 3, 2017, reads: "MR #TRUMP, SORRY YOU CANNOT BAN #MUSLIMS" (likes = 2,775). The Facebook page organizers even paid for an ad showing Clinton shaking hands with the 2011 Yemeni Nobel Peace Prize winner, Tawakkol Karman, to be posted six times. The ad is meant to frame Clinton as a savior of, or advocate for, American Muslim voters. Based on its description, the microtargeted audiences should be people aged 16–53 who know English (U.S. or U.K.) and/or Arabic and who live in Washington, D.C. The matching interests listed are Islam, Muslim world, Islamism, Muslims Are Not Terrorists, ProductiveMuslim, Hillary Clinton, or Muslim Brotherhood (U.S. House of Representatives 2018b).

Based on a qualitative examination of the available data, references to Islam and Muslims are framed as exclusively positive on the RTs' other Facebook pages, like those showing affiliation with Black Americans and the LGBTQ community. For instance, the Blacktivist Facebook page posted the following message on June 17, 2016: "America will not be destroyed by Muslims, undocumented workers, Blacks, Mexicans or Latinos. But rather by uncontrolled hatred, unethical politicians, misinformation" (Likes = 31,658), while the LGBTUN Facebook page posted the following on June 2, 2017: "It always amazes me how some people claim that bashing Christians is wrong, but it's totally OK bashing gays, Sikhs, Muslims, atheists" (Likes = 1,108).[2] All of these messages frame Muslims in a positive light and highlight the importance of showing sympathy toward them.

In sharp contrast, Facebook pages run by RTs that target Republicans and conservative audiences, including Secure Borders, Being Patriotic, Stop A.I. (All Invaders), and Heart of Texas, contain highly pejorative frames against Islam and Muslims, as illustrated by the negative paid ads run by these pages (U.S. House of Representatives 2018b and 2018c). There isn't enough space to include them all here, but a couple of ads should suffice to paint the picture. The Heart of Texas page, for example, paid for an ad that reads as follows: "The police report that the Black Lives Matter terrorist sniper Micah Johnson used buildings owned by Muslim Arabs to carry out his attack. If you think it was just a coincidence, you make a mistake. . . . Muslims seem to be not peace-loving as they say. And I don't want to see 10,000 potential terrorists here in Texas" (July 14, 2016). In this example Muslims are once again associated with Black Americans, but only to frame them negatively and to suggest that the two communities are involved in violence and chaos. The Being Patriotic Facebook page ran an ad on June 8, 2015, which read: "America should wake up before it's too late. Have you forgotten the fires burning in Europe because of very bad progressive ideas? It's always a bad idea to bring people with radical beliefs into the country. Muslims don't want to be friends with us, they should be deported back to their 7th century countries." All these paid ads on Facebook pages targeting right-wing audiences, especially those posted by the Stop A.I. page, framed Muslims negatively and contained many hateful and xenophobic messages. On these pages, former President Barack Obama, for example, was often

FIG. 4.5 A Facebook page paid ad on Stop A.I (All Invaders) showing Barack Obama as a Muslim leader. The paid ad was used twice on May 5, 2015. One ad targeted audiences in the United States, the other in the Netherlands.

labeled as a Muslim in order to demean him (Howard et al. 2018, 33) by associating him with foreignness and by implication with Islamist-inspired terrorism (figure 4.5). Overall, racist and highly divisive posts characterize the kind of messages sent by RTs during key election periods (Popken 2017a and 2017b).

On Instagram, RTs' materials have not yet been fully removed, as they continue to freely spread. This is true of the Heart of Texas group's Instagram account (Michel 2017a and 2017b), as well as many posts by @muslim_voice. This account, as noted earlier, is connected to the Facebook page of the United Muslims of America. They often use the same hashtag, #UnitedMuslimsofAmerica, and describe themselves as follows: "This is the community which unites all the muslims who live in the US." As with other cyberoperations by RTs, the account's name is also used by many other Muslim groups and individuals, and it appears to have been chose to help conceal the true identity of its sponsors and organizers. In relation to the observed message patterns, RTs once more connect Muslims with liberals, the LGBTQ community, and Black Americans. One popular post, for instance, on the RTs' Born Liberal Instagram account, reads as follows (Digi 2017b): "Labels are for clothes only. We are all 100% human. It's easy to blame Muslims for terror, gays for moral degradation, and blacks for rising crime rates. But it's much harder to accept the fact we are all the part of a problem, no matter what religion or skin color we have" (Likes = 977).[3] Here, Muslims and Islam are framed positively since the messages are tailored to fit with the targeted audiences' background. To sum up,

Russian trolls use religious disinformation as a wedge issue in order to further divide audiences who were targeted based on their race, ethnic backgrounds, and ideological views. As part of RTs' agitative propaganda efforts, carefully designed frames are disseminated to audiences to further enhance divisions among them. All of this has been facilitated by the increasingly sophisticated microtargeting features offered by different social media platforms.

To conclude, this chapter has dealt with the microtargeting of disinformation by Russian trolls with a focus on the way Islam and Muslims are framed. The findings reveal that RTs have been systematic in their framing of messages to microtargeted audiences on social media, who are largely categorized into two main camps. On the one hand, the Democrats and liberals are mostly connected to Muslims, Black Americans, LGBTQ community, Latinos, and refugees. On the other hand, the Republicans and conservatives are associated with White Christians, nationalists, populists, and people holding anti-Islam and anti-immigration stances. Based on a report released by Tech for Campaigns, the money spent by RTs on Facebook ads was mostly focused on targeting conservatives, followed by Black Americans, Muslims, Latinos, LGBT, liberals, and Native Americans (Chan and Dale 2018). Depending on the targeted camps, tailored frames are chosen to fit certain audiences' information preferences, while Islam is used as a divisive issue to further segregate and divide audiences. In their agitative propaganda efforts, concealed disinformation is employed through the spreading of false news, half facts, and sensational stories to move and influence audiences. The results also show that the majority of tweets are framed negatively toward Islam, while audiences are microtargeted with the use of certain hashtags and mentions.

RTs' disinformation is made more effective because it is carried out by meticulously concealing the identity of the senders in order to give the impression that the different social media posts are written and disseminated by ordinary individuals and/or grassroots organizations and associations. Mejias and Vokuev rightly observe that "information spread by governments or corporations can be skeptically dismissed," whereas "information produced and shared by regular users (or what are perceived to be regular users) acquires authenticity," possibly generating more "attention, popularity and visibility" (2017, 1029). Jessie Daniels (2009), furthermore, believes that one of the other goals of concealing such disinformation efforts is to evade deletion, calling such platforms "cloaked websites" which are often run by far-right hate groups and are popular on social media outlets like Facebook (Farkas, Schou and Neumayer 2017). RTs have indeed been very careful in their astroturfing activities, hiding their true identities for all of the above reasons. One Russian military guidebook on disinformation lists several ways to wage an information war, including spreading lies to foreign audiences, using ambiguous terms, stories, and words that can only confuse people, and disseminating negative news "which is more readily accepted by the audience than positive" (as cited in Giles 2016, 47–48).

In brief, the general objectives behind the Russians' troll factory and tailored messages on social media are to agitate diverse users, spread disinformation to confuse audiences, and enhance divisions among them. Unlike the conventional wisdom that RTs only supported Trump during the 2016 election, this chapter shows that its strategy was actually more complicated, aiming primarily to sow divisions by appealing to diverse audiences that are sometimes critical of Trump as part of online political disruption activities. All of these objectives have become more attainable due to the way concealed and astroturfing messages can spread virally online and the microtargeting features provided by social media platforms. Ben O'Loughlin argues that the overall intention behind Russia's information strategy is to "destabilize . . . audiences' sense of certainty about what is happening in world affairs . . . undermin[ing] the very fundamentals of information and credibility that informed debate are supposed to rest upon" (O'Loughlin 2015, 169). If that is the case, it's hard to argue Russia has not at least partially accomplished its mission.

5

Cyberwars and
Regional Politics

● ● ● ● ● ● ● ● ● ● ● ● ● ● ● ● ● ● ● ●

Regional political tensions are considered one of the driving forces behind hacking and other cyberoperations understood as situated within the horizontal form of online political disruption. This chapter discusses one case study centered around the 2017 Qatari crisis, which led to political tension and retaliation between Qatar and a few other Arab states.[1] The political tensions in the Middle East, it is important to understand, are not only the result of global conflicts and geostrategic competition but are also caused by regional political rivalries and tensions. Before looking at the specific case study on Qatar, it is important to sketch the contours of the wider and ongoing cyberwar in the region, which includes the online dimension of the Arab-Israeli conflict that has motivated hackers from Israel, the rest of the Middle East, as well as from outside the region to attack each other and the various state and nonstate actors involved. In addition to background on the Arab-Israeli conflict, what follows is an outline of some of the other cyberattacks that have been made in connection to other regional issues such as the ongoing sectarian tensions in the Middle East.

Just two months after the start of the second Palestinian Intifada, which began in September 2000, the Pakistan Hackerz Club attacked the website of the Israeli lobbying group AIPAC. Around the same time, UNITY, a British website that is part of ummah.net, attacked several Israeli online sites. Meanwhile, presumably due to the work of Israeli hackers, visitors to Hamas-affiliated websites were diverted to porn websites (Siapera 2012, 113). It is not clear whether these hacking groups were cyberwarriors—that is to say, groups affiliated with governments. If they were, these acts would be categorized as a horizontal form of online political disruption with the purpose of sending a political message through disturbance, interference, and intervention, as was discussed in chapter 1.

When the Israeli war with Lebanon erupted in 2006, online attacks went hand in hand with offline military operations. As one close observer put it, "Malware, DDoS attacks and general hacking defacements of websites—both official and civil—by both sides has been a growing and important feature of the struggle" (Richards 2014, 32). These attacks continued from different parts of the world, especially from Iran. On July 10, 2009, the Israel Defense Forces (IDF) declared that Iran and Israel were actually in a state of cyberwar due to the increasing number of cyberattacks between the two countries (Benham et al. 2012, 88). In January 2016, a Saudi man calling himself "xOmar" hacked the websites of the Israeli El Al airline and Stock Exchange and claimed to have released the credit card details of 200 Israelis (Alarabiya 2016). That hacking incident was widely seen by social media users as a victory for Saudi Arabia as a whole, although the hacker appeared to have been acting independently in a form of bottom-up online political disruption.

Later, when Israel attacked Gaza and killed Palestinian civilians in November 2012, it prompted the global hacktivist group Anonymous to launch "OpIsrael" DDoS attacks as part of its international bottom-up online political disruption. The operation by Anonymous resulted in the deletion of the database of the Israeli Ministry of Foreign Affairs and Bank of Jerusalem as well as the taking down of about 663 Israeli websites (Greenberg 2012; Sutter 2012). OpIsrael was relaunched by Anonymous in 2013 and again in 2014 following subsequent Israeli military attacks in Palestinian territories (RT 2013; Becker 2014). There are, furthermore, dozens of additional hacking groups that are actively trying to attack Israeli websites and other official targets such as embassies and diplomats. There was, for example, the case of Gaza Team Cybergang, which often used spearphishing techniques (Huffpost Arabi 2017h), as well as the case of the Saudi-led Nightmare group that hacked the Israeli stock market and El Al airline's websites in January 2012 (Knell 2012). Indeed, the cyberconflict between pro-Israeli and pro-Palestinian hackers has never stopped. It is an ongoing cyberconflict directly linked to the region's geopolitical developments. In 2016, the Israeli Knesset discussed a bill aimed at prohibiting the Islamic call for prayers with loudspeakers. In retaliation, pro-Palestinian hackers managed to take over control of two Israeli national TV channels and then the call for prayers while showing images of Islamic holy sites as well as Israeli wildfires that had occurred in the same year (Moore 2016).

It is widely believed that Anonymous has many members from the Arab world. When the organization launched its #OpIsrael attack in November 2012, as mentioned, it managed to hack about 600 Israeli sites, releasing personal information that belonged to high-ranking Israeli officials (The Wire 2013). In a newspaper interview, an Algerian member of Anonymous revealed a combination of nationalistic and religious motives for the attack on Israeli websites. The hacker claimed that their mission was to "wipe Israel from the map of cyberspace" and that "details of over 20,000 Facebook and 5,000 Twitter accounts and about 30,000 Israeli Bank accounts were released to the public" as part of the #OpIsrael operation (Budihan 2013).

On another cyber front, as a reaction to the ongoing cyberattacks against Iran, several cyberoperations were carried out by Iranian hackers targeting neighboring countries, especially those regarded as allies of the West. These acts are obviously conducted by state-affiliated hackers or cyberwarriors; hence, they can be categorized as horizontal online political disruption operations. For example, Iranian hacking groups like Shahin and the Cutting Sword of Justice claimed responsibility for cyberattacks on Saudi Arabia and Qatar in 2012 (Baldor 2012). As part of these attacks, the website of Aramco, a Saudi oil company, was hacked, with the hackers managing to destroy about 35,000 computers. Around the same time, they also attacked the Qatari website of RasGas (Goldman 2012) by using malware called Shamoon and by unleashing several digital bombs in many targets. The malware leaves the image of a burning American flag before the computer becomes inoperable (Greenberg 2017), leaving no doubt as to the political as well as economic motives behind the attack: a clear shot against the close alliance between the United States and both Qatar and Saudi Arabia and the presence of U.S. forces in those two Persian Gulf states. Iranian hackers also targeted official websites in many Arab Gulf countries, with a particular focus on Saudi Arabia in December 2016 and 2017, with Shamoon 2.0 malware (Riley 2016; alkhalisi 2017, Huffpost Arabi 2017a, 2017b; Perlroth and Krauss 2018). These actions prompted the Saudi government to enhance cybersecurity measures in the kingdom. The CEO of CISCO in Saudi Arabia even announced a $100,000 award for anyone who could provide security analysis on the Shamoon 2.0 virus, causing over 100 security experts and hackers to contact the company in less than 24 hours (Alanizi 2017). In 2016, another wave of cyberattacks in the Middle East was orchestrated by Iranian hackers using Shamoon 2.0 malware. These attacks destroyed thousands of computers, overwriting their drives with the photo of Aylan Kurdi, the 3-year-old Syrian refugee who tragically drowned in the Mediterranean (Greenberg 2017). The goal of the hacking attempt was to convey the message that some Arab Gulf countries like Saudi Arabia and Qatar, which provide military and financial support for Syrian rebels, are implicated in the killing and deaths of Syrian children fleeing the country.

After the 2016 execution of Nimr Al-Nimr, a Shiite preacher, by the Saudi authorities, several hacking attempts were made against targets located in the

Sunni monarchies of the Persian Gulf. These acts, motivated by religious ideology, can be classified as bottom-up political disruption. The Yemen Cyber
Army (https://www.facebook.com/yemencyberarmy/), for example, hacked
the Saudi Ministry of Foreign Affairs and leaked thousands of confidential diplomatic cables, which were published by WikiLeaks. This attack was in retaliation for the U.S.-led Al Hazm Storm military operation; the hacking group
used the hashtag #CyberDecisiveStorm and referred to their actions as "cyber
jihad" (https://twitter.com/YemeniCyberArmy). Team322, in addition, hacked
the website of the Qatari Ministry of Defense as a response to the execution of
Al-Nimr (Alsumaria 2016). And, in December 2015, other Shiite activists and
hackers from Lebanon and Bahrain hacked the website of the Saudi Al Arabiya
TV channel's website, posting a message that denounced the Saudi regime and
defended Al-Nimr (Antar 2016).

Cyberoperations have been waged on both sides of this bitter rivalry in the
Middle East. Saudi hackers, such as the Hazm Electronic Storm, who appear
to be affiliated with and/or supported by the Saudi government, conducted
hacking attacks on Iranian targets, including one on the Iranian Statistics
Department. This prompted some Iranian media outlets to claim that the tension between Saudi Arabia and Iran had become tantamount to a cyberwar
(Huffpost Arabi 2016). The sectarian dimension to these attacks is unmistak-
able. The term *Hazm* (decisive) refers to a Saudi-led military attack against the
Yemeni Shiite Houthi rebels who are supported by Iran. These horizontal
online political disruption acts were accompanied by other bottom-up activities. For example, the February 2013 hacking of the website of former Shiite
Prime Minister of Iraq, Nouri Al-Maliki, in which messages praising Iraqi
Sunni protesters were posted, clearly illustrates the highly sectarian dimension
to this cyberwar (Al Jazeera 2013). Maliki's website was defaced and hacked by
a group calling themselves "Team Kuwait Hackers," who posted messages comparing Maliki to Syria's Assad because of the Iraqi government's support for
Assad's regime and attacks against Sunni protesters. The statement hackers
posted on Maliki's website was not subtle: "You want to be like Bashar Assad . . .
Bashar is over" (Associated Press 2013). Having shared some practical examples
of the cyber fault lines in the Middle East, we now turn to a discussion of the
theoretical framework for understanding these cyberoperations.

As discussed in chapter 1, Kenneth Waltz's theory of structural realism and
power is useful for explaining international relations; power or its appearance
here serves to maintain the state's independence, give broader ranges of actions,
offer more safety and security, and provide the more powerful a bigger stake in
the political system. This is applicable in the context of hacking and regional
politics because nation-states' affiliated hackers and their cyberwarriors use
cyberoperations and their perceived impact to achieve many of these goals and
functions. They sometimes function as a deterrent or warning against future

cyberattacks by opponent states or they can be an exercise of technological power, projecting a public impression that the nation-state is superiorly equipped and has the upper hand. Cyberoperations as projections of power can also serve as tools of public diplomacy, positively influencing the nationalistic attitudes of nation-states' citizens and their trust in their state's image and capabilities. The following section will empirically examine the meaning of "electronic flies" by examining Arabic-language data taken from news sources and social media.

Electronic Flies and Regional Conflict

Using Netlytic, I collected 535,691 tweets posted by 157,980 unique users that referenced "electronic flies" in Arabic using two key terms, الذباب الالكتروني (flies) and التشبيح الالكتروني (ghosting). The data collection spanned one year, from July 13, 2018 to July 25, 2019. Based on the locations of users, self-identified by country, the highest number of Twitter users in this dataset are from Qatar and Saudi Arabia, followed by other countries like Kuwait, Oman, and the UAE. The greatest number of tweets (n = 7,840) were sent on October 19, 2018 (see figure 5.1), discussing the consequences of Jamal Khashoggi's murder and the decision to remove Saud al-Qahtani from his position.

The term *electronic flies*, interestingly, is not only used to refer to state-run trolls but also to fake accounts or sockpuppets that pretend to be on one side but are in reality supportive of the other side through the creation and use of fake social media accounts (Klotz 2007). For example, the most retweeted post (n = 655) on October 19, 2018, was from the currently suspended Twitter user @jassemalatiah who pretended to be a Qatari citizen expressing concern about the GCC blockade against Qatar. The same user, however, responded to himself saying that the situation is only getting worse. Attaching the screenshot of this error, one Qatari user posted this ironic message: "To the brothers in charge of the electronic flies operational room in Saudi Arabia and the UAE. You can find below one of your flies who forgot to change his fake accounts when he responded to himself. Please follow the required procedure and deduct the amount of money that is assigned to him https://t.co/RFlr9DyJK5." Another popular retweet on this date is a statement by Jamal Khashoggi stating that "electronic flies are a waste of public money."

Using Excel and QDA Miner WordStat 8, I quantitatively analyzed the dataset using a variety of methods. First, I identified the fifty most active users based on the frequency of their tweets. Interestingly, all of these users, except for one anti-Iranian user, are pro-Qatari accounts that tweeted a total of 24,732 tweets referencing electronic flies. In fact, their tweets constitute 4.6 percent of the total number of tweets in the whole dataset. Among the top fifty, there were ten pro-Qatari accounts that were suspended for violating Twitter's rules

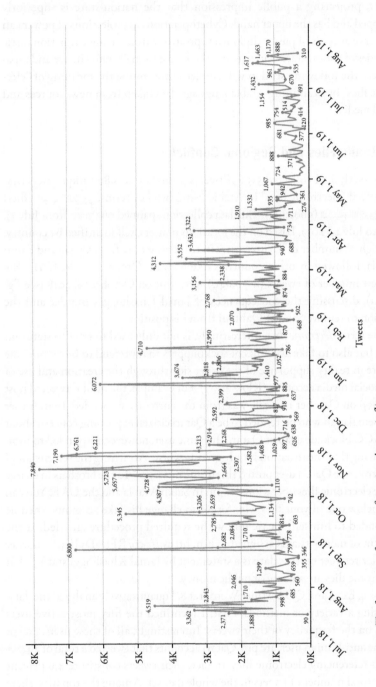

FIG. 5.1 The frequency of tweets referencing electronic flies.

Table 5.1

The Top Fifty Most Active Users Tweeting about Electronic Flies

No.	User	Frequency	No.	User	Frequency
1.	Falharami76	1,650	26.	alsada307	394
2.	Q_I979	1,628	27.	merdas54	378
3.	Alreemalqataria	1,374	28.	pass1216	375
4.	NassrQatar2022	898	29.	Beyda2_Qatar	358
5.	umsultan2022	815	30.	Majlesqatar11	357
6.	LightningsQatar	812	31.	u_sli	355
7.	AlAqatar	720	32.	Dala143I	346
8.	hassanalishaq73	707	33.	FkjfhWQsPGI02Wg	345
9.	Hudaalmohannad2	558	34.	alsulaitiabdull	344
10.	QATAR__4EVER	505	35.	Ahmad16339471	338
11.	Alhitmi79	504	36.	aj_althani72	338
12.	almarri_qt	488	37.	AbdallaQatar	337
13.	qatar_F9	464	38.	Asred4	332
14.	bofaisal9111	451	39.	patriot_QTR	329
15.	DrMannaiS	436	40.	talpha66	319
16.	A2016Hassa2016	434	41.	q_a974	311
17.	alalmass	421	42.	4QTr4EveR	310
18.	IssaSAlHitmi	421	43.	a_e00omr	306
19.	A__Alawadi	418	44.	Abosaad07714757	295
20.	SaeedAl99915814	405	45.	AhmadQatar	284
21.	AnaswahAlaa	402	46.	abuhilalah	279
22.	dar_altamimi	401	47.	q78qtr	271
23.	azizoxy	395	48.	VIP_AL_MANSOORI	263
24.	pJk0oqhaiCkF2Ne	395	49.	elbasiony_osama	262
25.	underrubble753	395	50.	lkis99	260

on automation and/or community standards such as harassing other users. In addition, two accounts deleted all their tweets to avoid detection after tweeting hundreds of messages that can be found in the collected database (see table 5.1). As for the pro-Qatari users, they mostly focus on attacking Saudi Arabia and its political figures like the crown prince, Mohammed bin Salman, and his troll manager, Saud al-Qahtani, while other attacks, though far fewer, are directed toward the UAE and Bahrain.

What is unique about the pro-Qatari users is that the majority have the photo of the Qatari Emir Tamim Bin Hamad as their Twitter profile image, while their descriptions for the most part include praise and declarations of loyalty for the emir's leadership and devotion to the state of Qatar. Members of this tightly knit online community routinely exchange details about other users whom they suspect of being anti-Qatari trolls or electronic flies. For example, Twitter user @Falharami76 retweets the following message: "RT @qatar_F9: صالح الديل ذبابه اللكترونيه ☺ @A2f77m #الذباب_الالكتروني https://t.co

/KODKMAmFMA" in which two users are allegedly identified as sockpuppets engaged in astroturfing activities. Twitter user @BoSALMAN_122 frequently lists the alleged fake accounts of people who are labeled as Dilaim (دليم), those who are presumably pretending to be Qataris but acting to support the Saudis. Flagging users in this way can be highly problematic because anyone can be labeled as an electronic fly, so the term has been weaponized and often used as a tool to silence any dissenting and genuine activists by accusing them of being sockpuppets or foreign agents.

By examining the top twenty most retweeted posts, we see a different picture (see table 5.2). Fifteen out of the top twenty posts are supportive of Saudi Arabia and the UAE, while the remaining five carry different messages. One of the popular retweets (n = 4,780) includes an online plea sent by @hureyaksa (toward freedom) in which the user urges his followers to support him by retweeting and replying to his messages because of the "aggressive and continuous campaign targeting my account for disclosing the corruption and crimes of Mohammed Bin Salman https://t.co/ZP8RE9MRYe." Another popular retweet (n = 1,516) states: "Electronic flies succeeded in: projecting a very negative image of our values and morals ... agitating other Arabs and turning them into our enemies ... burning our glorious and honorable past experience with the Palestinian cause ... spreading the poisons of isolationism, populism, chauvinism, and division https://twitter.com/KhaledBinW /status/1065340447743193088." The majority of the other top retweets, however, are pro-Saudi due to the large number of supportive users tweeting about electronic flies. Many of these users attempt to demean and discredit the Qataris and their supporters with the pejorative nickname "Qatari Zionists."

In terms of word frequency, "Saudi Arabia" and "Saudis" (in two formats) are the most mentioned in the dataset (n = 167,998) since the online attacks by pro-Qatari users are mostly focused on Saudi Arabia, while other users defending the kingdom also mention the term. "Qatar" comes second with 93,022 references, while "Mohammed bin Salman" comes third (n = 62,138), followed by "Khashoggi" (n = 46,618), "Turkey" (n = 37,844), "Al Jazeera channel" (n = 28,370), and "Hamadin," which is the term used by some Arab countries that opposed Qatar after the 2017 Gulf crisis (n = 22,368). It is important to mention here that Al Jazeera, which is based in Qatar, has been extensively trolled by pro-Saudi users who sometimes refer to it as Al Khanzirah (female pig) instead of Al Jazeera, a wordplay insult against the news channel. In terms of the most recurrent phrases, "Mohammed bin Salman" comes first (n = 28,043), followed by "Jamal Khashoggi" (n = 25,550), "Saudi electronic flies" (n = 18,686), "Al Hamadin regime" (n = 16,601), "Qatari Zionists" (n = 15,096), "Saud al-Qahtani" (n = 11,065), "Faisal Al Qassim" (n = 9,492), who is a famous journalist at Al Jazeera, "adversary accounts" (n = 9,336), "Qatari Intelligence" (n = 9,117), "attack on Saudi" (n = 8,571), and "Turkish Intelligence" (n = 8420). The term

Table 5.2
The Top Ten Most Retweeted Posts

No.	Tweet	Frequency
1.	لو أن هذا الفيديو في السعودية أجزم انه لن تبقى قناة اجنبية ولا منظمة حقوقية الا واصدرت بيانا حول ذلك وستخصص الجزيرة برامجها لمناقشته وسيواصل الذباب الالكتروني الليل بالنهار يغرد ويشتم ويطلق الهاشتاقات المسيئة.https://t.co/LDTcAUUuTR	9,245
	If this video was in Saudi Arabia, I'm pretty sure every foreign news channel and human rights organization would have issued a statement about it. Al Jazeera would air programs to discuss it while the electronic flies will tweet curses and insulting hashtags day and night. https://t.co/LDTcAUUuTR	
2.	الخزاعي يجلد فيصل القاسم جلد عراقي فاخر في الاتجاه المعاكس ويكشف اسرار الذباب الالكتروني 😊 @kasimf https://t.co/G3jaalotf9	5,361
	Al Khazaay giving an excellent Iraqi roasting to Faisal Al Kassem in the Opposite Direction program and reveals the electronic flies' secrets. 😊 @kasimf https://t.co/G3jaalotf9	
3.	متابعينا الكرام: حسابي يتعرض لحملة قوية ومستمرة منذ عدة أيام من قبل #الذباب_الالكتروني.. بسبب فضحنا لفساد وإجرام محمد بن سلمان بحق الشعب.. يرجى دعم الحساب بالريتويت والمتابعة والردود... فضلاً وليس أمراً 🌹https://t.co/ZP8RE9MRYe	4,780
	Our dear followers, my account has been strongly and constantly targeted for a few days by the #electronicflies because we exposed Mohamed Bin Salman's corruption and crimes against the people. Please endorse this account by following, replying and retweeting this account . . . This is a request and not an order. 🌹 https://t.co/ZP8RE9MRYe	
4.	بعد أن اظهرت سياسة الفيسبوك موقع الحسابات المعادية! . . #رامي_جان المنشق عن قطيع #الإخونج بتركيا يكشف طريقة عمل (الذباب الإلكتروني) الذي أسسه #صهاينة_قطر ويتخذ من تركيا مقرا له وبدار عبر #المخابرات_القطرية بحماية #المخابرات_التركية للهجوم على السعودية. . #فضيحة_الحسابات_المعاديةhttps://t.co/bHgbnw2Zao	4,645
	After Facebook's policy revealed the locations of malicious accounts!..#Ramy_Jan, a dissident of the #MuslimBrotherhood in Turkey reveals the way (electronic flies), which were established by #QatariZionists, function. They are located in Turkey and operated by the #Qatarintelligence and protected by the #Turkishintelligence to attack Saudi Arabia #themaliciousaccountscandal https://t.co/bHgbnw2Za0	
5.	إعلام #قطر أطلق على المغردين السعوديين #الذباب_الالكتروني حتى يدعي أنه لا يوجد سعودي يدافع عن قيادته ولما تخندقت شخصيات معروفة مع #السعودية كمشروع استراتيجي للعالم الإسلامي حرك جيوشه الإلكترونية كي تتهمهم بأنهم مرتزقة حتى يزعم أن كل #العرب ضد #المملكة. حذار من هذا المخطط المفضوح!	4,177
	#Qatar's media called Saudi twitter users #electronicflies to claim that there are no Saudis defending their leadership. When famous figures partnered with #Saudiarabia as part of a strategic project by the Islamic world, Qatar's media mobilized its electronic armies to accuse Saudi Arabians of being mercenaries so that they can claim that all #Arabs are against #thekingdom. Beware of this disgraced scheme!	

(continued)

Table 5.2
The Top Ten Most Retweeted Posts (*continued*)

No.	Tweet	Frequency
6.	تم التبليغ.. منشن كلنا أمن.. يجب محاسبته.. يجب إيقافه.. يجب إيقافه.. باسم الوطنية يرددونها وغيرها من جمل التشبيح الإلكتروني والترهيب لكل من يختلفون معه .. جو بوليسي قذر منتعش له فترة .. انعشوه الوطنجية الجدد Reported..Mention We Are All Security..He has to be prosecuted.. He has to be stopped..They say it in the name of patriotism and other phrases of electronic attacks and intimidation against all those who disagree with him.. A filthy police environment that has been around for some time..The neo-patriots revived it.	4,054
7.	الذباب_الالكتروني و اعلام #تنظيم_الحمدين وخلايا الاحباط ينشرون خزعبلات ان التحالف لم ينجد# حجور. . . وكثير من (المدرعمين) التحقوا بالحملة ولكن الحقيقة ان انزال أغذية وعلاج وسلاح قد تم# وهذا فيديو لطيران التحالف وهو يقضي على المهاجمين . . . انشروه بكثافة #كلنا_حجور و نحن_هنا_أين_أنتم#https://t.co/7oHF8fg2FV #Theelectronicflies and the media of #Hamdingroup and individuals promoting despair are spreading worthless news that the coalition did not #save Hajour . . . and a lot of the (supposed supporters) joined the campaign but the reality is that food, medicine and arms were sent and this is a video for the coalition's air forces eliminating the attackers . . . Spread it widely #WeareallHajour and #Weareherewhereareyou https://t.co/7oHF8fg2FV	3,742
8.	المصري #رامي_جان المنشق عن مرتزقة #صهاينة_قطر في تركيا قطيع #الإخونج_المفسدين الهاربين من اوطانهم يكشف طريقة عمل (الذباب الإلكتروني) الذي أسسه #صهاينة_قطر ويتخذ من تركيا مقراً له ويدار عبر #المخابرات_القطرية بحماية #المخابرات_التركية للهجوم على السعودية و مصر والدول المقاطعة لهم.https://t.co/H4nqN7Filx Egyptian #RamyJan who left #QatariZionist mercenaries in Turkey, part of the #CorruptBrotherhood herd who escaped their countries reveals the operations behind (the electronic flies) established by #QatariZionists. They are located in Turkey and operated by the #Qatariintelligence with protection from the #Turkeyintteligence to attack Saudi Arabia and Egypt and countries that boycott them. https://t.co/H4nqN7Filx	3,742
9.	الى #عبدالملك_الحوثي #حزب_الله #الحرس_الثوري #الحشد_الشعبي #عيال_شريفة #تنظيم_الحمدين #الذباب_الالكتروني وصلنا عمق صعدة و #محمد_العرب امام مسجد الصحابي الجليل معاذ ابن جبل رضي الله عنه https://t.co/hQoJtLA574 To #AbdelmalekAlHouthy #Hezballah #The revolutionaryguard #popularmobilizationforces #Sharifachildren #Hamdingroup #electronicflies we reached downtown Sa'dah and #mohamedelarab in front of the mosque of the Prophet's companion Muadh ibn Jabal, may Allah be pleased with him.	2,827

Table 5.2
The Top Ten Most Retweeted Posts (*continued*)

No.	Tweet	Frequency
10.	منى عبد الحميد أبو سليمان.. مثال نفتخر فيه ويحتذى فيه لكل بنات الوطن ، -اول سفيرة سعودية في- تعرضت في الاونة الاخيرة لهجوم غير مبرر من الذباب الالكتروني من - الامم المتحده للنوايا الحسنة فيه حاجة حلوة لكم تحت التغريدة المقتبسة تستاهل منا كل الدعم - اعداء اي نجاح لاي ٬٬سعودي https://t.co/oLTTkSc95q	2,680
	Mona Abdelhamid Abu Soliman..A role model for all women in our country and an icon we're proud of, -the first female Saudi Goodwill Ambassador for the United Nations - was subjected lately to unjustified attacks by the electronic flies who are enemies of any Saudi success. There is a nice surprise for you in the quoted tweet. https://t.co/oLTTkSc95q	

"Qatari Zionists" is strongly associated with Turkey, suggesting that many pro-Qatari trolls are allegedly based in Turkey. In terms of hashtags, #Saudi is the second most recurrent one after #electronicflies (n = 32,268), #Qatar (n = 21,905), #QatariZionists (n = 14,401), #Hamadin regime (n = 12,586), and #Jamal_Khashoggi (n = 11,700). These results give us the outline of two distinct online communities. On the one hand, the majority of users who refer to Hamadin, Al Jazeera or Al Khanzirah, Qatari and Turkish Intelligence, Qatari Zionists as well as Faisal Al Qassim are pro-Saudi users who routinely attack Qatar and its polices. On the other hand, the majority of users who refer to MBS (Mohammed bin Salman), Khashoggi, and Saudi electronic flies are pro-Qatari and anti-Saudi.

When it comes to the most frequently mentioned users, we find Faisal Al Qassim, @kasimf, at the top of the list (n = 11,589). As of late July 2019, Al Qassim had 5.2 million followers on Twitter. The second most mentioned user is Saud al-Qahtani, @Saudq1978 (n = 2,818), who is known as the "Minister of Electronic Flies" and has 1.3 million followers. In third place is Al Jazeera Arabic channel, @AJArabic (n = 2,548), partly because they air Al Qassim's show on electronic flies, followed by Al Jazeera Arabic's principal presenter Ghada Oueiss, @ghadaoueiss (n = 2,082), and Jamal Rayyan, @jamalrayyan (n = 1,823), another TV presenter at Al Jazeera. Except for Saud al-Qahtani, all the other top users are based in Qatar and are frequently trolled by pro-Saudi users.

As for Arab news media coverage, I searched Factiva for all Arabic-language news stories that referenced electronic flies and found 961 news stories from 76 different outlets that included the term (see table 5.3). The majority of these news stories (n = 588) were published in 2018; only one story using the term appeared in 2012, rising sharply to 125 stories in 2013. The peak of discussion on electronic flies occurred in 2018, particularly after the assassination of Jamal Khashoggi.

Table 5.3
The Top Ten Arabic-Language News Sources That Covered Electronic Flies

No.	Source	Count
1.	Al Sharq (Qatar)	234
2.	Al Watan (Qatar)	124
3.	Al Alam News (Iran)	98
4.	Al Arab (Qatar)	94
5.	Al Rayah (Qatar)	78
6.	Al Jazeera Arabic	33
7.	Al Arab	23
8.	Al Ittihad (United Arab Emirates)	22
9.	AlArabiya.net (United Arab Emirates)	17
10.	FARS News Agency (Iran)	17

As can be seen in table 5.3, Qatari and Iranian news sources, for political reasons, have been very active in reporting on electronic flies. Both countries oppose Saudi Arabia's polices in the region. As with the analysis of the Twitter data, the same digital tools were used. In terms of the most frequently mentioned terms and figures, "Khashoggi" comes first (n = 575), followed by "al-Qahtani" (n = 464), "Mohammed bin Salman" (n = 356), "Saudi" (n = 380), "Qatar" (n = 220), "Al Jazeera" (n = 166), "murder" (n = 113), and "Turkey" (n = 111). As for the top-ranked phrases, the first one is "crown prince" (n = 196) followed by other terms similar to those above in that they mostly related to events surrounding Khashoggi and his murder. As noted, the majority of news stories that included discussion of electronic flies mentioned them in association with the horrific murder of Jamal Khashoggi. This was especially true of stories from Qatari and Iranian outlets.

The term *electronic flies*, in summary, has been useful in identifying and conceptualizing potential bots and trolls; however, it has also become a weaponized term used by online users to demean and undermine the credibility of anyone who politically opposes them and expresses dissent. Our empirical analysis of news and tweets clearly shows that there is a regional trolling war waged by state-run actors and nationalists who feel that their duty is to virtually defend their state against online attacks from other belligerent nations. Two distinct online communities are very apparent: one pro-Saudi and one pro-Qatari. For the nationalists, some members seem to be ordinary citizens who are concerned about their nation's well-being and are willing to spend time and effort in identifying astroturfing actors or flies and reporting them in order to block them on Twitter. Qatari trolls tend to be far more organized and active than others, since they systematically identify opponent flies and continuously retweet each other's supportive messages. This is illustrated in our examination of the most active users. Overall, however, the majority of what is being retweeted, mentioned, and hashtagged is pro-Saudi due to the high number of pro-Saudi users who routinely attack Qatar and its supporters, many of whom are labeled as Zionists, as well as its leaders, whom they identify as the Hamadin regime and Al Jazeera channel and its prominent journalists and presenters like Faisal Al Qassim. As for the news coverage, electronic flies were mostly discussed in association with the killing of the Saudi dissident journalist Jamal Khashoggi. There is a clear bias in the majority of news reports written and disseminated by Qatari and Iranian news outlets. In the final section of this chapter, we discuss other trolls from the Middle East and their cyberoperations in the region.

Saudi, Emirati, and Egyptian Trolls

In September 2019, Twitter released a small dataset containing 340 tweets sent by six different users, detailing the activities of Saudi trolls (Twitter 2019). The tweets were mostly sent in English and were supportive of the Saudi government's positions regarding different issues like its stance against Iran and Qatar. For example, one troll going by the handle @KSAToday, tweeted the following on May 29, 2017: "#Saudi Prince Slams #Iran's Supreme Leader with a verse @abdulrahman." This same user had an active website (www.ksatoday.net) which publishes promotional news about Saudi Arabia, and, as of December 2019, it also has a Telegram app account (https://telegram.me/s/KSAtoday). Another Saudi troll calling itself "the Globus" tweeted the following false claim on April 2, 2019: "Reports say that several of the so-called national security experts at CNN have direct links to #Qatar 'a terror-funding, Islamist enclave in the Middle East that has placed itself on the warpath against America's most important regional allies.'" This tweet is clearly a malicious attack on liberal news media such as CNN, falsely associating it with Qatar, which is accused of being a terrorist state. This kind of false accusation is in line with the content coming from troll accounts we will be discussing in the rest of this chapter.

Another dataset released by Twitter in April 2019 contained 214,898 tweets from 271 accounts identified as Emirati and Egyptian trolls (Twitter 2019). Of these users, the overall largest number of them self-identified their geographical locations as Libya, followed by Qatar and Saudi Arabia. As we would have expected, an analysis based on the most retweeted posts found that the trolls promoted Emirati and Saudi internal and regional achievements, prominent figures, and policies in the region. The analysis also revealed significant overt support for Khalifa Haftar, the Libyan military commander who has received support from the Emirati, Saudi, and Egyptian governments. Haftar has been repeatedly accused of human rights violations and war crimes (Cohen and

Berlinger 2019). To boost Haftar and his war efforts, these trolls retweeted messages sent by several accounts, including @LyOffSpokesman, @QatariLeaks, which was focused on attacking Qatar, and @HaftarOfficial, which as you can imagine was dedicated to promoting Haftar. Before it was suspended by Twitter, the latter account was allegedly the official Twitter account of Khalifa Haftar. One troll, for example, tweeted the following: "RT @binlibyaa: شعب #ليبيا يقف خلف #الجيش_الوطنى_الليبى بقياده المشير خليفه #حفتر ڧ حربه ضد الإرهاب الممول من #تركيا و #قطر" ("The Libyan people support the Libyan National Army led by Field Marshal Khalifa Haftar in his war against the terrorism that is sponsored by Qatar and Turkey"). It is clear here that the animosity against Qatar and Turkey stems from alliance of those states with the Muslim Brotherhood organization, as well as their support for the Libyan Government of National Accord (GNA), an interim government formed in 2015 under the supervision of the United Nations. In other words, there is a proxy war waged in Libya with Turkey and Qatar on one side and Saudi Arabia, Egypt, and the UAE on the other. In terms of the hashtags used, the most frequently referenced is #Qatarileaks (n = 33,528), followed by #Qatar (n = 21000), #Doha (n = 11101), #Doha_exposed (n = 9,803), #Othmanli (n = 9,151), in reference to Turkey, and #Qatar_commits_suicide (n = 7,601).

Figure 5.2 shows an example of the kind of attacks received by Qatar and its Al Jazeera channel, in which its correspondents were compared to flies, or unscrupulous mercenaries, gathering around the channel's logo for the sake of getting rich. Other hashtags include insults against Qatar like #Qatar_sponsors_terrorism (n = 5,297), #Tamim_the_dishonorable (n = 5157), in reference to the Qatari emir, and #Enough_Qatar (n = 4,760), while other hashtags reference Turkey, the Muslim Brotherhood, and Iran (see figure 5.3).

Evidence of another regional proxy cyberwar can be found in the dataset, which clearly shows these trolls paying close attention to Sudanese protests and to a lesser extent the Mauritanian government by repeatedly retweeting posts sent by Twitter users @mohamedghezwny and @sudanAlyoum2. Regarding Mauritania, the UAE and Saudi Arabia financially support the country's government in return for its anti-Qatari stance and its fight to uproot the Muslim Brotherhood from the country (Reuters 2017; Egypt Today 2018). Once again, we see how regional offline politics are mirrored in online trolling activities. The UAE and Saudi Arabia also supported popular protests against the former Sudanese president Omar Hassan al-Bashir because of his alliance with Islamic parties as well as Qatar (Georgy, El Dahan, and Abdelaziz 2019). In the third dataset released by Twitter, in March 2019, which contains 1,325,529 tweets posted by 4,248 Emirati trolls, the war in Yemen against the Houthis, popular protest in Sudan, and attacks on Qatar were among the most retweeted messages. In terms of the most used hashtags, #Yemen comes first (n = 63,435), followed by #UAE (n = 50,725), #Qatar (n = 25,069), and #Houthi (n = 21,318) (see figure 5.4).

FIG. 5.2 A visual posted by Emirati/Egyptian trolls attacking the Al Jazeera channel.

Finally, in December 2019 Twitter released 29,273,179 tweets posted by 5,929 Saudi trolls that were representative of the core network of over 88,000 accounts. Most of these accounts were managed by a Saudi social media company called Smaat, and they were all suspended for their spamming activities. The author's examination of the top retweets and users did not show any new patterns, other than the promotion of Saudi Arabia's national events and issues. Twitter revealed that these accounts were "amplifying messages favourable to Saudi authorities, mainly through inauthentic engagement tactics such as aggressive liking, retweeting and replying. While the majority of the content from this network was in Arabic, a portion of it related to events relevant to Western audiences, including amplification of discussion around sanctions in Iran and appearances by Saudi government officials in Western media" (Twitter Safety 2019). Twitter's findings are similar to what is presented here on the subject of how spamming and trolling by electronic flies occurs. Nevertheless, the

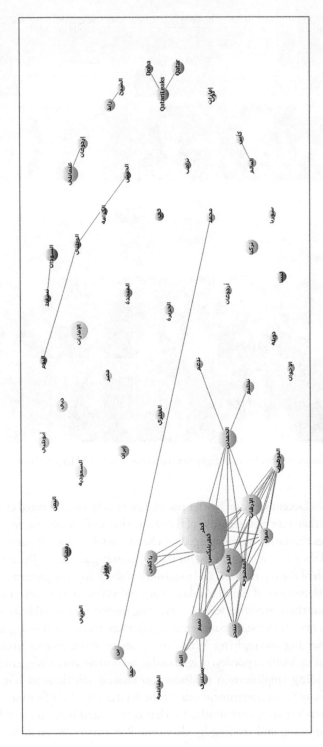

FIG. 5.3 The top 70 most recurrent hashtags sent by Egyptian and Emirati trolls.

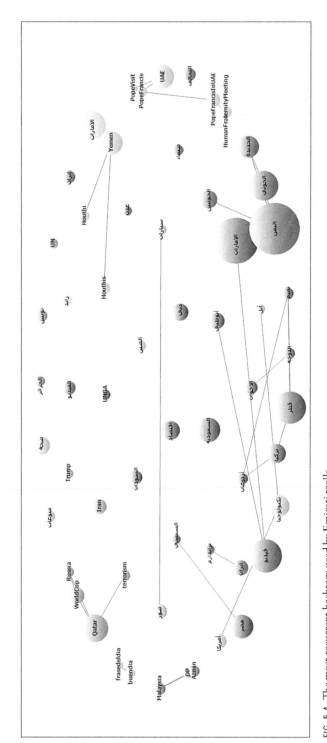

FIG. 5.4 The most recurrent hashtags used by Emirati trolls.

majority of Saudi users who are members of the Salmani Army are still active on the platform despite the removal of all the accounts just mentioned.

On October 2, 2018, Jamal Khashoggi was assassinated inside the Saudi consulate in Istanbul. The examination of all the datasets released by Twitter on Saudi Arabia shows that Saudi trolls launched a Twitter campaign on the same day he was killed using the hashtag Jamal_Khashoggi_scandals in two different formats in Arabic such as "فضائح_جمال_خاشقجي" (n = 78) and "فضائح_جمال_خاشقجي" (n = 141). These hashtags were never used before, and the Saudi trolls attacked the former *Washington Post* journalist by accusing him of being a foreign agent for Turkey and Qatar and stating that his disappearance was fake orchestrated by Turkey. Several other hashtags were used to make the latter false connection, such as #hey_Turkey_where_is_Khashoggi or #hey_Erdogan_where_is_Khashoggi. Other disinformation activities by Saudi trolls included sharing fake videos and links showing that Khashoggi left the consulate safely and that he was probably kidnapped, as well as accusing his fiancée of being a Turkish spy by sharing a well-designed infographic from another Saudi troll's Facebook page that is incidentally still active (https://www.facebook.com /blackhands515/) (see figure 5.5). The timing of this disinformation campaign shows the close coordination between the Saudi trolls and the political establishment responsible for the assassination of Khashoggi. In the next section, we turn our attention to the activities of Iranian trolls and their Arabic-language messages and astroturfing activities in the region.

Iranian Trolls and Regional Conflict

In order to understand the nature of Iranian trolls and their activities directed toward the Arab world, I examined 1,491,125 Arabic tweets extracted from a total of 9,859,437 ones released by Twitter in a total of five different datasets. The tweets were posted between April 13, 2011, and April 17, 2019. As can be seen in figure 5.6, the largest number of tweets (n = 3,462) were sent on June 21, 2017, while the second busiest day (n = 3,438) was May 15, 2017. Most of these tweets focused on attacking Israel, coinciding with the International Quds (Jerusalem) Day, which is an annual event initiated by Iran in 1979 to show opposition toward Zionism and call for the establishment of an independent Palestinian state.

Examination of the most recurrent words in the dataset, furthermore, shows that the following countries are the most referenced: Bahrain (Arabic n = 92,404 and English n = 81,216), Yemen (n = 39,851), Saudi Arabia (n = 31,319, Saud n = 16,737, Saudi n = 15,939), Iraq (n = 22,614), Sudan (n = 18,565), Palestine (n = 18,514, Al Quds n = 16,160), and Syria (n = 15,935). Mohammed bin Salman (n = 21,695) is the most referenced person, while Daesh is the most mentioned entity (n = 19,503). Iranian trolls show clear preference toward Shiite-majority

FIG. 5.5 A Facebook Infographic attacking Khashoggi's fiancée, Hatice Cengiz.

nations, with the exception of Sudan. This corresponds with Iran's strategic interests in the region, which are focused on supporting Shiite rebel movements in Bahrain, Yemen, and Saudi Arabia, and that are also manifested in its media strategies of highlighting sectarian and divisive political issues (Al-Rawi 2015 and 2017; Baghernia and Mahmoodinejad 2018). Iranian trolls on Twitter also have a clear tendency to support Syria's dictator Assad (Elswah, Howard, and Narayanan 2019), as well as the Houthi rebels in Yemen. A Reuters news investigation found about seventy disinformation websites run by the Iranian government focusing on a dozen countries without disclosing the true identity of their sponsors. The countries most frequently targeted by these astroturfing

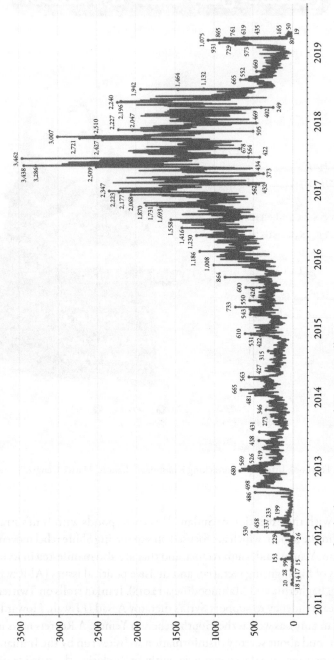

FIG. 5.6 Frequency of Arabic-language tweets sent by Iranian trolls.

FIG. 5.7 Anti-Saudi visuals posted by Iranian trolls on Twitter.

activities include Yemen, Syria, Afghanistan, and Pakistan (Stubbs and Bing 2018). The Iranian-designed reports mostly counter the official version of news to promote Iran's agenda in the region; this is done, partly, by routinely retweeting news reports produced by Iranian state channels like Al-Alam (Arabic) and PressTV (English). Iranian trolls on Facebook often focus on the Middle East region, connecting their public Facebook pages to state-run news outlets like Press TV in order to disseminate news coverage favorable to Iran and its strategic interests, such as supporting Syria's Assad, Palestinians, and Houthis in Yemen and expressing criticism against Saudi Arabia including, to take just one example, by creating a fake Facebook page that supports Saudi women's rights (Facebook Newsroom 2018).

In addition to Saudi Arabia and Israel, the United States remains Iran's archenemy, which explains the popularity of some antagonistic phrases and hashtags in the Twitter dataset. Iranian trolls often associate and link these three countries together, as seen in some of the visuals used by the trolls (see figure 5.7). Some of the news stories that Iranian trolls spread are fake, meant to spread mistrust in the region regarding some national governments and coalition forces. One of the popular stories on social media in the Arab world that got largely disseminated with the help of Iranian trolls and users involved allegations that U.S. forces helped ISIS by supplying it with weapons and ammunitions (Sly 2015). In relation to the most frequently used phrases and terms in the dataset examined here, aside from some popular Shiite supplications, "Al Quds [is] Palestine's eternal capital" (in different formats) comes first (n = 1,905), followed by "Al Hashd Al Muqadas" (the sacred mobilization army) (n = 1,879), which is a reference to the regional Shiite militias that fought ISIS in Iraq and Syria. The adjective "sacred" is used to add reverence and respect for the members of these militias that are often known for their violent tactics (Al-Rawi and Jiwani 2017). The next most frequent terms were "Saudi aggression" (n = 1,811), "Mohammed bin Salman" (n = 1,797), "Bahraini people" (n = 1,741), and "Yemeni people" (n = 1652). When it comes to the most frequent hashtags, they are as follows: #Bahrain (English n = 71,396, Arabic n = 49,006), #Yemen (n = 11,811), #Saudi Arabia (n = 9,255), and #thepiercingstar (n = 5,973), which is a reference to the Yemen Houthi rebels' rocket that was used against Saudi targets. Coinciding with these tweets, several anti-Saudi billboard campaigns in Lebanon and Iraq were initiated by Iranian authorities using the label "the cursed tree" (الشجرة الملعونة) in reference to the House of Saud (Brown and Daraghai 2016; El-Bar 2016), especially after the death of several hundred Iranian pilgrims during the Mina stampede in 2015 (DW 2015). The same term was also used as a hashtag on Twitter to attack Saudi authorities and figures, especially the king and the crown prince. Iran's Supreme Leader Ayatollah Ali Khamenei himself, in fact, used this hashtag in 2016 to attack Saudi authorities in relation to the issue of Iranian pilgrims (Shiloach 2016).

As for the most referenced user, it is @Netnthnews or Najam Thaqib (Piercing Star) (n = 9,289), a suspended channel that focuses on news about the Houthi rebels, followed by @Alwasatnews (n = 7,530), a newspaper suspended by the Bahraini government in 2017. This is followed by the oppositional Bahraini TV channel The Pearl, @Lualuatv (n = 8,665), which is based in London, and other Bahraini oppositional figures and entities like Alwefaq National Islamic Society, @Alwefaq (n = 7,530), and Said Al Muhafdah, @Saidyousif (n = 6,869). As can be seen, there is a clear emphasis on supporting Shiite opposition in the Persian Gulf region in order to promote the interests of the Iranian authorities.

Finally, our examination of the top twenty most frequently retweeted posts yields similar results to what is presented above. There are direct attacks against Saudi Arabia, which is accused of supporting terrorism in Syria and Iraq mostly using the hashtags #Saudis_are_ pilgrims_ killers and #the_devil_launches_ rockets_against_Yemen's_Muslims (English translation of hashtag). The other frequently targeted country is Bahrain, whose monarchy is accused by the trolls of killing and torturing Shiite oppositional figures. Iranian trolls, furthermore, provide solidarity and support for active Shiite militias and lesser known news channels in the region, such as Ahrar TV (@QanatAhrar), for example by posting their Twitter handles and asking others to follow them. At the same time, they urge followers to join closed Twitter groups like Imam "Abbas' Lovers Group," and they disseminate supportive hashtags such as #their_nightmare_ is_Hezbollah (English translation of hashtag), #we_are_the_black_shirts (English translation of hashtag), #martyrs, and #resistance, all of which are meant to create the impression of a unified Shiite nation or ummah (Al-Rawi and Jiwani 2017).

Although the raw data is not available, Facebook announced in 2018 and 2019 that it removed hundreds of public Facebook pages and groups as well as Instagram accounts for what it described as "coordinated inauthentic behavior."

These nefarious online activities were managed by Iranian trolls, mostly targeting people in the Middle East and Southeast Asia. The main objectives were to shape public opinion and sow division regarding political and race issues, as the "Page administrators and account owners typically represented themselves as locals, often using fake accounts, and posted news stories on current events" (Gleicher 2018 and 2019a). Some of these public pages include "The Ahwazi Saudi channel" and "The Scandals of Al Saud," which were meant to show opposition to the Saudi government (Gleicher 2019b). The Saudis themselves, for their part, have been involved for many years in sponsoring counter news outlets and social media campaigns focused on supporting the independence of Arab Iranians and establishing an Ahwazi state within Iran (Al-Rawi and Groshek 2015). In the following section, a discussion is provided on the ongoing cyberconflict in the region, providing various details on the way horizontal online political disruption can create regional tension and impact policy.

The Qatari Hacking Crisis

There are only a scant few academic studies that address hacking in the Middle East, despite its importance in directly and indirectly impacting geopolitical developments in the region and beyond (Powers and Jablonski 2015). One of the most significant recent cyberconflicts in the region was the Qatari hacking crisis, which occurred in the context of tension between some Gulf Cooperation Council (GCC) countries and the state of Qatar, involving regional rivalries, jealousies, and competitions (Lenderking, Cammack, Shihabi, and Des Roches 2017). The first and most important source of tension is Qatar's well-known, long-term support of the Muslim Brotherhood and other Islamic conservative political groups and parties, such as Hamas in the Palestinian territories. The Muslim Brotherhood are regarded as terrorists in Egypt, Saudi Arabia, and the United Arab Emirates (UAE). Qatar, for example, actively supported Muhammed Mursi's rule in Egypt before he was toppled and replaced by military rule headed by Abdulfatah el-Sisi. One of the leaders of the Muslim Brotherhood, Yussif Al-Qaradawi, lives in Qatar where he became known for his Al Jazeera TV show *Shariah and Life*, which stopped broadcasting in 2013, and for his website, Islamonline.net. In 2003 and 2004, Qatar made a series of secret agreements with its Gulf neighbors "barring support for opposition and hostile groups in those nations, as well as in Egypt and Yemen" (Sciutto and Herb 2017). Some GCC countries, however, have accused Qatar of violating these agreements while siding with Iran and Hezbollah, two significant Shiite adversaries of Saudi Arabia, Bahrain, and the UAE (Sciutto and Herb 2017). In other words, Qatar is seen by some of the Arab states as a rogue nation due to its frequently oppositional stances against their geopolitical interests (Hedges and Cafiero 2017).

A second major source of tension is the fact that Qatar runs the Al Jazeera TV channel, which has been a divisive issue since it was launched in 1996. Arab countries have filed hundreds of complaints against the channel, blaming Al Jazeera for causing or inflaming regional tensions with the way it handles and covers sensitive topics and taboos (Al-Rawi 2017a). The channel's coverage was one of the causes of the 2014 withdrawal of GCC ambassadors from Qatar (Al Arabiya 2014), who charged Al Jazeera with biased coverage, due to ideological or political differences, of various events and issues related to the Arab Spring (Al-Rawi 2017a). Not for the last time, and in addition to other demands, the countries forming the 2014 anti-Qatari alliance wanted Al Jazeera indefinitely shut down.

Finally, a few other more minor factors have contributed to diplomatic tension, including the fact that Qatar, despite opposition from other GCC countries, paid approximately $1 billion in ransom in April 2017 to free Qatari hostages taken by a Shiite militia in Iraq (Solomon 2017). This Iraqi militia has close connections with Iran and Hezbollah (Arango 2017). Other issues contributing to tensions in the region include the UAE's failed bid to cohost the 2022 World Cup with Qatar (Grim and Walsh 2017), the Qataris' refusal to buy $100 billion of Saudi Aramco stocks in the event they were to be offered on the New York Stock Exchange (HuffPost Arabi 2017g), and Jared Kushner's failed attempt in 2015 to obtain a $500 million loan from a Qatari emir, which reportedly prompted the U.S. president's son-in-law to pressure Trump into taking a hard line against Qatar (Swisher and Grim 2018). Relatedly, it is widely known that Kushner has an excellent relationship with the Saudi crown prince, Mohammed bin Salman, whom he has visited on a number of occasions (Zakheim 2017).

Some Arab states—especially Saudi Arabia and the UAE—had experienced periods of tense diplomatic relations with Qatar long before the 2017 hacking crisis (Ulrichsen 2017), which appears to have been part of a multipronged campaign. In April 2017, the Qatari government pointed to a series of fourteen op-ed articles in a number of U.S. newspapers attempting to implicate Qatar with supporting terrorist groups; this media blitz occurred just before the hacking operation (Kirkpatrick and Frenkel 2017). As will be explained later in more detail, the leaked emails of Yousef Al Otaiba, the UAE ambassador to the United States, revealed that the UAE actually wanted to tank Qatar's economy by hitting its currency hard. The goal was to force Qatar to share the 2022 soccer World Cup by highlighting Qatar's alleged "dwindling cash reserves" that presumably would prevent it from building the required infrastructure (Grim and Walsh 2017). The leaked emails also revealed some of the UAE's public relations efforts, including awarding about $20 million to the Middle East Institute, a well-known U.S. think tank, to criticize Qatar (Grim 2017). Other leaked documents, provided by people sympathetic to Qatar, indicate that former Al Jazeera journalist Mohamed Fahmy received $250,000 from Al Otaiba to cover his legal fees for suing the channel for $100 million over its actions—and inactions—before and after Fahmy was arrested and imprisoned by Egyptian authorities for allegedly supporting the Muslim Brotherhood (Kirkpatrick 2017). Anti-Qatari sentiment had been increasing for a number of reasons in the GCC region and elsewhere in the Arab world long before the hacking incidents, which appear to have been related to other overt and covert moves against Qatar.

Shortly after Donald Trump's visit to Saudi Arabia in May 2017, former White House chief strategist Steve Bannon confirmed that the visit had led to the escalation of regional tension with Qatar (Middle East Eye 2017). Indeed, at this point both Saudi Arabia and the UAE seemed to be waiting for the U.S. administration's green light to turn up the heat politically and economically on Qatar. On June 5, 2017, Saudi Arabia, the UAE, Bahrain, and Egypt—and later the Maldives, Mauritania, Yemen, and Libya as well—fully severed diplomatic and economic ties with Qatar. Saudi Arabia also announced that Qatari troops would no longer be part of the GCC unified army stationed in Yemen, while the UAE sent strong warnings to its citizens and residents to refrain from publicly sympathizing with Qatar. Some observers believe the diplomatic tensions were so severe that Saudi Arabia was planning a military invasion of Qatar. Due to the diplomatic efforts of U.S. Secretary of State Rex Tillerson, any such plans Saudi Arabia had were thwarted (Emmons 2018). The BBC obtained the leaked emails of U.S. businessman Elliott Broidy, a close aide to Donald Trump and the UAE leaders, which revealed that Broidy had lobbied the Trump administration in October 2017 to fire Tillerson due to his stance on Qatar. Broidy disparaged Qatar as "a television station with a country," in reference to Al Jazeera (Kianpour 2018). Trump fired Tillerson in March 2018.

The diplomatic rift between Qatar and other GGC states has manifested on social media. Many pro-Qatari Twitter users, and trolls or flies, changed their profile pictures to show the image of the emir of Qatar accompanied by the statement "We are all Hamad," while anti-Qatari users employed various hashtags and slogans to condemn Qatar, such as #Qatar_supports_terrorism (قطر_تدعم_الأرهاب) or calling the emir's father "the Gulf's Qadaffi." Saudi Arabia's information minister claimed that Qatar had hired 23,000 Twitter users to sow division in the region (HuffPost Arabi 2017c). Although this specific claim was difficult to prove, political trolls, whether hired by the state or not, have been identified in many regions, not least the Middle East. Whether they are called online seminars (Darwish, Alexandrov, Nakov, and Mejova 2017), political trolls (Bradshaw and Howard 2017), troll armies, electronic armies, electronic flies, or electronic ghosts, their main purpose is to intensify cyberconflicts by spamming and disseminating pro-state propaganda.[2]

In summary, there were myriad motives and causes to the severe diplomatic tension between Qatar and some GCC countries. At the center of the conflict were Qatar's unilateral policies and reluctance to follow Saudi Arabia's regional strategies. Having outlined the reasons for the GCC cyberconflict, we now examine in more detail the cyberoperations and state surveillance in the region.[3]

In terms of surveillance and offensive cyber capabilities, as noted in chapter 1, the UAE and Saudi Arabia are undoubtedly ahead of many other Arab countries (Perlroth 2016). This leading position stems from significant investments motivated by a concern over their national and economic security as well as their shared desire to quell internal political dissent. One of the first controversies related to electronic surveillance was related to the use of BlackBerry devices in the UAE. In 2010, the state pressured Research in Motion, the Canadian maker of the mobile device, to hand over their encryption software in order to monitor emails and messages. The UAE also asked to "maintain servers within the country so that, when it identifies someone who is acting suspiciously, it can find out what else he or she has been up to" (Gapper 2010). Saudi Arabia demanded similar measures be taken in the kingdom. As part of its current surveillance and cyber offensive strategies, the UAE hired the services of DarkMatter to monitor all Emirati citizens and foreigners visiting and/or working in the country (McLaughlin 2016).[4] Another UAE hacking company, the Royal Group, is made up of "a conglomerate run by a member of the Al Nahyan family, one of the six ruling families of the Emirates" (Perlroth 2016). The company's spyware was sold by FinFisher and HackingTeam. Invoices from 2015 show that the UAE paid HackingTeam alone more than $634,500 to use the spyware against 1,100 targets (Perlroth 2016).[5]

These and other surveillance and spying technologies used by the UAE and Saudi Arabia have been deployed in the hacking attempts against opposition figures. The UAE government sought a spying software update from NSO Group, a company based in Israel that sells Pegasus, a government-exclusive intercept spyware product (Menn 2016), in order to monitor perceived opponents and enemies of the state. The Emirati government, seeking evidence that the software actually worked, requested phone recordings of the Qatari emir, the prime minister of Lebanon, a Saudi prince, and the editor of an Arabic newspaper based in London. The company offered two phone recordings as evidence, according to leaked emails provided by a Qatari journalist to the *New York Times* (Kirkpatrick and Ahmed 2018). These hacked emails reveal the UAE government monitored the phone devices of 159 members of the Qatari royal family as well as other officials. Later, an assistant to the chairman of the UAE intelligence agency emailed his director to confirm that the devices were infected with the Pegasus spyware (Kirkpatrick and Ahmed 2018).

Ahmed Mansoor, a well-known Emirati human rights advocate, has repeatedly been targeted with cyberattacks attempting to steal information from his electronic devices and ultimately silence him (Groll 2016). Often called the "million dollar dissident" because of the estimated exorbitant amount of money spent to hack his electronic devices, Mansoor was targeted with spyware sold by FinFisher and HackingTeam (Franceschi-Bicchierai 2016). As a consequence, he was "jailed and fired from his job, along with having his passport confiscated, his car stolen, his email hacked, his location tracked and his bank account robbed of $140,000. He has also been beaten, twice, in the same week" (Perlroth 2016). What happened to Mansoor is an example of vertical (top-down) online political disruption practiced by a state against a dissident citizen to disrupt and create chaos in the person's life, both online and offline. As the hacking and other threats severely curtailed Mansoor's political activism, other human rights activists were targeted by emails sent from a fake organization called the Right to Fight, asking them to click on suspicious links related to human rights issues in the UAE (Perlroth 2016).

In Saudi Arabia, the assassination of Khashoggi in October 2018 revealed more details about the surveillance and hacking activities of the Saudi government against him and many other human rights activists. As noted earlier, the Saudi government hired the services of several Western hacking companies to train Saudi intelligence agents to spy on Saudi citizens. One of the prominent figures who led the Saudi kingdom to purchase spying tools and hire trolls and hackers is Saud al-Qahtani, a media adviser to the Saudi crown prince who previously worked at the Center for Media Monitoring and Analysis at the Saudi royal court. Earlier, al-Qahtani had shown interest in hacking culture as an active member of the Hack Forums online community. In 2016, one year after the leak of their emails, HackingTeam was about to go bankrupt. Al-Qahtani convinced the Saudis to purchase 20 percent of the company's shares in order to keep it alive (Franceschi-Bicchierai 2018). Though al-Qahtani was recently fired, he is still known as Saudi Arabia's Steve Bannon (Al-Arabi 2017), Mr. Hashtag (Franceschi-Bicchierai 2018), or the Prince of Darkness (Kerr, Raval, and England 2018) due to his covert efforts to create an army of bots and trolls or electronic flies to combat state dissidents and supporters of Qatar. These cyberoperations were not confined to the Saudi kingdom; the Citizen Lab reported that Omar Abdulaziz, a Saudi human rights activist and friend of Khashoggi's who resides in Montreal, was successfully targeted by the Saudi government with Pegasus spyware (Marczak et al. 2018). Also, UN experts revealed that MBS himself was implicated in hacking the phone of Amazon's CEO, Jeff Bezos, who also owns the *Washington Post*, where Khashoggi wrote his critical articles against Saudi Arabia (Kirchgaessner 2020).

Again, this is typical of the kind of vertical (top-down) online political disruption used by the Saudi government against human rights activists, aiming to disrupt their lives and silence them. Al-Qahtani was also responsible for creating the viral Arabic hashtag #TheBlacklist on August 17, 2017 (Khashoggi

2018), a few months after the Qatari crisis, asking Saudis to add the names of any Qatari sympathizer or "traitors" to the infamous Twitter list (Al Ali, 2018). Finally, it is believed that al-Qahtani masterminded the killing of Khashoggi at the Saudi consulate in Istanbul, giving orders to his aides over Skype (Reuters 2018). One of the assassins was a Saudi intelligence officer named Maher Abdulaziz Mutreb, or "dark face," who was trained to use spying technologies in Riyadh and presumably in Italy by the Hacking Team (BBC News 2018c). In brief, the UAE and Saudi Arabia are not alone in using sophisticated spying tools to monitor foreigners and citizens. Hacking electronic devices to gain valuable political information is a method of state surveillance largely at the disposal of autocratic states for use against their opponents, internal and external. To further ground our discussion of the Qatari hacking crisis, the next section provides an account of the concepts of hacking, cyberwar, and cyberconflict.

Cyberoperations and the Qatari Hacking Crisis

As mentioned earlier, Valeriano and Maness (2015) show that many cyberconflicts occur among rival neighboring states—a circumstance that applies to this case study. The conflict between Qatar and some GCC countries did not escalate into more of a full-fledged cyberwar because the intention behind the hacking of the Qatari News Agency (QNA) website seems to have been focused on influencing or changing diplomatic relations between the countries (Valeriano and Maness, 2015); that is to say, our case study appears to have remained within the bounds of cyberconflict. The hacking of the QNA website is a form of horizontal political disruption intended to destabilize the diplomatic relations among GCC states.

The geopolitical context described above ultimately paved the way for the hacking of QNA's website and its social media outlets shortly after Donald Trump's visit to Saudi Arabia. According to multiple reports, the hacking, which occurred at 12:13 a.m. on May 24, 2017, was engineered and orchestrated by the UAE and Saudi Arabia and used as a pretext to cut diplomatic ties with Qatar (Kareem and Ryan 2017). Senior Emirati officials allegedly discussed the details of the hacking plan the day before its execution (DeYoung and Nakashima 2017), and the Qatari Interior Ministry claimed that the hacking was traced to two IP addresses located in the UAE, from where the hackers exploited a security vulnerability and installed a malicious program on the QNA site.[6] Doha later claimed that it identified 122 people implicated in the hacking incident, including hackers living in Turkey and some Arab countries such as Egypt and Saudi Arabia (Al Jazeera 2017a). The fake news story posted by the hackers referenced the emir of Qatar, Sheikh Tamim Bin Hamad al-Thani, alleging that the Qatari ruler had praised Hamas and Iran and suggested that Trump might not last long in office (DeYoung and Nakashima 2017; CNBC 2017). Within twenty minutes, an unusually and surprisingly fast turnaround, Saudi and Emirati TV channels started airing credulous reports of the fake news story and began "interviewing long lines of well-prepared commentators to expound on the perfidy of Qatar" (Kirkpatrick and Frenkel 2017). Given the timing, and the logistical difficulties of obtaining such hardline responses in a region known for its official media censorship and sensitive political environment, observers viewed this media response as further evidence that the hacking operation was carefully planned and coordinated by the UAE and Saudi Arabia.

Other decisive diplomatic measures quickly followed the hacking, in an attempt to further isolate Qatar. Saudi Arabia blocked access to the Qatari websites of Al Jazeera, Asharq, Al-Raya, and Al-Arab the next day (HuffPost Arabi 2017f), and the UAE, Bahrain, and Egypt followed the Saudis' lead (DeYoung and Nakashima 2017). During the crisis itself, Al Jazeera TV's website and social media outlets were subjected to multiple hacking attempts (McKernan 2017). Another fake news story, this one claiming that "six Arab nations had demanded Fifa strip Qatar of the 2022 World Cup," (Harwood 2017) appeared just days later, on May 28. Online spammers succeeded in virally disseminating the fake story, causing Reuters and a Swiss news agency to publish it (Harwood 2017). Hacking incidents and the spreading of fake news have continued since 2017, and these can be regarded as escalations of regional cyberconflict and online political disruption. Hacked mobile audio and text messages from Zayed bin Saeed al-Khayareen, Qatar's ambassador to Iraq, were published on April 28, 2018, by the *Washington Post*. The messages detailed the huge ransom paid by Qatar to free its nationals who had been held hostage in Iraq. Though the identities of the hackers were not disclosed, the following statement appeared in the report: "The intercepted communications also include cellphone conversations and voice-mail messages in Arabic that were played for Post reporters for authentication purposes, on the condition that the name of the foreign government that provided the materials not be revealed" (Warrick 2018). The foreign government involved in this hacking incident is most likely either Saudi Arabia or the UAE, since both Gulf states have a clear motive for disseminating such information. Because these cyberoperations involved the use of bots and spamming and the spreading of fake news, and because they were orchestrated and conducted by states and/or their affiliates against Qatar, they represent a horizontal form of online political disruption.

Meanwhile, Qatar has taken a number of cyber measures to counter these attacks. Qatar seems to have explored the option of hiring mercenary hackers who freelance "for all sorts of different clients, and adapting their skills as needed" (Kirkpatrick and Frenkel 2017). For example, Al Otaiba's email was hacked on June 2, 2017, by hackers using phishing techniques to lure their

victim into clicking on certain links. Other Emirati diplomats and public figures in the Gulf region received similar messages in the same time period
(Kirkpatrick and Frenkel 2017). Al Otaiba's leaked emails—which were
handed over to the Intercept, the Daily Beast, Al Jazeera, and HuffPost (Jilani
and Emmons 2017)—were released by GlobaLeaks, which is affiliated with
the DCLeaks website. This incident did not appear to be a coincidence,
because the hacked emails were "distributed by a group apparently sympathetic to Qatar" (Kareem and Ryan 2017) and defended the Qatari state against
various accusations. Incidentally, this was not the first time that leaked documents from the UAE emerged publicly. In 2015, internal emails hacked from
the Emirati foreign ministry were provided to the *New York Times* from an
Arab intermediary with ties to Qatar (Kirkpatrick and Frenkel 2017). The
emails revealed that "the U.A.E. was knowingly violating a United Nations
resolution by shipping weapons to Libyan militias" (Kirkpatrick and Frenkel
2017). Some of these emails appeared in the *Guardian* newspaper and on
Qatari-sponsored sites. These leaks were clearly intended to pressure the UAE
to change its policies in Libya, which were not aligned with Qatari policies.
These hacking incidents were meant to disclose embarrassing information
and potentially help clear Qatar from any terrorism-related charges; they also
revealed the cyber vulnerability of the UAE (and Saudi Arabia).[7] The email
account of Elliott Broidy, as noted above, was also allegedly hacked by Qatari-
affiliated hackers (Mazzetti, Kirkpatrick, and Haberman 2018), as cybersecurity experts found similarities between this incident and the one involving
Al Otaiba's hacked emails (Kianpour 2018). Figure 5.8 shows how the online

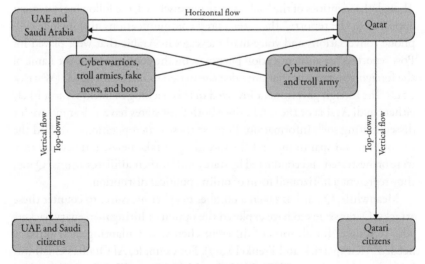

FIG. 5.8 Online political disruption model applied to the GCC context.

political disruption model applies to the Qatari crisis. There is a clear form of horizontal disruption among some nation-states as they attempt to pressure each other's governments and influence policies. On the other hand, there is a vertical (top-down) flow of online political disruption and surveillance practiced by nation-states against their own citizens to monitor, disrupt, and curb dissent and political activism.

In brief, the Qatari QNA website was hacked by the UAE in coordination with Saudi Arabia as a means to politically and diplomatically isolate and pressure Qatar and undermine its influence in the region. This hacking incident coincided with the new wave of foreign policies implemented by Saudi Arabia's crown prince, which included intensifying diplomatic pressures against Iran (Zilber 2017). Indeed, the majority of Arab countries—especially the wealthy ones in the Gulf region—have purchased, used, or employed cyber offensive measures, surveillance tools, and spying techniques to hack their rivals as well as monitor and target dissidents and human rights activists. Several Arab countries created offensive cyber divisions to gather intelligence and hack their enemies—mostly their neighbors—as part of their horizontal political disruption operations that are manifestation of power relations between neighboring countries (Waltz 2010). The UAE and Saudi Arabia, in particular, seem to be more advanced than the others in the area of offensive cyberoperations, but neighboring states such as Qatar that maintain an opposite stance on some political issues have also actively used hacking methods to undermine one another and exert online and, subsequently, offline power.

Overall, there is an ongoing political disruption in the region that closely aligns with different geopolitical developments and power balances. This closely corresponds with geopolitical developments in the region, and it "has the potential to escalate" (Valeriano and Maness 2015, 96). Tensions in the Middle East are likely to increase in magnitude and multitude due to rapid developments in spying tools and increasing demands for hacked data by autocratic states that continuously seek to quell external dissent from other countries in the region. The ongoing cold war—which occasionally takes the form of hot or proxy war—between Iran and a few other regional players, especially Saudi Arabia, is partly manifested in the media and in the multileveled cyberconflicts between these regional powers.

6

Arab Hackers and
Electronic Armies

●●●●●●●●●●●●●●●●●●●●●●

This chapter provides an overview of the different Arab hackers and cyber armies that are active online. The international, regional, and national dimensions often overlap, given that the activities of these hackers and online armies are geographically diverse. Using data collected from social media and multiple news reports, this chapter empirically analyzes public discourses on these hackers and cyber armies. Special attention is paid to the Syrian Electronic Army (SEA), which, I argue, is not a hacktivist group but rather consists of cyberwarriors closely connected to the Syrian regime in order to serve two main roles: to disseminate propaganda for the Syrian regime, drawing the world's attention to the Assad government's official version of events taking place in the country, and to provide a hacking tool to undermine Syrian oppositional groups.[1] First, we need to examine the current state of Arab hackers and electronic armies in the Middle East.

Arab Hackers

This chapter delves into an under-researched subject: the state Arab hackers and the nature of their activities. Building on the theory of bottom-up online political disruption, this chapter argues that these hacktivist acts are ultimately an outgrowth of, or a response to, government corruption, nepotism, and injustice, and they can be considered as part of the cyberwarfare waged to create or advocate for social reforms, to popularize a cause, change state policies, and ultimately to enhance democracy. The author has previously attempted to interview some of the hackers in the MENA region, but he has not pursued these efforts for many reasons. First, there are many instances of criminal cyber activities, such as hacking for money, thrill, or fun, which are carried out by the same people hacking for political goals, so it becomes difficult to parse the motivations of particular hackers. Additionally, as noted in the introduction, there are many hackers who appear to be primarily cyberwarriors or merce-naries, directly or indirectly supporting their respective authoritarian govern-ments. Many Arab hackers seem to have nationalistic objectives. They might deface certain websites run from their respective countries just to highlight security vulnerabilities and provide advice on how to fix them while expressing national sentiments, such as the case of the Jordanian Cyber Army hackers. Finally, a concern for the physical safety of relevant political hackers also played into the author's considerations about attempting to contact and inter-view, given the risk their true identities might have been disclosed by mistake. The accounts below have been drawn from several sources, such as the hackers' own social media platforms, the zone-h.org archive that lists the history of website defacements, and news reports about and interviews with some hack-ers that provide a better understanding of the nature, motivations, and appeals of their activities. Before proceeding, it is important to note that there are hundreds of Arab hacking groups, whose details can be found in the zone-h .org archive, so it is not possible to discuss them all here (see the appendix for a selected list of hacking groups).

In the Middle East, there is a thriving do-it-yourself (DIY) hacking culture which manifests in the abundance of YouTube video tutorials, online guides, forums, and numerous private Facebook groups that allege to teach online users the means to carry out hacking, including ethical hacking operations. Adel Troy, for example, is an amateur Arab hacker focused on national targets and explaining DIY hacking tools through his YouTube channel (Hack Webs 2016). Other hackers who periodically post DIY video tutorials and promotional materials to meticulously explain how to hack include Syrianoo Hacker, an anti-Assad Syrian group which focuses on hacking Syrian and Russian government websites (Syrianoo Hacker 2012), Alamdar, which targets national and inter-national sites (Alamdar Hacking Organization 2016), Sheret Hacker, an Iraqi DIY hacker (Sheret Hacker Iraq 2019), and the Shiaa Hacker Boys (2012). Some of these DIY hacking channels, which also offer online security tips, are pri-vate groups on mobile apps like WhatsApp and Telegram, including @HACK_ SAiF, @pupgeg, and @bandanas600. For this study, the author collected 1,990,779 tweets that referenced the Arab word for "hack" and its derivations from January 2, 2018, to October 26, 2019, using Netlytic. Interestingly, the most frequently retweeted posts are related to guidelines covering how to pro-tect one's WhatsApp and social media accounts, whereas other popular tweets focused on reports about the hacking of a Saudi sports club and famous individuals. Some of the most active users include self-proclaimed ethical hackers like @hkar_hkar, who allegedly provides services to assist online users hacked by others. These online discussions, groups, and forums assist in disseminating information about online safety and security. Some human rights activists in Saudi Arabia, UAE, Bahrain, and Iraq have become more tech savvy when it comes to understanding the risks of state surveillance and therefore now often download virtual private networks (VPNs) to protect themselves at key times, such as during the popular protests in Iraq in October 2019. Others seek collaboration with international groups, linking up with the efforts of groups like the Citizen Lab, which developed a tool called Himaya (protection) to identify spying software and malware on mobile phones (Perlroth 2016).

Due to the proliferation of the Internet and social media, politically independent and individual hackers are increasing in number in the Middle East. Counter to the common perception that these hackers are young people merely seeking online adventure (Communication Technologies, Inc. 2004), there is evidence suggesting this proliferation of hackers could be emerging from diverse age groups and backgrounds. Similar to the more organized hacking groups, many of these individual hackers have political motives when targeting the websites of their own national governments. Among the main reasons for these hacking and cyberoperations are to create better employment opportunities for citizens, to highlight state corruption and injustice, and possibly to reshape a political system built on authoritarian and dictatorial rules. Arab states often practice what is known as networked authoritarianism, a phenomenon that emerges when "an authoritarian regime embraces and adjusts to the inevitable changes brought by digital communications" (MacKinnon 2011, 33). This description, indeed, applies to the majority of Arab states, including Saudi Arabia, Bahrain, Syria, Algeria, Egypt, Iraq, Qatar, and the UAE. In Saudi Arabia, the government even engages in deleting certain trending Arabic hashtags that are critical of the kingdom, such as, to take one unsubtle and lengthy hashtag as an example, #StopalSheikFromWastingTheNationsMoney (Maza 2017). Networked authoritarianism, however, is more sophisticated than just deleting or censoring tweets. "States that practice networked authoritarianism do not strictly censor online dissent: they compete with it, making an example out of online dissenters in order to affirm the futility of activism to a disillusioned public" (Pearce and Kendzior 2012, 284). During the 2019 protests in Algeria, which ultimately resulted in the resignation of President Abdelaziz Bouteflika, there was a high level of activity by state-sponsored electronic flies or trolls targeting human rights activists and their outlets, such as the Collective of Activist Youth's Facebook page (Silva 2019). Political trolls in Iraq, to take another example, are routinely hired by Iraqi officials and religious parties to silence opposition and dissent through the use of systematic and organized efforts, often involving mean-spirited comments, insults, and curses on social media (Alaraby 2017).

In relation to the national dimension of cyberwars and online political disruption, we can find ample evidence of how hacking is used to influence internal politics. During the October 2019 protests in Iraq, which were mostly organized by students (both male and female), some Iraqi hackers defaced the website of the Ministry of Telecommunication and posted a message in Arabic, stating: "We are the people who refuse any foreign intervention in Iraq's internal affairs. Our mission is to fight the enemies like foreign agents and the corrupt inside the country . . . Again and again . . . this is a free people's revolution . . . and our weapon is our ideas . . . the website of the Ministry of Telecommunication was shut down by the people's orders" (Arabi21 2019). The protests, which led to the killing of hundreds of civilians all over the country and to the resignation of Prime Minster Adel Abdul Mahdi, also coincided with other hacking attempts. One group hacked the Twitter and Facebook accounts of the Iraqi Anti-Terrorism Squad Force and posted a false message announcing the arrest of the former prime minister, Mahdi, in order to disrupt and weaken trust in the country's political leadership. This is another example of the kind of bottom-up online political disruption that occurs within a particular country. Around the same time, an Iraqi hacker known as "M4X Pro" defaced thirty Iraqi websites (*Kurdistan 24* 2019) including one belonging to the Iraqi Hezbollah group (https://www.kataibhezbollah.com; the website is currently inactive as it was seized by the US government in October 2020).

The hacker revealed to the public that this group uses spying software to monitor the social media outlets of Iraqi human rights activists. In another hack, he revealed the corruption, blackmail, and embezzlement practiced by the Iraqi National Cyber Security Team, which was established in 2017. His main purpose appears to be to reveal state corruption and malpractice, while showing clear support for the protesters, especially those who died, such as Safaa Al Sarai (https://www.zone-h.org 2019).

In February 2017, anti-corruption rallies were organized in Iraq, resulting in the death of several innocent civilians (Al Jazeera 2017a). In the aftermath, a group calling themselves "Cyb3r-Shia & Ghost IQ" hacked the website of the Iraqi Electoral Committee and posted a message stating that the hacking was an act of revenge for the martyrs who fell in peaceful demonstrations: "They persecuted the protestors and the right to protest . . . persecuted the constitution and laws. They killed protesters and tomorrow will kill the right to protests and freedom of expression." In 2017, another Iraqi hacker, named Hussein Mahdi,[2] defaced twenty Iraqi government websites, including the sites of former Iraqi prime minister Nouri al-Maliki, Speaker of the Iraqi Parliament Salim Abdullah al-Jabouri, Iraqi MP Hanan al-Fatlawi (El-Taaey 2017), and the Iraqi National Security Advisory (INSA), accusing the group of corruption following a major suicide attack in Baghdad in 2016 that killed over 300 people. Mahdi blamed INSA for wasting public money in their efforts to monitor Friday prayer sermons, expressing surprise that this included spying on Shiite mosques. Mahdi was arrested by Iraqi authorities later in 2017. In response, several other Iraqi hackers, including one known as Uruk Team,[3] formed a collective and defaced ninety-six Iraqi websites, including the Ministries of Construction, Youth and Sports, and Municipalities, as well as Basrah University, in an attempt to pressure the government to release Mahdi (El-Taaey 2017).

When it comes to political hacking in Egypt, the internal political tension between the Muslim Brotherhood and the government created fertile ground for the emergence of several hacking groups. The Arabic term *Rabaa* (four) has become a distinguishing word that refers to Muslim Brotherhood members, many of whom were killed in the protests that followed President Abdel Fattah El-Sisi's ascension to power in 2014. To take a couple of examples, Dr. Afndena is an Egyptian hacker associated with the Anonymous Rabaa hackers group (Cimpanu 2015) and the AnonCoders group (Raincoaster 2015) who once hacked the website of the Ministry of the Environment in Costa Rica, defacing it to post a video about the 2013 Rabaa Square massacre in Cairo (Cimpanu 2015). Another group calling themselves Anonymous Rabaa hacked the websites of Cairo Airport and the Egyptian presidency (Aboulkheir 2015) to express their rejection of El-Sisi's government. As for Saudi Arabia, a hacking group called Team 04HrB hacked the website of Riyad Bank in June 2010 demanding the resignation of the ruler of the Madina region of the country due to his alleged corruption and inadequate provision of public services. The hackers sent a message addressing the broader public and appealing to the king of Saudi Arabia to remove that official (WikiLeaks 2010): "The Campaign to expel the ruler of Medina (Apologies the thief of Medina)."

As for the regional dimension of cyberwars and Arab hackers, we can find numerous cases of cyberconflict, including several already discussed at length in earlier chapters, that occur due to offline political tensions and sectarian divisions. The Yemen Cyber Army (YCA), for instance, hacked the website of the Saudi Ministry of Foreign Affairs and handed over all the classified documents to WikiLeaks in 2015. The YCA also hacked the website of the Saudi-run *al-Hayat* newspaper in 2015 (Al Arabiya 2015). Figure 6.1 shows a defaced Saudi website from 2018 wherein a photo of the Saudi king, Salman Al Saud, is posted showing him handcuffed in hell with a Quranic verse that has the same meaning as the image. These hacking attempts and messages are in reaction against the Saudi military intervention in Yemen, known as Operation Decisive Storm. Although there is no conclusive evidence, YCA would appear to be an Iranian-backed hacking group using the name of Yemen as a cover under which to wage a proxy cyberwar with Saudi Arabia (Frenkel 2015).

FIG. 6.1 A defaced Saudi website hacked by the Yemen Cyber Army.

A small group calling themselves Rab3oun is another example of a hacking group that directs most of its attention to regional powers, namely Israeli and Iranian websites. Due to historical political tension with Israel, many Arab hackers see it as a preferred target. Rab3oun left the following messages on Israeli websites: "It's just the beginning" in English, and "Who will walk on your limbs in battle" in Hebrew. At the same time, a completely different offensive message was posted on the Iranian website, indicating the sectarian dimension of this hacking activity.

The same kind of rhetoric is found in the messages used by the Saudi hacker Crazy-3r3r, who often advises hacked Saudi and Emirati websites to update their online security procedures while at the same time attacking Iran, the United States, and Israel with offensive language. On one occasion he complained about the lack of employment opportunities when he hacked a Saudi government website, while the messages he left on Israeli websites were of an entirely different nature, such as, "Crazy Arar- Fuck Israel—Done" or "Play began . . . penetrate all Israeli sites . . . by pirate Arabia . . . down with Israel." On Iranian websites, he would leave crude messages such as "Go Fuck your Iran" and post images accompanied with religious texts that defended Sunni Islam and condemned Shiite doctrine (see figure 6.2).

On the other side of the Middle East's sectarian divide, there are dozens of Shiite hacking groups like Shia, Shia Cobra, Shia Hackers, Shia SHielD, Shia TeaM, Shia-root, shia.sec, shiaghost, shialectures, ShiaCyb3rArmy, all of which tend to focus on regional targets related to Sunni-Shiite tensions. The Yemen Cyber Army, discussed above, is one example, and the ShiaCyb3rArmy is another. In 2017, the latter group defaced a Sunni religious website

FIG. 6.2 An Iranian website defaced by a Saudi hacker called Crazy-3r3r.

(https://www.ibn-jebreen.com) with the following message in Arabic: "A hacking gift to the courageous Iraqi Army, Popular Mobilization, and Islamic resistance groups in Iraq as well as the wounded Yemeni people, Hezbollah, Egypt's Shiites, and to every honest Shiite on this globe- https://www.facebook.com/ShiaCyb3rArmy." In summary, Arab political hackers have diverse religious and national backgrounds and motivations, but they have many common features when it comes to how their attacks are directed inside their respective countries in order to disclose and expose malpractices, state corruption, and social injustice. We now turn to a more detailed discussion of Arab cyber armies, with a focus on the Syrian Electronic Army.

Arab Cyber Armies

The author collected 46,944 Arabic tweets that made reference to "electronic armies" for over a year, from April 19, 2018, until July 21, 2019, using Netlytic. Figure 6.3 shows the frequency of tweets that mention electronic armies in Arabic. The highest number of messages using this term (n = 1,612) were posted on June 22, 2018, followed by June 14 (n = 1,603) and October 26 of the same year (n = 811). During the busiest day, the most retweeted post (n = 52) was a tweet related to the 2018 Iraqi election ironically stating that Iraqi political parties and their electronic armies have diverse interests which would only converge once commissions from Iraq's oil were shared. This post and its popularity reveal a perceptive public cynical about political parties. It's also a reminder that it's not only nation-states that have their own electronic armies; this phenomenon

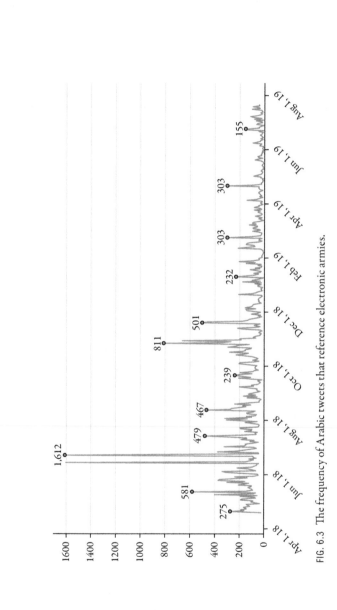

FIG. 6.3 The frequency of Arabic tweets that reference electronic armies.

extends to political parties, especially in Iraq and Lebanon where several active political groups are also extremely present online.

One of the busiest days for tweets about electronic armies, June 14, we find that the most frequent terms in the 100 most retweeted posts are related to the Saudi Electronic Army, also known as "Salmani's Army," which was established in 2016.[4] The content of many of the tweets wishes the Saudi national football team victory during the FIFA world cup competition in Russia, using the trending hashtag "#the electronic army supports you green [team]" (#الجيش_الالكتروني_معاك_ياالاخضر) in reference to the color of the Saudi national team's shirts. Interestingly, the most active user on this day, @Conan_011, who sent eighteen tweets, is allegedly himself a member of the Saudi Electronic Army, based on his profile page, which carries its logo and a link to one of its official accounts. His tweets revolve around trolling the state of Qatar and praising the Emirati ruler, Zayd Bin Nahyan, the UAE, and Saudi Arabia's Mohammed bin Salman. Examining the dataset as a whole, we also see the prominence of the Saudi users. One interesting finding is that the highest number of retweets are attributed to a story praising Saud Al-Qahtani (n = 1,970 in two formats), who was in charge of the Saudi electronic flies, the Saudi Electronic Army, and allegedly responsible for the killing of Jamal Khashoggi. The popular tweet contains a video report made by the Saudi-run MBC channel that describes Al-Qahtani as a "savior" who "heroically rescued" the kingdom of Saudi Arabia from the electronic attacks from Qatar and other opponents. The original tweet reads as follows: "The Consultant at the Royal Assembly who noticed the danger of electronic armies and the Internet war, Saud Al Qahtani. He managed in a very short period of time to create a strong internal front through which the lies of Al Jazeera channel and its sister media outlets were silenced in a professional and organized manner. . . . https://twitter.com/MBCinaWeek/status/1010129481552613376."

An examination of the other most frequently retweeted posts shows a varied picture. There are some ironic or humorous messages meant to attack the existence of electronic flies and armies in the Arab world, taking aim at the Saudi Electronic Army. Tweets by journalists from Al Jazeera, Ghada Oueiss, and Faisal Al Qassim attacked these armies for trolling their opponents. The two journalists' posts got 990 retweets. Other popular retweets were related to the same trolling problem that plagues Twitter, with references to Omani Lebanese, Iraqi, and Houthi electronic armies (see table 6.1). As mentioned, the main focus of the tweets are the Saudi trolls and their army, who in addition to official Twitter accounts have their own Snapchat and Telegram as well. One of their popular posts (n = 232) includes news about hacking the Twitter account of a Yemeni TV channel (@almasirah) due to its anti-Saudi coverage, as well as reference to the hacking of an Iranian company's website that sells carpets by a Saudi user using the handle @DrBassam_. Most pro-Saudi trolls use the

Table 6.1
The Top Ten Most Retweeted Posts

No.	Retweets	Frequency
1.	المستشار في الديوان الملكي الذي انتبه لخطر الجيوش الإلكترونية وحرب الانترنت ، سعود القحطاني .. استطاع خلال فترة وجيزة صناعة جبهة داخلية قوية استطاعت اسكات اكاذيب الجزيرة واخواتها عبر عمل ممنهج واحترافي .. تقرير: مالك الروقي @saudq1978 https://t.co/3PXLdrMN4o The Royal Court advisor who noticed the dangers of the electronic armies and cyber wars, Saud Al Qahtani.. He managed to establish a strong inner front in a short period of time that managed to shut down Al Jazeera and its siblings' lies through systematic and professional work. Report by: Malek Elroky https://t.co/3PXLdrMN4o	1507
2.	كيل الشتائم الذي يمارسه الجيش الإلكتروني العماني لكل من يتحدث عن سلطنة عمان..لا يخدم الصورة المعروفة عن الشعب العماني حسن السمعة والأخلاق The amount of insults coming from the Omani electronic army towards anyone who talks about the Sultanate of Oman..does not serve the good and well-known reputation of the Omani people.	950
3.	د. أنور مالك: تم تجييش وسائل إعلام وشبكات من الجيوش الإلكترونية لضرب السعودية والانتقام منها ومحاولة إشغالها بنفسها https://t.co/5kJ8XWuq5h #المراقب_24 #السعودية Dr. Anwar Malak: The media and electronic armies have been mobilized to avenge and attack Saudi Arabia, and distract the country. #Saudiarabia #themonitor24 https://t.co/5kJ8XWuq5h	715
4.	تحت اسم احمد وبصورة ولي عهد السعودية وعلم المملكة يستمرّ ذباب المجرم قحطاني في السباب والطائفية والعنصرية. هذا مستوى الجيش الالكتروني الذي يعمل لمحمد ابن سلمان ويجهل او يتجاهل ان ترمب وابنته حلبا خزينة المملكة وهما ليسا مسلمين! فليطّلع العالم على مستوى من يدافع عن ابن سلمان https://t.co/pI76IgMicS Under the name of Ahmed and using the picture of the Crown Prince of Saudi Arabia and the Kingdom's flag, the flies of the criminal Al Qahtani continue to spread insults, racism and sectarianism. This is the debased level of the electronic army which works for Mohamed Bin Salman who is ignorant about or ignores the fact that Trump and his daughter milked the Kingdom's treasury thoguh they're not Muslims! Let the world see how those who defend Bin Salman are like. https://t.co/pI76IgMicS	593

(continued)

Table 6.1
The Top Ten Most Retweeted Posts (*continued*)

No.	Retweets	Frequency
5.	المضحك ان من يتشفى في انخفاض العملة التركية و الاقتصاد التركي . . .	485
	كان يذهب للسياحة في تركيا . . . .و ملابسه تركية وقهوته تركية ويعشق الشاورما والبقلاوة التركية ..وحتى حمامه تركي. . . .☺	
	.المنتج المحلي الفالح فيه هو الجيش الإلكتروني . . .	
	لا أعرف من يستحق الشفقة 🤭	
	What's funny is that those who are happy about the decline of the Turkish currency and the Turkish economy . . .	
	Used to visit Turkey as a tourist . . . his clothes are from Turkey, his coffee is Turkish, loves Turkish shawarma and baklava and even his spa is Turkish. . . . ☺	
	His only local product he is successful with is the electronic army I don't know who deserves more pity here 🤭	
6.	فيديو	المستشار في الديوان الملكي الذي انتبه لخطر الجيوش الإلكترونية وحرب الانترنت.. سعود القحطاني.. الرجل الذي وحد الصف وأخمد الفتن ضد بلاده في تويتر. @saudq1978 https://t.co/L8yrGyVy7v	400
	Video | Royal Court advisor who noticed the threat of electronic armies and cyber war..Saud Al Qahtani..The man who united fronts and put off attacks against his country on Twitter. @saudq1978 https://t.co/L8yrGyVy7v	
7.	هذا المقطع يذكرني بالذباب الالكتروني أو الجيوش الالكترونية بتاع المخابرات والمباحث. . . يحسبون كل صيحة عليهم وعلى اسيادهم، فينبحون جوقة واحدة.https://t.co/EMOVu0Zz55	397
	This video clip reminds me of the general intelligence services or the state security's electronic flies or electronic armies..They record every shout against them and then they all bark back at the same time. https://t.co/EMOVu0Zz55	
8.	طعنت عرضي وسلطت كلابك ليفعلوا مثل فعلك ولا زالت إساءتك لي على اليوتيوب بفبركة الجيش الالكتروني لطعن الأعراض موجودة حتى الآن ..	331
	اسأل الله تعالى الأعلم بصدقي وبكذبك والأعلم بغيري على ديني وعفتي ومحافظتي على نفسي ودناءتك، أن يعاملك بعدله وأن ينتقم منك أشد انتقام وكل من يؤيدكhttps://t.co/KNwpQRkN7w	
	You tarnished my reputation and sent your dogs to do the same. Your insults are still on YouTube till today with the help and manipulation of the electronic army to tarnish people's reputation. . . . I ask Allah to take revenge. . . . https://t.co/KNwpQRkN7w	
9.	بأنك سوف تقوم@ALTrendALsauoditتتحدث باسم الجيش الالكتروني وتهدد في الواتس وفي خاص حساب بحمله سبام علي ..	295
	ساعدتك في رفع هشتاقين من باب الأخوه فقط ولكن انت لايثمر فيك المعروف ابداً فحبيت ابين لك شي للعالم والله على قول شهيدhttps://t.co/ASCV6oia4I 🤚	
	You speak on behalf of the electronic army and send threats privately and on WhatsApp that you will start a spam campaign on @ AlTrendALsauodi.	
	I helped you promote two hashtags out of kindness only but you don't value favors at all so I wanted to show the world everything and Allah is my witness.	
	🤚 https://t.co/ASCV60ia4I	

Table 6.1
The Top Ten Most Retweeted Posts (*continued*)

No.	Retweets	Frequency
10.	https://t.co/rCCbSGRo3e "SA" هاشتاق بدأ تداولة في كذلك في: دول الخليج 📌 #حجب_يوتيوب_في_السعوديه • "الترند السعودي خبراء التسويق والنشر" @AlTrendAlsaudi #الجيش_الالكتروني https://t.co/rCCbSGRo3e A hashtag that was promoted in "SA" and the Gulf countries 📌#block-YoutubeinSaudiArabia "The Saudi trend experts in digital marketing and publishing" @AlTrendAlsaudi #Electronicarmy	279

image of Mohammed bin Salman as their profile picture, similar to the way pro-Qatari users tweet about electronic flies with weaponized slogans and hashtags like "Great Saudi" or "Saudi Arabia is a red line," which implies that any criticism against the kingdom is frowned upon. Other popular hashtags include "Khamenei's tails," a reference to anti-Saudi users who are routinely accused of being supporters of Shiite Iran in order to silence them.

The focal point of discussion is the Saudi Electronic Army, whether it's being referenced to attack or to praise its members. The activities of the Saudi users are not exclusively about hacking; mostly it is about supporting and protecting its members through liking their tweets and increasing their number of followers in order to keep them active on Twitter. Other key objectives of the Saudi trolls include spamming, trolling, and reporting on any opponent who expresses views that do not align with what the Saudi government promotes. Examination of this dataset shows, interestingly, that the Syrian Electronic Army is no longer a significant factor in the Twitter discussion.

The second level of analysis involved investigating the identity of the fifty most active users in the dataset (see table 6.2). Except for three users (Iraqi, Kuwaiti, and Lebanese), all the top users are pro-Saudi, although only some of them, like @d_77b, publicly state that they belong to the Saudi Electronic Army. Sixteen out of the forty-seven Saudi accounts were suspended, mostly for violating Twitter's community guidelines, so the only way to examine them was through examining the tweets already collected. Three active accounts, furthermore, had no public tweets since they had all been removed by the users; this is a common tactic to avoid detection or suspension from the online site. Finally, a couple of users, @sa77_7md (Kuwaiti) and @SS_XX_ss123, appeared to be bots, based on the nature and frequency of their repeated messages. The latter account, in fact, labels itself as a "trending account" whose main purpose

Table 6.2
The Most Active Twitter Users Who Reference "Electronic Armies" in Arabic

No.	User	Freq.	No.	User	Freq.
1.	nn05324176131	314	26.	frsan	36
2.	m6mp3	142	27.	K990F	35
3.	binanaad	132	28.	marsadiraq	34
4.	abinbandr2	125	29.	Mansour907	33
5.	Ai_5jl	114	30.	SS_XX_ss123	32
6.	d_77b	87	31.	M6n51	31
7.	FKSA1111	87	32.	2090Sfsfsf	30
8.	shawhkhi	86	33.	lO8IO	30
9.	abm3722	85	34.	sam7mut	29
10.	abm3733	85	35.	7zB6noooo o5	28
11.	gragosh221	76	36.	alshorea	27
12.	l_lmss1	65	37.	azizusu	27
13.	sa77_7md	65	38.	Abo_Salem_1976	26
14.	N_alarrak	61	39.	14yzon	25
15.	Abo1_1rakan	58	40.	dooooly1400	25
16.	Conan_011	54	41.	kd53	24
17.	Allal2011Seri	50	42.	pp100pp300	24
18.	S6ll8	49	43.	Q2I9I	24
19.	2ow	47	44.	Toni_naeo	24
20.	koooldh	46	45.	Vo5Ge9	24
21.	Mrkiller1111	46	46.	ksairh	23
22.	sehr_harout	44	47.	m6no5	23
23.	l_lmss	42	48.	monzerhakeem	23
24.	semfo990	41	49.	R14000000	23
25.	ksa__halo	38	50.	Rayan9200	23

is to magnify pro-Saudi messages. In summary, the most active users and the most frequently retweeted posts are related to praising Saudi Arabia and its electronic army, demonstrating that Twitter is dominated by such users, unlike the results on electronic flies we discussed in chapter 3.

Based on a qualitative examination of the top users, we find that members of the Saudi Electronic Army do not often engage in successful hacking attempts. Instead, they primarily wage information warfare against their opponents by spamming and reporting on other accounts, an action they refer to as squishing (دعس). This usually plays out in a process following several steps. First, they identify users whose accounts need to be targeted or closed due to their opposition to Saudi Arabia. Second, a number of like-minded users are contacted using their handle names and instructed to report on these opponents' accounts by following six instructions, which were visually illustrated by @Brave_ksa in one of his posts (see figure 6.4). Emojis can even be used to guide the actions of members of the electronic army (✗👇✗👇✗👇✗👇👆).

FIG. 6.4 Steps followed by the Saudi Electronic Army to report on opponents' Twitter accounts. The post can be retrieved from the following link https://twitter.com/Brave_ksa /status/1061616162465812480.

Members of the Saudi Electronic Army will sometimes try to game the online system by claiming that accounts they disapprove of, such as those supportive of Houthi Yemenis and Qataris, actually belong to terrorists, often shaming those responsible if no action is taken. Some pro-Saudi users report to Twitter and its founder, Jack Dorsey (@jack), about reinstating the accounts of their own community members and/or removing the accounts of their opponents. This weaponization of a social media platform's reporting procedures will be discussed further when we look in more detail at online spamming.

Regarding the most frequent words and phrases in the tweets, and leaving aside the word "electronic," we find that "Saudi" (in two formats) is the most frequent word (n = 167,986), followed by "Qatar" (n = 93,017), "Salman" (n = 62,133), and "Khashoggi" (n = 46,598). As for phrases, "Salmani Army" is the most frequently used (n = 5,081), followed by "Saudi Electronic Army" (n = 2,644) and "Saud Al Qahtani" (n = 2,507). The other electronic armies that are referenced in tweets include the Omani (n = 950), the Lebanese free patriotic movement (n = 608), which seems to belong to President Michel Aoun, as well as the Iranian (n = 510), and the Southern Yemeni (n = 359) armies. The latter has its own Twitter account, @Jnoob_Army, and Facebook page (https://www.facebook.com/AdeniLED/), although they do not seem to have any large following and their main messages are supportive of the Saudi-led coalition against the Houthi rebels and hopefully about the possibility of achieving independence from Yemen. As of February 2021, its Twitter account got suspended and its Facebook page contained no posts at all.

Regarding the most used hashtags, and leaving aside #flies, #Saudi comes first (n = 39,759), followed by #Qatar (n = 34,768), #intelligence (n = 16,786), and #Jamal (n = 16,674). Also among the top ten hashtags is #Qatari-Zionists (n = 14,449), which as we have seen is a reference to trolls that is often used to describe Qatari sympathizers. The association with Zionism is meant to discredit the Qatari cause and frame the state of Qatar as one that is supportive of—and supported by—Israel. As can be clearly seen from the most-referenced words, phrases, and hashtags, there is a clear binary division between Saudi Arabia and Qatar in relation to electronic flies, pointing again to the regional dimension of this conflict. Many of the posts again involved reference to the Saudi activist Khashoggi, as well as the activities of the Saudi and Qatari trolls.

In terms of the Arabic news coverage, the author retrieved all the stories from Factiva, which referenced the term "electronic armies." In total, there were 1,403 news stories from 100 Arabic-language sources, and the year 2018 saw the highest number of stories, mostly due to the killing of Khashoggi (see table 6.3). The most frequent relevant words include "Daesh" (the Arabic acronym of ISIS), which comes first (n = 178) in relation to its Cyber Caliphate Army, followed by "Saudi" (n = 134), "Syrian" (n = 91), "social" media (n = 81), and "hacking" (n = 70). Regarding the most frequent phrases, "social media" is the most recurrent combination of words (n = 65), followed by "electronic army" (n = 57), "Daesh group" (n = 36), "Saudi Foreign Ministry" (n = 31), "USA" (n = 30), "Syrian Electronic Army" (n = 28), and "Yemeni Electronic Army" (n = 26). The latter refers to the Yemen Cyber Army (@YemeniCyberArmy) which was involved in #OpSaudi that succeeded in hacking the Saudi Ministry of

Table 6.3
The Distribution of News
Stories Referencing
"Electronic Armies"

Year	Frequency
2011	32
2012	49
2013	120
2014	76
2015	94
2016	101
2017	314
2018	416
2019	201
Total	**1,403**

FIG. 6.5 The Twitter profile of the Yemen Cyber Army.

Foreign Affairs in 2015. The group tweeted just a few times in 2015 after the hacking attempt, stating that they are "a group of Yemeni youth who were divided in the past due to their political alliances while united today because of the Saudi aggression against our country." The group's Twitter profile contains the popular hashtags they often use, but it's worth noting there are stark differences between the Arabic and English ones. The Arabic hashtags include some hostile ones like "Death to America," "Allah curse Saud's family," Death to Israel," and "Jews' brother" (see figure 6.5). The latter term is regarded as a pejorative description assigned to the Saudis for bombing Yemen.

Another electronic army that used to be more popular is the Egyptian one. First established in 2014, the Egyptian Electronic Army's Twitter account was changed from @egyptianarmy30 to @RamezEladala. This was probably due to the number of reports targeting the account, whose Twitter profile read as follows: "The Egyptian Army is fire against the aggressor and peace for those

Table 6.4
Most Active Twitter Users Referencing
Spam in Arabic

No.	User	Frequency
1.	@alamrikiya_001	450
2.	@gragosh221	330
3.	@MGWVc	197
4.	@r_alwadaan	152
5.	@__ssq_	148
6.	@Abo1_1rakan	130
7.	@AlbrqAlshmali	129
8.	@vip_kingahrose	107
9.	@R333m67	97
10.	@A_BINSAAD_	93
11.	@pp100pp300	91
12.	@Abdullah_alslmi	82
13.	@KSA_MBS_2030	82
14.	@aishaaraby	81
15.	@amal22315	75
16.	@Ai_5jl	70
17.	@Soo_12f	66
18.	@zm298	66
19.	@goorryyi	60
20.	@ksa_halo	59

who conform. We warn those who challenge us." It seems that its initial mission was hacking the websites and social media accounts of ISIS. Using Crimson Hexagon, the author downloaded all 346 tweets posted between November 16, 2014, until December 1, 2014. Some of the tweets are linked to a fake Facebook page that has since been deleted. Other posts urge followers to like the aforementioned Facebook page or follow its Twitter account to avoid it being deleted, while still others attack Al Jazeera or discuss hacking Egyptian opposition figures, especially Muslim Brotherhood leaders and activists, labeling them as agents for Israel and the United States. Another popular theme in their tweets is the feud with Anonymous in which they accuse some its members of being mercenaries, while hacking some Turkish websites due to Turkey's support for Egypt's Brotherhood as well as Qatar. One of the group's tweets succinctly justifies their cyberoperations: "You have freedom of expression, while I have freedom of hacking."

To add another level of analysis regarding Arab cyber armies and their weaponization of social media, the author used Netlytic and collected 165,331 tweets sent by 101,698 unique users. The tweets that referenced the Arabic word for "spam" were collected from the period between April 6, 2018, and November 12,

FIG. 6.6 A list of pro-Saudi spam and anti-spam supporters compiled by @MGWVc.

2018. Similar to the findings above, the regional political tensions are evident on Twitter. Table 4.4 shows the top active users are mostly Saudi or pro-Saudi and are part of the Salmani Army, which expresses opposition to any Twitter user who shows animosity toward Saudi Arabia and especially toward Qataris, Iranians, and Houthi Yemenis. As Twitter offers the ability to report accounts that spam others with messages (Twitter 2019), this feature was weaponized by various users in order to remove political opponents from the platform. In other words, those users have gamed the online system to serve their political agenda. For example, the second-most active user, @gragosh221 (n = 330) had his account deleted because of the high number of spam reports received about him. The third-most active user in our sample, @MGWVc (n = 197), a supporter of the Salmani Army, had his account deleted for similar reasons. Figure 6.6 shows the same user's coordinating role in bringing a networked community of pro-Saudi users together to support affiliates in their defensive, anti-spam efforts or to spam opponents themselves. The most retweeted posts show that many users ask for help form their network when they get notified by Twitter that their accounts have been repeatedly reported as spam and might be deleted. In these cases, those users ask for more followers, retweets, and replies in order to show that their accounts are legitimate and to avoid deletion. The famous Al Jazeera journalist Jamal Al-Rayan tweeted this message to his 1.5 million followers: "I am subjected to a spam attack by the electronic flies. Please support #Gulf, #Egypt, #North_Africa https://t.co/nXkyS4jGvE." This message was retweeted over 2,814 times, and the spam campaign was indeed obviously politically motivated due to the Qatari-Saudi regional conflict. Another popular retweet (n = 1,808) called for taking action against one specific Twitter user: "Guys and girls, we need to shut down and remove this account since he spoke against Saudi Arabia @amer_hallal." Incidentally, the account, which belonged to a Lebanese man who expressed anti-Saudi sentiments, is, as of December 2019, suspended.

Finally, and although they have still not made the full dataset publicly available, Facebook announced for the first time in August 2019 the existence of coordinated inauthentic behavior in Egypt, the UAE, and Saudi Arabia. The social media company removed hundreds of Facebook pages and Instagram accounts that were administered by front companies like New Waves in Egypt and Newave in the UAE acting on behalf of the above Arab governments and posting about "local news, politics, elections and topics including alleged support of terrorist groups by Qatar and Turkey, Iran's activity in Yemen, the conflict in Libya, successes of the Saudi-led coalition in Yemen, and independence for Somaliland." Some of their targets included the Muslim Brothers, Al Jazeera, and the questioning of Amnesty International's reports. Some of the fake Facebook pages that were removed include "Mohamed Bin Salman's Life" and "I'm the son of Libya, who are you?" which often praised the Emirati-supported Libyan leader, Khalifa Haftar (Gleicher 2019). In the following section, we look at another case study, featuring a detailed discussion of the Syrian Electronic Army (SEA).

The Syrian Cyberwar

The Syrian conflict has been ongoing since 2011 and quickly escalated into a civil war, leading to one of the worst refugee and humanitarian crises in recent world history. Syrian Sunni rebels are opposed to the Alawite government of Bashar Assad, but the rebels are also divided into numerous factions, including the Free Syrian Army, al-Qaeda, and Daesh (also known as "the Islamic State," ISIS, and ISIL); a number of the rebel groups have been, at various times, fighting each other as well as the Assad regime. The Syrian Observatory for Human Rights estimated that about 450,000 men, women, and children had been killed and 2 million injured between the beginning of the civil war in Syria and December 2016 (Syrian Observatory for Human Rights 2016). This section deals with the cyber battlefield, more specifically the government-run Syrian Electronic Army (SEA) and some of its cyber opponents.

It is known that the Syrian government operates the Syrian Electronic Army (SEA) (https://twitter.com/official_sea16) as a tool for propaganda, espionage, hacking Western websites, and gathering information from oppositional groups and undermining their efforts (Al-Rawi 2014). The Syrian government felt an urgent need to counter the various cyberattacks against its websites, so it created and supported SEA. Established around May 2011, SEA is a hacking group that claims to be independent from Assad's Syrian government. SEA, however, is not a hacktivist group that defends or fights for some causes on their own initiative, but rather a community of cyberwarriors who are defined as people possessing "the characteristic of being sponsored by states and being subject to the oversight of their governments" (Baldi, Gelbstein, and Kurbalija 2003, 18). The Syrian government uses SEA as a propaganda tool to serve its own interests. The organization's ongoing denial of its strong connection to Assad's regime has three main advantages. First, if SEA fails in its activities, for example by having its website hacked, no one can claim a victory over the Syrian government itself. Second, this kind of vague link or association between the two "gives the Syrian government some protection from the legal and political consequences of SEA's attacks" (FireEye Intelligence 2013); effectively, the SEA strives to retain "plausible deniability" of their association with Assad. Finally, keeping the link to the Syrian regime ambiguous and unofficial helps SEA's organization in getting more recruits, including the type of "script kiddies" or "thrill seekers" who seek fame and would not want to be associated with Assad's government but who are nonetheless excited to be part of a "small" organization that is sometimes able to attract the world's attention. Aside from the hacking operations conducted by Anonymous, as explained further below, other attacks against Syria included the email leaks by Syrian opposition activists, including the disclosure of emails from Bashar Assad and his close aides and family members, which were published by the *Guardian* (Booth and Mahmood 2012).

It is important to note that SEA is not only made up of a group of cyberwarriors who are supported by and affiliated to the Syrian government, but is also aided by what are called "patriotic hackers" (FireEye Intelligence 2013) and "cyberjoyriders" (Weimann 2006, 41). SEA, despite its claims to independence and a nonhierarchical structure, is in fact a highly organized group. There is a well-defined leadership and hierarchy, unlike the case of Anonymous, which is made up of loosely connected networks of hackers from all over the world. The TV channel Al-Mayadeen, for instance interviewed the leader of SEA on September 26, 2013. The head of SEA, who is a young Syrian man living in Damascus, framed his group as hacktivists who are defending a cause, stating: "We have Syrian members who live outside the country in case the Internet connection is shut down. As an organization, we are proud to be on the same [FBI terrorist] list with that of the armed wing of Hezbollah" (SEAOfficial-Channel 2013c). This was also confirmed by Anonymous. When it initiated its #OpSyria operation, Anonymous hackers managed to disclose the identity of some of SEA's members living in Romania and Russia and its leader, who is nicknamed Deeb (meaning wolf in Arabic) (Murphy 2013). Finally, a pro-Syrian TV channel, Dunya, interviewed a young Syrian man called Tareq on May 23, 2011, who claimed to be the head of SEA. Dunya revealed that the group consists of hackers living inside the country and others in the diaspora. Tareq emphasized that some Syrians living abroad are helping with translating the organization's messages into different languages (YouTube, 2011b). Due to this hierarchical management structure, I argue that SEA is an extension of the Syrian political establishment. SEA's core members are performing these services for the Assad government, because they adhere to the same ideological beliefs and show great support for the regime and its political system. Second, those practitioners must show "confidence of top management in order to recommend needed adjustments to organizational policies and procedures" (Freitang and Stokes 2009, 5). SEA members largely act in this manner, more evidence that the hierarchical structure is well established and respected.

In relation to its direct connection to the Syrian government, Reporters without Borders identified several countries that it called "Enemies of the Internet," including Syria, in part because of its use of the Syrian Electronic Army as an official intelligence tool. SEA is known to use malware to collect information on oppositional groups (Reporters without Borders 2013). These malware programs and Trojan applications include "Blackshades, DarkComet, Fynloski, Rbot, Xtreme RAT and Zapchast" and have "key logging, document and data stealing, and audio eavesdropping capabilities" (FireEye Intelligence 2013). SEA's actions against opposition members can be extreme and wide-ranging. SEA, for example, published the names and passwords of 11,000 opposition members in July 2012 (Reporters without Borders 2013, 33), and this information was sent to a "computer address lying within Syrian government-controlled internet protocol (IP) space for intelligence collection and review" (FireEye Intelligence 2013). SEA also hacked and stole valuable information from Truecaller, Tango, and Viber, which are all free Internet messaging and telephone services widely used by Syrian opposition members (FireEye Intelligence 2013).

SEA's attacks, furthermore, are also and primarily directed against the social media channels of traditional media outlets as well as against Syrian oppositional websites and Facebook pages. This means that SEA is one of Assad's key international and regional media and propaganda tools, because since the beginning of the rebellion and civil war it has become difficult for the Syrian government to express its views to the world. There are numerous examples of SEA's hacking operations that were mostly directed against Qatar, Saudi Arabia, Canada, the United States, and the U.K. due to their political opposition to Assad's regime. These attacks included hacking Al Jazeera mobile and sending false mobile texts claiming that the Prince of Qatar was subjected to an assassination attempt (Associated Press 2012). SEA also hacked the Facebook and Twitter accounts of the Qatar Foundation on February 28, 2013, posting messages claiming that Qatar supports terrorism (YouTube 2013b). Dozens of other media outlets like the *Washington Post*, the *New York Times*, and The Onion, or the Twitter accounts belonging to the Associated Press, NPR, and Reuters, have also been hacked by SEA. On the Associated Press's Twitter account, SEA once wrote that the White House was bombed and that Obama was injured; this fake news actually made the stock market drop (Memmot 2013; Scharr 2013; FireEye Intelligence 2013). Furthermore, one of the Twitter accounts that belongs to BBC Weather was hacked by SEA, which posted sarcastic messages like "Earthquake warning for Qatar: Hamad Bin Khalifah about to exit vehicle," ridiculing his past obesity, or "Hazardous warning for North Syria: Erdogan orders terrorists to launch chemical weapons at civilian areas" (Deans, Plunkett, and Halliday 2013). Other SEA hacking operations included distributed denial-of-service (DDoS), phishing, and domain name system (DNS) attacks in the case of the *New York Times* (Scharr 2013). Sometimes, a website or an app is hacked, as happened to the Canadian CBC news outlet (Sparks 2014). Finally, one cyberattack involved defacing the U.S. Department of State's website following Ambassador John Ford's visit to Syria in July 2011 to show support for anti-Assad protesters (Valeriano and Maness 2015, 104).

The SEA, it is important to mention here, has not been active since the beginning of 2016, and the last tweet the SEA sent was in December 2015. As for its VK account (https://vk.com/syrianelectronicarmy, a Russian social networking site), the last post made was in March 2016. There are two main reasons that can explain this inactivity. The first relates to the increasing challenges faced by SEA online, as the majority of their sites and social media outlets were attacked and hacked. Additionally, three members of SEA are on the FBI "most wanted" list, because of their roles in targeting U.S. websites, and a reward of $100,000 has been offered for information leading to their arrest (FBI 2016). Some former members of the SEA went on to create fake pages on social media, especially after the Russian intervention in the Syrian conflict (Jaber 2017). Secondly and most importantly, Syria has been relying extensively on other regional powers, especially Russia and Iran, to counter its enemies, and this reliance extends to the cyber battlefield. For example, Iranian hackers are believed to have targeted Syrian dissidents living inside and outside the country with various malware in order to steal valuable information from them, which can lead to death or torture for the dissidents (Scott-Railton et al. 2016; Deibert 2016). Many Russian websites, as well as hackers based in or supported by Russia, have supported Assad's efforts to maintain power and influence in cyberspace (Jaber 2017).

SEA's SNS and Online Presence

The Syrian Computer Society, which was established by Bashar Assad's brother Bassel in 1989 and was headed later by Bashar himself before he became president, hosted and registered the SEA's websites, which indirectly reveal its government affiliation (Scharr 2013). SEA's old website (syrian-es.org/) is no longer functioning due to U.S. web service restrictions (Scharr 2013). On their Instagram account (instagram.com/official_sea/), which was active in 2013, the first image that the SEA posted was of Bashar Assad, with the text: "Every year and you're the nation's leader." On its Twitter page (https://twitter.com/Official _SEA16),[5] however, SEA describes itself as neutral from the state or any political faction: "We are not an official side and do not belong to a political party. We are Syrian youths who responded to the call of duty after our homeland, Syria, was subjected to cyber attacks. We decided to respond actively under the name of Syrian Electronic Army SEA" (Syrian Electronic Army 2013a). It is impossible for the SEA to operate inside the government-controlled areas without the direct knowledge of, and direction from, the totalitarian government of Syria.

The SEA later created another website (sea.sy/index/en) that was hosted in Russia, which could be confirmed because the public email associated with the site ends with .ru. This website, however, was attacked and abandoned shortly after it started. In June 2011, Assad praised some of his supporters and highlighted the hacking operations of the SEA, which he said "has been a real army in virtual reality" (Scharr 2013).

According to its old website, the SEA attributes its existence to the anti-Assad stance taken by many Arab and Western media channels. It claims that these channels "started to support terrorists groups that killed civilians and members of the Syrian Arab Army as well as destroying private and public properties. These media outlets functioned as an umbrella for these groups to continue their acts by ignoring the coverage of terrorism in Syria and accusing the Arab Syrian Army to be behind everything" (Syrian Electronic Army n.d.). It seems that the SEA's Facebook page has been routinely and continuously removed by Facebook administrators (Syrian Electronic Army, 2013c). On its 252nd Facebook page (facebook.com/SEA.252),[6] the SEA wrote in the following three word in the "About" section to describe the group: "Homeland ... Honor ... Loyalty." This is the same slogan used by Assad's Syrian Arab Army. By closely examining the 253rd Facebook page (facebook.com/SEA.253), which was created on December 10, 2013, and removed shortly afterwards, I observed that the page was heavily moderated by its creators and only contained instructions on where to attack Syrian oppositional groups or report abuse or hate speech to Facebook administrators in order to shut them down.

Another Facebook page was called "The SEA Fourth Division." It was created on December 5, 2013, and had over 2,546 likes in less than five days (facebook.com/SEA.P.252); it too was removed from Facebook in short order. One comment, posted on December 10, 2013, mentioned that the Facebook page was being reported as being in violation of Facebook guidelines; the person running the page instructed his followers to like or comment on some of its posts in order to help avoid being shut down, urging: "Please don't let me down, Shabiha." The term *Shabiha* is used to refer to militia members affiliated with Assad's regime (Al-Rawi, 2014a). Other instructions were directed toward hacking Facebook pages or reporting abuse in relation to Facebook pages that opposed Assad, such as Al-Yarmouk Camp (facebook.com/NewsOfYarmouk ?fref=ts) and Imam Dhahabi Divisions (facebook.com/kalidbrkat.ahmad.1). Later, the SEA announced on its website that its 260th Facebook page had been created:

> They have been hurt by the blows of the SEA, so they fought us with everything that they have and shut down our Facebook page hundreds of times. Now, learn and let your masters learn, too. We swear that if you shut us down millions of times, you will neither affect our determination nor perseverance. This is our arena and you know this well. Wait for us for you who boast of freedom of speech. We do not need any funding from any side because there is only a need to have a computer and an Internet connection. (Syrian Electronic Army n.d.)

As of late 2014, the SEA also had three YouTube channels: syrianeso, syrianes1, and SEAOfficialChannel. Since its Facebook page was getting removed continuously, as explained, YouTube became one of the only sources where the group could post its videos. These three YouTube channels contained similar videos, but they are believed to have been created in order to archive the SEA's activities in case one of the channels was removed. syrianes1 was the first YouTube channel created by the SEA, on May 11, 2011 (YouTube 2011a). It had 225 videos, 4,436 subscribers, and 1,535,068 views as of January 6, 2014.[7] SEAOfficialChannel had 49 videos, 1,851 subscribers, and 51,844 views and was created on April 9, 2013 (YouTube 2013a). The third YouTube channel is syrianeso, which was created on June 7, 2011. It had 284 videos, 3,245 subscribers, and over 1,600,000 views (YouTube 2011c). As of December 2017, the latter two are the only channels that the SEA has on YouTube.

The video that had the highest number of views showed a group of captive Syrian soldiers wearing civilian clothes being allegedly freed by Assad's army.[8]

The clip was taken from footage aired by the pro-Assad TV station Al-Dunya, and most of the comments on YouTube mocked the video and alleged it was a fake production (YouTube 2012c). The next most popular video was posted on the syrianes1 channel, and featured a famous Syrian female singer, Assalah Nasri, referring to the Syrian national anthem. The video clip is framed as if she belittled the anthem (YouTube 2012b).[9] Many comments on the post make reference to "sexual jihad," a term repeatedly used by pro-Assad commentators to discredit opposing views. This was in reference to a controversial fatwa issued by some Salafi Muslim sheikhs, and rejected by the majority of Sunni imams, that allows Muslim women to have sex with the rebel fighters as part of their efforts to establish an Islamic state (BBC News 2013). On the other hand, hundreds of other users leaving comments who oppose Assad and the SEA often make references to "Mutt'ah," which means "pleasure marriage," a derogatory term used by some Sunnis to discredit the Shiite doctrine. The Alawite regime of Bashar Assad is regarded as an offshoot of Shiism, and the above term suggests that some Shiites are born as a result of illegitimate marriages (Haeri 1989).

Another popular term used in the audience comments was the word "mule" (Jahsh in Arabic) to refer to Assad, whose name means lion in Arabic; the mule is associated with stupidity and dullness, in complete contrast to the ferociousness and bravery of the lion. Since the conflict in Syria has had regional implications for several other countries, such as Lebanon and Iraq, there were other political usages of the word "Jahsh." For example, a Saudi film producer, Mohammed Al-Qahtani, announced his plan to make an "Al-Jahsh" film to depict the villainy and violence practiced by the Assad family throughout their rule. The Saudi film was planned as a reaction to the making of an anti-Saudi film, *King of the Sands*, made by the Syrian director Najdat Anzour, which was screened in several cinema theaters in Damascus and negatively depicts the life of King Saud of Saudi Arabia (Al-Qudus Al-Arabi 2014).

In brief, the case of the Syrian Electronic Army can be applied to the several other totalitarian regimes, possibly includes the likes of North Korea's authoritarian government, that use cyberwarriors as an online tool either to steal information from opposition groups or hack websites and SNS outlets aiming at creating an image of a sophisticated and undefeatable regime. These all form part of the cyberwar tactics that are used for offensive and defensive purposes. The SEA effectively used cyberspace to defend, support, and popularize the Assad regime, and some of its strategies were unorthodox. The SEA's case, it is critical to mention, remains unique due to the special circumstances that led to its creation. The phenomenon of the SEA prompted similar reactions from other countries that are close to Assad's regime, including Algeria and Tunisia. For example, the Algerian Electronic Army appeared in 2013. On its Facebook page, a slogan similar to that used by the SEA is posted: "Loyalty. . . . Sacrifice . . . Commitment" (Algerian Electronic Army 2013).

The Tunisian Cyber Army (TCA) was also created in 2013 (Tunisian Cyber Army 2013). Like other governments worldwide, the Syrian government uses cyberwar as part of its offensive tools to protect its own interests. The SEA is one of Assad's government means to attack vital targets in cyberspace, adding prestige and enhancing its image as a sophisticated regime that is able to create havoc in the West. This image has an impact on the propaganda efforts directed at the Syrian public, in particular, and the Arab and international public more generally.

Syrian oppositional groups also have their hacking teams, including the Supreme Council of the Revolution group, which leaked Assad's emails in 2012 (Booth, Mahmood, and Harding 2012), and a group calling itself the Revolutionary Syrian Electronic Army (RSEA) (https://www.facebook.com/SERA.official/), which once hacked the Lebanese National television website and posted an angry message as a protest against the alleged mistreatment of Syrian refugees in Lebanon in 2017 (HuffPost Arabi 2017j). RSEA's main goal is to hack pro-Assad websites and their social media outlets. However, the organization and the impact of these hacking groups cannot be compared to the SEA, which is far more effective in various ways. Finally, Anonymous has also targeted the SEA. One of its famous operations was called Syria—Fighting for Freedom, which included the hacking of the Syrian Customs website (customs.gov.sy) (Anonymous 2013). The Syrian Electronic Army reacted by hacking a Dutch website affiliated with Anonymous and posting a video announcement: "Our integrity is equivalent to the integrity of our territory. If you approached us even a little bit then you should await your complete annihilation" (YouTube 2012a). One commentator on this video, MrKilian555, replied: "You will pay. Believe me. Expect us!" As a reaction, Anonymous initiated operation #OpSyria that allegedly succeeded in exposing the names of five members of the SEA, including some of those who live in Romania and Russia, such as its leader, who is known as Deeb (Murphy 2013). Indeed, the SEA used to be a highly organized group of cyberwarriors whose goal was to serve Assad's government by either stealing sensitive information for intelligence purposes that could help in combating the Syrian rebel groups or hacking the websites of international media outlets or their social media channels in order to draw international attention to Assad's cause. SEA uses all the available tools at its disposal to spread the word on the activities of Assad's Syrian army and to distort the image of Syrian rebels, which is similar to the general objectives of the official Syrian media outlets. It is reasonable to think that SEA's future will always be linked to the fate of Bashar Assad and his Baath government.

In conclusion, there are certain Arab electronic armies, existing primarily on social media, that are very organized and systematic. Currently, the most active one is the Saudi Electronic Army, whose members seem to be closely affiliated with the Saudi government though there still seem to be some ordinary

Saudis showing support for the king and the crown prince, motivated by nationalistic sentiments. Unlike the advanced hacking techniques of the Syrian Electronic Army, what is occurring on social media today is mostly related to spamming and trolling opponents, including reporting on them in order to "squish" or delete their online accounts. The Saudi Electronic Army seems to be ahead of the rest in showing support for its members to keep them active on Twitter while reporting on their opponents and gaming the Twittersphere by accusing everyone they disagree with of being a terrorist. Indeed, the ongoing trolling and online harassment against activists and independent journalists prompted Jamal Khashoggi to propose creating a grassroots online movement comprised of "electronic bees" who can deter and possibly stop the state-sponsored activities of the electronic flies and armies (Shaban 2018). Unfortunately, Khashoggi was murdered before his vision was implemented, and it is doubtful that such an initiative can be effective now given the organized and continuous state-sponsored efforts to undermine online and offline dissent in autocratic countries like Egypt, the UAE, Bahrain, and Saudi Arabia.

Conclusion

• •

This book, which deals with cyberwars in the Middle East, considers hacking and other forms of cyberoperations as forms of online political disruption, which is a militaristic and aggressive public communication inherently powerful due to its use of advanced technology and potential influence. Drawing from Kenneth Waltz's theory of structural realism in international relations and borrowing from Manuel Castells's discussion of power and counterpower, I developed a model that examines the communication flows shaping our networked world. On the one hand, nation-states, the hacking groups of terrorist organizations, and their affiliates or cyberwarriors represent the hegemonic communication powers, employing hacking as offensive and defensive mechanism toward other nation-states and citizens. Due to their inherent power that is represented by using advanced technological means, this type of communication is considered a horizontal flow of online political disruption. In other contexts, these nation-states use spying tools and surveillance mostly inside their territories as a vertical flow (top-down) form of online political disruption to target political activists and perceived opponents.

On the other hand, independent national hackers and global hacktivist groups stand for the counterpowers, practicing a form of vertical (bottom-up) political disruption as a reaction against corruption and the internal politics of their states. However, we also find examples of a horizontal form of online political disruption when hackers target ordinary citizens for a variety of reasons. In the Middle East and elsewhere, cyberoperations activities are conducted along three dimensions: international, regional, and internal. There will certainly be some overlap along these dimensions because the Internet cannot be confined to one geographical region.

The second chapter of the book discussed the horizontal and vertical political disruption that often involves nation-states' cyberoperations. Based on the international dimension of the online political disruption model, the third and fourth chapters provide case studies of U.S. and Russian cyberoperations involving and/or targeting the Middle East region. For example, the U.S. Department of State's Digital Outreach Team (DOT) initiative and other astroturfing online campaigns against terrorism fall within the category of vertical online political disruption (top-down). I argued that the identities of the campaigns' sponsors were concealed due to the general mistrust in the U.S. intentions in the region, and I concluded by stating that the U.S. astroturfing communication approach was not effective because Arab audiences largely viewed it as miscalculated propaganda.

As for the Russian cyberoperations via political trolls, they were more advanced than the U.S. cyberoperations, especially in microtargeting their Western versus Muslim Arab audiences due to using the affordances of social media. Through a discussion of issues surrounding Islam and immigration, the fourth chapter examined the Russian trolls' online political disruption where differences in the English and Arabic messages were highlighted. In English posts, Russian trolls mostly associated Islam with liberals and the Black Lives Matter movement. Yet, the religion is negatively presented when far-right groups are microtargeted. On the other hand, the Arabic-language messages do not show the same animosity toward Islam, which is, instead, framed in a positive way. The overall goal of the Russian trolls is to divide, distract, and possibly mobilize audiences, often giving the false impression that these messages are sent locally in a bottom-up approach (grassroots). The reality, however, is that these cyberoperations are international in dimension and conducted using a vertical (top-down) method.

Chapter five focused on regional politics where cyberoperations are situated within the horizontal form of online political disruption. After closely examining the 2017 Qatari crisis, I showed evidence that most Arab countries have either purchased or used offensive cyber measures and surveillance tools to hack their regional rivals and spy on political activists inside their territories. Specifically, the UAE and Saudi Arabia obtained more advanced spying tools and technologies than other Arab countries, but none of them can compete with Israel's capabilities and to a lesser extent that of Iran.

Finally, the last chapter offered an understanding of a selection of Arab hackers as well as electronic flies and cyber armies, with a focus on the Syrian Electronic Army (SEA). The goal of these cyber armies is to disseminate pro-regime propaganda and attack political opponents, activists, and critics. While SEA was active a few years ago, it became highly invisible in recent years. Instead, the Saudi Cyber Army (Salmani Army) has become the most organized trolling group with the assistance of its former manager, Saud al-Qahtani. Through coordinated and systematic spamming, trolling, and reporting (squishing), cyber armies often succeed in limiting the number of opponent Twitter accounts for short periods of time. These are ongoing cyberoperations that are akin to war skirmishes. For the cyber army members, the outcome of their actions remains unknown but still thrilling to witness. As for independent Arab hackers, we find a thriving DIY online culture that hacktivists engage with to learn how to hack in order to expose government corruption and nepotism. This aspect of cyberwar is waged to create social justice and is theoretically situated within the vertical (bottom-up) online political disruption model.

Finally, I conclude that we have been witnessing an ongoing political disruption in the Middle East region, which corresponds with the current geopolitical developments and diplomatic relations. I also caution that the present cyberwars that are manifested in different forms are likely to continue following the evolving nature of spying technologies and the political tension among regional rivals. As long as the political establishments in the Middle East remain the same, online political disruption will not cease.

With the introduction of my cyberwar model, I am hoping that other scholars, experts, and practitioners find it relevant in studying other geographical regions and contexts. In terms of future research in this area, there remain many under-researched aspects, such as understanding the inner workings of political trolls, which can be done by interviewing them. We also do not know much about the possible offline and online outcomes of cyberoperations. Finally, we need to continuously examine and compare other case studies, especially new ones, to better understand the ever evolving phenomenon of online political disruption.

Appendix: Selected List of Arab Hacking Groups

● ● ● ● ● ● ● ● ● ● ● ● ● ● ● ● ● ● ● ●

YMH: A Yemeni hacker with regional hacking targets. His main hacking attempts include the Egyptian Military Technical College, the Tourist Development Authority and the Egyptian Armed Forces Training Authority (Kovacs 2014a), often stating on the defaced websites: "Long live Yemen."

Libyan Cyber Army: A Libyan hacking group with regional and international targets. The group focuses on attacking websites in the United States, the United Kingdom, and Israel but has also hacked Egypt's Ministry of Information (Kovacs 2014b).

Al Rashedon: A Syrian hacking group with regional targets. The group is pro-Assad and their main hacking attempt is defacing Qatar's Al Jazeera Arabic TV Channel (Kumar 2012).

Zombi3_Ma, SQL_Master: A Moroccan hacker who is part of the Moroccan Hackers team, with regional and international targets. Their main hacking attempts include defacing the Google Oman domain (Wei 2013).

Cyber of Emotion: Group of hackers or one Saudi hacker with national targets (*Alriyadh* 2015). Their main activities include hacking twenty-four Saudi government websites and the Twitter account of the Saudi Ministry of Justice.

Moroccan Kingdom Hackers: A pro-government Moroccan hacker group with regional targets, especially against Algeria. The main activity is hacking a popular Algerian website for web developers (Gobran 2011).

AnonGhost: A group of Palestinian hackers with regional targets focusing on Israeli websites. Their main activity includes hacking the official UN website designated for the Kingdom of Jordan (Dunn 2018).

DZ27: An Algerian hacker with regional targets. His main activities include hacking a number of Saudi Arabian government websites, including the Saudi Ministry of Media and Culture (*Mobtada* 2013).

Sy-Soldier: An avid supporter of Bashar Assad who defaced several websites in the region, including some based in Lebanon (zone-h.org).

Hussein X-Bomb: A Tunisian hacking group with nationalistic objectives, affiliated with the Tunisian Cyber Army and Al Fallaga Team (zone-h.org).

Notes

Chapter 1 Toward a Theoretical Framework of Cyberwars

1   The HackingTeam video tutorial for RCS Galileo is freely available on YouTube
    and is used for promotional purposes (https://www.youtube.com/watch?v
    =HcfuIwQOqoQ#t=6.730952). On its website (http://www.hackingteam.com
    /solutions.html), the company states the following in relation to this tool: "Our
    historical solution, Remote Control System, is used by 50+ major governmental
    institutions for critical investigations, in more than 35 countries."

Chapter 2 Cyberwars and International Politics

1   Members of Anonymous also run a Twitter account @Op_Israel that used
    hashtags like #FreePalestine and #AntiZionism.
2   It is also known that Hollywood has been used for decades in promoting the
    United States around the world as well as in projecting a positive image of many
    U.S. agencies, including the U.S. Army (Robb 2004; Valantin 2005; Sussman
    2010; Boyd-Barrett, Herrera, and Baumann 2011; Jenkins 2016). For example,
    Karen Hughes "persuaded Disney in 2005 to produce a feel-good 'Portraits of
    America' film that was shown in airports and U.S. embassies" (Miller and
    Higham 2015). Also in February 2016, the U.S. secretary of state, John Kerry, met
    with several Hollywood producers to encourage them to produce anti-ISIS films,
    stating: "Hollywood can help optimize what they do and told us they are eager to
    do so. They have audiences in these places and would like to help. Hollywood is a
    very powerful voice" (Gaouette and Labott 2016). These U.S. efforts were part of
    the Global Engagement Center activities that focused on countering ISIS
    ideology.
3   I would like to sincerely thank Mr. Corey Walters, a graduate student at George-
    town University, for kindly sending these declassified documents to me in
    August 2019. The documents contained hundreds of pages of detailed U.S.
    strategic communication in Iraq, and the details provided here are mostly taken
    from these documents.

Chapter 3 U.S. Cyberoperations in the Middle East

1   This chapter is partly adapted from previously published papers written by the author: Al-Rawi, "US Public Diplomacy in the Middle East and the Digital Outreach Team," *Place Branding and Public Diplomacy* (2019): 1–25; Al-Rawi, "The Anti-terrorist Advertising Campaigns in the Middle East," *Journal of International Communication* 19, no. 2 (2013): 182–195.

2   The IIP website states the following: "IIP communicates with foreign opinion makers and other publics through a wide range of print and electronic outreach materials published in English, Arabic, Chinese, French, Persian, Russian, and Spanish. IIP also provides information outreach support to U.S. embassies and consulates in more than 140 countries worldwide." With the help if IIP, the U.S. Department of State runs other Arabic campaigns such as "USA in Arabic" (2016) targeting Arabic media outlets, Amreekani (2016), and Al Amreekania (2016). The latter is described as follows: "Al Amreekania is an American female persona who engages Arabic-speaking publics on women's rights issues, human rights and Entrepreneurship with a focus on women along with Americana style of information and public diplomacy topics."

3   The Global Engagement Center YouTube account was terminated by YouTube for violating YouTube's community guidelines.

4   There is only one Iraqi YouTuber calling himself "Iraqi Sumer" (in Arabic), who uploaded twenty-six relevant videos entitled "Iraqi Advertisement" collected from this campaign as well as "Future of Iraq" (Iraqi Sumer 2009). However, he does not seem to be directly affiliated with the campaign as he uploaded various other irrelevant videos.

Chapter 4 Russian Trolls, Islam, and the Middle East

1   On July 31, 2018, Facebook announced that it removed thirty-two accounts from Instagram and Facebook, labeling them "bad actors" for their involvement in the Russian-based Internet Research Agency (IRA) or troll factory (Facebook 2018).

2   Another Russian troll's Facebook page called Black Matters mentioned the following on June 19, 2015: "Unfortunately, American tolerance is not what we think it is. U.S. public is swapping patriotism for nationalism, tolerance for Islamophobia, racism and anti-immigrant sentiment."

3   According to SocialBlade (2018), this account had 76,952 followers and had uploaded 3,458 images into Instagram. The same Instagram account is also an RT's Facebook page called Born Liberal, which targets people who have interests in "Bernie Sanders, Social democracy, Liberalism or Democratic Party" (U.S. House of Representatives 2018b).

Chapter 5 Cyberwars and Regional Politics

1   This chapter is partly adapted from a previously published paper written by the author: Al-Rawi, "Cyberconflict, Online Political Jamming, and Hacking in the Gulf Cooperation Council," *International Journal of Communication* 13 (2019): 1301–1322.

2   Ghosting (التشبيح) is a reference to the infamous Bashar Assad's Alawite militia responsible for the kidnapping, blackmail, torture, and killing of many Syrian

civilians and members of the opposition. The word stems from the nickname "ghost" given to the Mercedes cars often driven by members of this militia.

3   The political tension among GCC countries has extended to cultural productions. Television songs, for example, were swiftly written and produced to criticize Qatar by the Saudi-run channel Rotana as part of this cultural war (Freer 2017).

4   Faisal Al Bennai, the chief executive officer of DarkMatter, used to work as the country's vice president of National Electronic Security Authority (NESA), which is responsible for providing sensitive intelligence to the state. Currently, DarkMatter and NESA work closely together in cyberespionage as the former has employed "an army of cyberwarriors from abroad to conduct mass surveillance aimed at the country's own citizens" (McLaughlin 2016). The company is allegedly interested in "exploiting hardware probes installed across major cities for surveillance, hunting down never-before-seen vulnerabilities in software, and building stealth malware implants to track, locate, and hack basically any person at any time in the UAE" (McLaughlin 2016).

5   The UAE government allegedly provided the Egyptian leader Abdulfatah El-sisi with a French-made spying tool to monitor Egyptian citizens. The UAE is interested in supporting the current Egyptian government because both countries oppose the Muslim Brotherhood, who are regarded as a security threat. The espionage tool was estimated to be worth about €10 million (HuffPost Arabi 2017i).

6   The hackers managed to take control of the news agency's social media outlets and posted a fake news story and a YouTube video. At 3:00 a.m., Qatari authorities regained control of the website, and at 7:00 p.m., they managed to restore the social media outlets. The Qatari interior ministry claimed that an iPhone device with a European phone number was used in the hacking (HuffPost Arabi 2017e).

7   Qatar also created a "Lift the Blockade" website in September 2017 to target audiences to send countermessages to those prepared by their Saudi and Emirati counterparts (Freer 2017). Qatar also filed a lawsuit against SkyNews Arabia and Al Arabiya in London because the news outlets continued to air "fake news" about Qatar even though the country strongly denied any connection on its QNA website (HuffPost Arabi 2017d).

Chapter 6   Arab Hackers and Electronic Armies

1   This chapter is partly adapted from a previously published paper written by the author: Al-Rawi, "Cyber Warriors in the Middle East: The Case of the Syrian Electronic Army," *Public Relations Review* 40, no. 3 (2014a): 420–428.

2   Originally from Basra city, he started hacking in 2009 by targeting Sunni terrorist groups and defacing Iraqi government websites to draw attention to their weak security (El-Taaey 2017).

3   Uruk Team often deface and hack Iraqi government websites, including that of Hanan Fatlawi and Humam Hamoudi (Al Masalah 2016), highlighting state corruption and inadequate public services.

4   The current leader of Salmani's Army on social media is Aziz Al-Qahtani together with Saad Al-Qahtani.

5   SEA posted 1,071 tweets and had 29,128 followers as of December 2017. The first tweet was sent on July 31, 2013.

6   The Facebook page was created on May 12, 2013, and had 2,779 likes. It is no longer available.

7   The account is no longer available. A YouTube message states: "This account has been terminated due to multiple or severe violations of YouTube's policy against spam, deceptive practices, and misleading content or other Terms of Service violations."

8   It had over 870,000 views and over 1,400 comments as of December 11, 2013, and was posted on the syrianes1 channel.

9   The video had over 1,045,000 views and 1,174 comments as of December 11, 2013.

References

Abdelhamid, A. 2015. "The Founder of the Egyptian Cyber Army Escapes an Assassination Attempt." Al Arabiya, January 29. https://goo.gl/9LUeRs.

Abo Sharar, G. 2008b. "Terrorism Has No Religion-4." http://www.youtube.com/watch?v=DwRCH6ylXy4.

Aboulkheir, R. 2015. "Egyptian Govt Websites Briefly Hacked: Official." Al Arabiya, October 25. http://english.alarabiya.net/en/media/digital/2015/10/22/Egyptian-govt-websites-briefly-hacked-official.html.

Advisory Commission on Public Diplomacy. 1983. *1983 Report of the United States Advisory Commission on Public Diplomacy.* https://archive.org/stream/ERIC_ED242622#mode/2up.

Agence France Presse. 2020. "US Government Agency Website Hacked by Group Claiming to Be from Iran." *Guardian*, June 23. Retrieved from https://www.theguardian.com/world/2020/jan/05/us-government-agency-website-hacked-by-group-claiming-to-be-from-iran.

Aghathkom1. 2008. "Dirty Wahhabism—Know Your Enemy." March 19. http://www.youtube.com/watch?v=MhfgRTuuOkM.

Al Ali, N. 2018. "Fired Saudi Royal Court Adviser Drops All Titles in Twitter Bio." Bloomberg, October 24. https://www.bloomberg.com/news/articles/2018-10-24/fired-saudi-royal-court-adviser-drops-all-titles-in-twitter-bio.

Alamdar Hacking Organization. 2016. "Hacking Government Website Backed by America by Alamdar." November 1. https://www.youtube.com/watch?v=oj-2k6b6GCA.

Al Amreekania. 2016. Facebook home page. Retrieved December 1, 2019, from https://www.facebook.com/AlAmreekania.

Al-Arabi, S. 2017. "Who Is Saud al-Qahtani, Saudi Arabia's Steve Bannon?" The New Arab, August 23. https://www.alaraby.co.uk/english/indepth/2017/8/23/who-is-saoud-al-qahtani-saudi-arabias-steve-bannon-.

Al Arabiya. 2008. "Arab Americans." June 12. http://www.alarabiya.net/views/2008/06/12/51387.html.

Al Arabiya. 2014. "Why Did the 3 GCC Countries Withdraw Their Ambassadors from Qatar?" March 5. https://goo.gl/CGkyuU.

Al Arabiya. 2015. "Pan-Arab Newspaper al-Hayat Hacked by Yemen 'Cyber Army.'"
April 14. http://english.alarabiya.net/en/media/digital/2015/04/14/Pan-Arab
-newspaper-al-Hayat-hacked-by-Yemen-Cyber-Army-.html.

Al Arabiya. 2016. "Saudi Hackers Attack the Israeli Stock Market Website and
Threaten to Ignite a Cyber War." January 16. https://www.alarabiya.net/articles
/2012/01/16/188614.html.

Al Arabiya. 2017. "Technical glitch temporarily unblock Al Jazeera, beIN Sports in
Saudi Arabi." July 24. https://english.alarabiya.net/media/digital/2017/07/24
/Technical-glitch-temporarily-unblocks-Al-Jazeera-beIN-Sports-in-Saudi-Arabia.

Algerian Electronic Army. 2013. Facebook page. https://www.facebook.com
/AlgerianElectronicArmy.

Ali, L. 2006. "This Is Your Street Mid-Bombing: A Hollywood Budget Public Service
Announcement Aims at Discouraging Suicide Attacks in Iraq and Elsewhere."
Newsweek, June 20.

Al Jazeera. 2013a. "Hacking of Nouri Al-Maliki's Website." February 2. https://goo.gl
/9QtuVv.

Al Jazeera. 2013b. "Report: US Hacked Al Jazeera Communications." September 1.
http://www.aljazeera.com/news/middleeast/2013/09/20139113658335421.html.

Al Jazeera. 2017a. "Violence Grips Protest Rally in Baghdad." February 11. https://
www.aljazeera.com/news/2017/02/protesters-killed-violence-grips-baghdad-rally
-170211140644671.html.

Al Jazeera. 2017b. "Turkey Arrests Five Persons Suspected of Being Involved in
Hacking the Qatari News Agency." August 25. https://goo.gl/4kvVid.

Alkashefo1. 2011. "Jihad, I'm a Muslim; I'm with It." July 12. http://www.youtube.com
/watch?v=D-ebD_Dgf8U.

Alkhalisi, Z. 2017. "Saudi Arabia Warns of New Crippling Cyberattack." CNN Tech,
January 26. http://money.cnn.com/2017/01/25/technology/saudi-arabia
-cyberattack-warning/.

Alkhouri, L., A. Kassirer, and A. Nixon. 2016. "Hacking for ISIS: The Emergent
Cyber Threat Landscape." *Flashpoint*. https://fortunascorner.com/wp-content
/uploads/2016/05/Flashpoint_HackingForISIS_April2016-1.pdf.

Al Masalah. 2016. "Hackers Who Hacked al-Fatlawi's Website Strike Again on
Humam Hamoudi." August 21. http://tiny.cc/7me3ez.

Al-Quds Al-Arabi. 2013. "After Announcing the Al-Jahyesh Film, Syrian Authorities
Ban the Entrance of ALL SAUDI CARS into the Country." January 1. http://
www.alquds.co.uk/?p=118920.

Al-Rawi, A. 2012a. "'Campaign of Truth Program': US Propaganda in Iraq during the
Early 1950s." In *Religion and the Cold War: A Global Perspective*, edited by Philip
Muehlenbeck, 113–138. Nashville, TN: Vanderbilt University Press.

Al-Rawi, A. 2012b. *Media Practice in Iraq*. Hampshire, UK: Palgrave Macmillan.

Al-Rawi, A. 2013. "The Anti-Terrorist Advertising Campaigns in the Middle East."
Journal of International Communication 19 (2): 182–195.

Al-Rawi, A. 2014a. "Cyber Warriors in the Middle East: The Case of the Syrian
Electronic Army." *Public Relations Review* 40 (3): 420–428.

Al-Rawi, A. 2014b. "Framing the Online Women's Movements in the Arab World."
Information, Communication and Society 17 (9): 1147–1161.

Al-Rawi, A. 2015. "Sectarianism and the Arab Spring: Framing the Popular Protests in
Bahrain." *Global Media and Communication* 11 (1): 25–42.

Al-Rawi, A. 2016. "Facebook as a Virtual Mosque: The Online Protest against Innocence of Muslims." *Culture and Religion* 17 (1): 19–34.

Al-Rawi, A. 2017a. "Assessing Public Sentiments and News Preferences on Al Jazeera and Al Arabiya." *International Communication Gazette* 79 (1): 26–44.

Al-Rawi, A. 2017b. *Islam on YouTube: Online Debates, Protests, and Extremism.* London: Springer.

Al-Rawi, A. 2018. "Video Games, Terrorism, and ISIS's Jihad 3.0." *Terrorism and Political Violence* 30 (4): 740–760.

Al-Rawi, A. 2019. "US Public Diplomacy in the Middle East and the Digital Outreach Team." *Place Branding and Public Diplomacy,* 16 (1): 18–24.

Al-Rawi, A., and J. Groshek. 2015. "Arab Iranians and Their Social Media Use." *CyberOrient* 9 (2).

Al-Rawi, A., and J. Groshek. 2018. "Jihadist Propaganda on Social Media: An Examination of ISIS Related Content on Twitter." *International Journal of Cyber Warfare and Terrorism (IJCWT)* 8 (4): 1–15.

Al-Rawi, A., J. Groshek, and L. Zhang. 2019. "What the Fake? Assessing the Extent of Networked Political Spamming and Bots in the Propagation of #fakenews on Twitter." *Online Information Review* 43 (1): 53–71.

Al-Rawi, A., and Y. Jiwani. 2017. "Mediated Conflict: Shiite Heroes Combating ISIS in Iraq and Syria." *Communication, Culture and Critique* 10 (4): 675–695.

Al-Rawi, A., and Y. Jiwani. 2019. "Russian Twitter Trolls Stoke Anti-immigrant Lies Ahead of Canadian Election." *The Conversation,* July 23. https://theconversation .com/russian-twitter-trolls-stoke-anti-immigrant-lies-ahead-of-canadian-election -119144.

Alriyadh. 2015. "Saudi Hacker Hacks 24 Government Websites in Two Hours." August 15. http://www.alriyadh.com/1073358#.

Al-Sulami, M. 2017. "Saudi Arabia Accuses Qatar of Using Twitter to Stoke Dissent." *Arab News,* July 7. https://www.arabnews.com/node/1125646/saudi-arabia

Alsultany, E. 2007. "Selling American Diversity and Muslim American Identity through Nonprofit Advertising Post-9/11." *American Quarterly* 59 (3): 593–622.

Alsumaria News. 2016. "Hacking of the Qatari Ministry of Defense as a Revenge Against the Execution of Sheikh Nimr." December 4. https://goo.gl/dQEocq.

Anonymous. 2013. "Syria—Fighting for Freedom." August 28. http://vimeo.com /75158017.

Arabi21. 2019. "Hackers Write 'Shut Down by the People's Order' After Hacking an Iraqi Ministry." November 19. https://arabi21.com/story/1223804.

Arango, T. 2017. "Big Ransom and Syria Deals Win Release of Royal Qatari Hunters." *New York Times,* April 21. https://www.nytimes.com/2017/04/21/world /middleeast/big-ransom-and-syria-deals-win-release-of-royal-qatari-hunters.html.

Arango, T., J. Risen, F. Fassihi, R. Bergman, and M. Hussain. 2019. "The Iran Cables: Secret Documents Show How Tehran Wields Power in Iraq." *New York Times,* November 18. https://www.nytimes.com/interactive/2019/11/18/world/middleeast /iran-iraq-spy-cables.html.

Arce, A. 2014. "U.S. Secretly Created 'Cuban Twitter' to Stir Unrest." Associated Press, April 3. https://www.apnews.com/904a9a6a1bcd46cebfc14bea2ee30fdf.

Arquilla, J. 1996. *The Advent of Netwar.* New York: RAND.

Arquilla, J., and D. Ronfeldt. 1993. "Cyberwar Is Coming!" *Comparative Strategy* 12 (2): 141–165.

Arthur, C. 2013. "Symantec Discovers 2005 US Computer Virus Attack on Iran Nuclear Plants." *Guardian*, February 26. http://www.theguardian.com/technology /2013/feb/26/symantec-us-computer-virus-iran-nuclear.

Ashqiraqi. 2007. "Terrorism. . . . Iraq." December 30. http://www.youtube.com/watch ?v=7iFYPifTqwk.

Assakina. 2012. "A Special Study by Assakina: Terrorists' Websites Lose their Scientific Glamour." July 30. http://www.assakina.com/news/news3/17085.html.

Associated Press. 2018. "ISIS Hackers' Threats against U.S. Military Wives Actually Came from Russian Trolls." NBC News, May 8. Retrieved from https://www .nbcnews.com/storyline/isis-terror/u-s-military-wives-threatened-russian-hackers -posing-isis-n872251.

Associated Press. 2019. "US Launched Cyber Attack on Iranian Rockets and Missiles _Reports." June 23. Retrieved from https://www.theguardian.com/world/2019/jun /23/us-launched-cyber-attack-on-iranian-rockets-and-missiles-reports?CMP =Share_iOSApp_Other.

Awad, O. 2018. "How Israel Is Becoming the World's Top Cyber Superpower." Vice News, March 13. https://www.vice.com/en_ca/article/evmyda/how-israel-is -becoming-the-worlds-top-cyber-superpower.

Baghernia, N., and E. H. Mahmoodinejad. 2018. "Al-Alam Versus Al-Arabiya: Iran and Saudi Arabia's Media Propaganda Tools." *Asian Politics and Policy* 10 (2): 388–391.

Bailey, O., B. Cammaerts, and N. Carpentier. 2007. *Understanding Alternative Media*. London: McGraw-Hill Education.

Baldi, S., E. Gelbstein, and J. Kurbalija. 2003. *Hacktivism, Cyber-Terrorism and Cyberwar: The Activities of the Uncivil Society in Cyberspace*. Msida, Malta: DiploFoundation.

Baldor, L. 2012. "US: Hackers in Iran Responsible for Cyberattacks." Yahoo! News, October 12. http://news.yahoo.com/us-hackers-iran-responsible-cyberattacks -072429280--finance.html.

Balnaves, M., S. H. Donald, and B. Shoesmith, B. 2008. *Media Theories and Approaches: A Global Perspective*. London: Palgrave Macmillan.

Bamford, J. 2007. *Body of Secrets: Anatomy of the Ultra-Secret National Security Agency*. New York: Random House.

Baram, A. 2005. "Who Are the Insurgents? Sunni Arab Rebels in Iraq." United States Institute of Peace. Special Report No. 134, April 2005.

Barnes, J. 2019. "U.S. Cyberattack Hurt Iran's Ability to Target Oil Tankers, Officials Say." *New York Times*, August 29. https://www.nytimes.com/2019/08/28/us /politics/us-iran-cyber-attack.html.

Bartlett, J. 2017. *Radicals: Outsiders Changing the World*. London: William Heinemann.

Baxter, K., and S. Akbarzadeh. 2012. *US Foreign Policy in the Middle East: The Roots of Anti-Americanism*. London: Routledge.

BBC News. 2013. "Tunisia's 'Sexual Jihad'—Extremist Fatwa or Propaganda?" October 26. http://www.bbc.co.uk/news/world-africa-24448933.

BBC News. 2015. "Malaysia Arrests Kosovo Man for 'Hacking US Files for IS.'" October 16. http://www.bbc.com/news/world-asia-34546793.

BBC News. 2018a. "Data-Stealing Spyware 'Traced to Lebanon.'" January 19. https://www.bbc.com/news/technology-42746772.

BBC News. 2018b. "US Sanctions Iranian Hackers for 'Stealing University Data.'" March 23. https://www.bbc.com/news/world-us-canada-43519437.

BBC News. 2018c. "Jamal Khashoggi: Saudi Murder Suspect Had Spy Training." October 19. https://www.bbc.com/news/world-middle-east-45918610.

BBC News. 2019a. "Pulwama Attack: Google Searches 'Hijacked' to Link Pakistan Flag to Toilet Paper." February 18. https://www.bbc.com/news/technology-47279252.

BBC News. 2019b. "'If You Google the Word Idiot, a Picture of Donald Trump Comes Up?'" December 12. https://www.bbc.com/news/av/technology-46533217.

Becker, O. 2014. "Hacktivist Group Anonymous Launches #OpIsrael Attacks." Vice News, April 8. https://news.vice.com/article/hacktivist-group-anonymous -launches-opisrael-attacks.

Benham, A., E. Edwards, B. Fractenberg, L. Gordon-Murnane, C. Hetherington, D. A. Liptak, and A. P. Mintz. 2012. *Web of Deceit: Misinformation and Manipulation in the Age of Social Media*. New York: Information Today.

Bennett, D. 2013. "Exploring the Impact of an Evolving War and Terror Blogosphere on Traditional Media Coverage of Conflict." *Media, War and Conflict* 6 (1): 37–53.

Berton, B., and P. Pawlak. 2015. "Cyber Jihadists and Their Web." *European Union Institute for Security Studies Brief* 2. https://www.files.ethz.ch/isn/187823/Brief_2 _cyber_jihad.pdf.

Bob, C., J. Haynes, V. Pickard, T. Keenan, and N. Couldry. 2008. "Media Spaces: Innovation and Activism." In *Global Civil Society 2007/8: Communicative Power and Democracy*, edited by M. Albrow, A. Helmut, M. Glasius, M. Price, and M. Kaldor, 198–223. Thousand Oaks, CA: SAGE.

Booth, R., and M. Mahmood. 2012. "How the Assad Emails Came to Light." *Guardian*, March 14. http://www.theguardian.com/world/2012/mar/14/how -assad-emails-came-light.

Booth, R., M. Mahmood, and L. Harding. 2012. "Exclusive: Secret Assad Emails Lift Lid on Life of Leader's Inner Circle." *Guardian*, March 14. https://www .theguardian.com/world/2012/mar/14/assad-emails-lift-lid-inner-circle.

Born, K., and N. Edgington. 2017. *Analysis of Philanthropic Opportunities to Mitigate the Disinformation/Propaganda Problem*. Hewlett Foundation. https://www .hewlett.org/wp-content/uploads/2017/11/Hewlett-Disinformation-Propaganda -Report.pdf.

Bouzis, K. 2015. "Countering the Islamic State: US Counterterrorism Measures." *Studies in Conflict and Terrorism* 38 (10): 885–897.

Boyd-Barrett, O. 2014. *Media Imperialism*. Thousand Oaks, CA: SAGE.

Boyd-Barrett, O., D. Herrera, and J. Baumann. 2011. "Hollywood, the CIA and the 'War on Terror.'" In *Media and Terrorism: Global Perspectives*, edited by D. Freedman and D. Thussu, 116–133. Thousand Oaks, CA: SAGE.

Boyd, D. A. 1999. *Broadcasting in the Arab World: A Survey of the Electronic Media in the Middle East*. Ames: Iowa State University Press.

Bradshaw, S., and P. Howard. 2017. *Troops, Trolls and Troublemakers: A Global Inventory of Organized Social Media Manipulation*. Working Paper no. 2017.12. Computational Propaganda Research Project. Oxford Internet Institute. https:// comprop.oii.ox.ac.uk/wp-content/uploads/sites/89/2017/07/Troops-Trolls-and -Troublemakers.pdf.

Bratich, J. 2011. "User-Generated Discontent: Convergence, Polemology and Dissent." *Cultural Studies* 25 (4-5): 621–640.

Brennan, M. 2017. "Qatar Denies Being Hacked by Russia, Accuses Gulf Countries of Cyberattack." CBS News, June 28. https://www.cbsnews.com/news/qatar-denies -being-hacked-by-russia-accuses-gulf-countries-of-cyberattack/.

Brewster, T. 2019. "Chinese Hacker Crew Stole NSA Cyber Weapons In 2016—A Year Before They Were Leaked Online." *Forbes*, May 7. https://www.forbes.com /sites/thomasbrewster/2019/05/07/chinese-hacker-crew-stole-nsa-cyber-weapons-in -2016—a-year-before-they-were-leaked-online/#894b09e237b4.

Broadcasting Board of Governors. 2014. *Annual Report 2014*. https://www.bbg.gov /wp-content/media/2016/06/annual-report__2014.pdf.

Brown, H. 2014. "Meet the State Department Team Trying to Troll ISIS into Oblivion." Think Progress, September 18. https://archive.thinkprogress.org/meet -the-state-department-team-trying-to-troll-isis-into-oblivion-3927b7c6492/.

Brown, H., and B. Daraghai. 2016. "There's a Whole Bunch of Anti-Saudi Posters Popping Up in Iraq." Buzzfeed, September 9. https://www.buzzfeednews.com /article/hayesbrown/theres-a-whole-bunch-of-anti-saudi-posters-popping-up-in-ira.

Brown, J., and L. Markovitz. 2015. "The Hacktivist Encyclopedia: Enemies of Anonymous, from ISIS to the KKK." Vocativ, November 24. http://www.vocativ .com/news/253884/history-of-anonymous/.

Browning, N. 2017. "Iran Blames Trump for the Worst Rift in the Arab World in Years." Reuters, June 5. http://www.businessinsider.com/iran-blames-trump-for -the-worst-rift-in-the-arab-world-in-years-2017-6.

Bryman, A., and R. G. Burgess, eds. 1994. *Analyzing Qualitative Data*. London: Routledge.

Budihan, Y. 2013. "Algerian Hacker Details Cyber Attack on Israel." Asharq Al-Awsat, April 15. https://eng-archive.aawsat.com/yassin-boudhaan/news-middle-east /algerian-hacker-details-cyber-attack-on-israel.

Bureau of Investigative Journalism. 2016. "Pentagon Paid for Fake 'Al Qaeda Videos." *Daily Beast*, January 10. https://www.thedailybeast.com/pentagon-paid-for-fake-al -qaeda-videos.

Burton, M. J., W. J. Miller, and D. Shea. 2010. *Campaign Craft: The Strategies, Tactics, and Art of Political Campaign Management*. New York: Praeger.

Cacciatore, M. A., D. A. Scheufele, and S. Iyengar. 2015. "The End of Framing as We Know It . . . and the Future of Media Effects." *Mass Communication and Society* 19 (1): 7–23.

Cameron, D. 2013. "Jeremy Hammond Supporters Share List of Countries the FBI Allegedly Used Him to Hack." Daily Dot, November 16. http://www.dailydot.com /news/jeremy-hammond-fbi-foreign-governments-list/.

Cammaerts, B. 2007a. "Jamming the Political: Beyond Counter-Hegemonic Practices." *Continuum: Journal of Media and Cultural Studies* 21 (1): 71–90.

Cammaerts, B. 2007b. "Political Jamming." In *Global Civil Society 2007/8: Communicative Power and Democracy*, edited by H. Anheier, M. Glasius, and M. Kaldor, 214–215. London: SAGE.

Campbell, D. E., ed. 2007. *A Matter of Faith: Religion in the 2004 Presidential Election*. Washington, DC: Brookings Institution Press.

Campbell, R., C. Martin, and B. Fabos. 2014. *Media and Culture: Mass Communication in a Digital Age*. Boston: Bedford/St. Martin's.

Cary, P. 2010. *The Pentagon, Information Operations, and International Media Development*. Center for International Media Assistance. November 23. http://www.cima .ned.org/wp-content/uploads/2015/02/CIMA-DoD-Report_FINAL.pdf.

Castells, M. 2007. "Communication, Power and Counter-power in the Network Society." *International Journal of Communication* 1 (1): 29.

Castells, M. 2013. *Communication Power*. Oxford: Oxford University Press.

Chan, A., and G. Dale. 2018. "How Russian Trolls Won American Hearts and Minds." Medium, May 21. https://medium.com/techforcampaigns/how-russian-trolls-won-american-hearts-and-minds-30037e1e13b7.

Chin, J. 2017. "Jack Posobiec, Rebel Media Washington Bureau Chief, Linked to French Election Hacking Scandal." HuffPost Canada, May 10. http://www.huffing tonpost.ca/2017/05/10/jack-posobiec-rebel-media-macronleaks_n_16539470.html.

Chomsky, N., G. Achcar, and S. R. Shalom. 2015. *Perilous Power: The Middle East and US Foreign Policy Dialogues on Terror, Democracy, War, and Justice.* London: Routledge.

Ciampaglia, G. L. 2018. "Fighting Fake News: A Role for Computational Social Science in the Fight against Digital Misinformation." *Journal of Computational Social Science* 1 (1): 147–153.

Cimpanu, C. 2015. "Anonymous Hacks Costa Rican Website Associated with Jurassic Park Island." Softpedia. December 25. https://news.softpedia.com/news/anonymous-hacks-costa-rican-website-associated-with-jurrasic-park-island-498087.shtml.

CNBC. 2017. "United Arab Emirates Reportedly Behind Hacking of Qatari Media that Incited Crisis." July 16. https://www.cnbc.com/2017/07/16/united-arab-emirates-reportedly-behind-hacking-of-qatari-media-that-incited-crisis.html.

Cohen, Z., and J. Berlinger. 2019. "Libyan General Praised by Trump Accused of Possible War Crimes." CNN, May 15. https://www.cnn.com/2019/05/15/politics/libya-war-crimes-allegations-intl/index.html.

Coleman, G. 2012. "Phreaks, Hackers, and Trolls: The Politics of Transgression and Spectacle." In *The Social Media Reader*, edited by M. Mandiberg, 99–119. New York: New York University Press.

Coleman, G. 2014. *Hacker, Hoaxer, Whistleblower, Spy: The Many Faces of Anonymous.* New York: Verso Books.

Collin, B. 1997. "The future of cyberterrorism: Where the Physical and Virtual Worlds Converge." *Crime and Justice International 13* (2), 15–18.

Collins, B., K. Poulsen, and S. Ackerman. 2017. "Exclusive: Russians Impersonated Real American Muslims to Stir Chaos on Facebook and Instagram." Daily Beast, September 27. https://www.thedailybeast.com/exclusive-russians-impersonated-real-american-muslims-to-stir-chaos-on-facebook-and-instagram.

Conway, M. 2003. "Hackers as Terrorists? Why It Doesn't Compute." *Computer Fraud and Security* 12:10–13.

Corbin, J. M., and A. Strauss. 1990. "Grounded Theory Research: Procedures, Canons, and Evaluative Criteria." *Qualitative Sociology* 13 (1): 3–21.

Corera, G. 2019. "Russian Hackers Cloak Attacks Using Iranian Group." BBC, October 21. https://www.bbc.com/news/technology-50103378.

Cottee, S. 2015. "Why It's So Hard to Stop ISIS Propaganda." *Atlantic*, March 2. http://www.theatlantic.com/international/archive/2015/03/why-its-so-hard-to-stop-isis-propaganda/386216/.

Crawford, B.C.H. 1999. "Information Warfare: Its Application in Military and Civilian Contexts." *Information Society* 15 (4): 257–263.

CSIS. 2002. *Assessing the Risks of Cyber Terrorism, Cyber War and Other Cyber Threats.* Center for Strategic and International Studies (CSIS). December. http://csis.org/files/media/csis/pubs/021101_risks_of_cyberterror.pdf.

CSO Online. 2017. "Saudi Arabia Again Hit with Disk-Wiping Malware Shamoon 2." January 24. https://www.csoonline.com/article/3161146/saudi-arabia-again-hit-with-disk-wiping-malware-shamoon-2.html.

Cull, N. J. 2008. *The Cold War and the United States Information Agency: American Propaganda and Public Diplomacy, 1945–1989*. Cambridge: Cambridge University Press.

Cull, N. J. 2009. "Public Diplomacy: Lessons from the Past." *CPD Perspectives on Public Diplomacy*, issue 2.

Cull, N. J. 2012. *The Decline and Fall of the United States Information Agency: American Public Diplomacy, 1989–2001*. London: Palgrave Macmillan.

Digi. 2017a. "Itemized Posts and Historical Engagement—6 Now-Closed FB Pages." Tableau, October 5. https://public.tableau.com/profile/digi#!/vizhome/FB4/TotalReachbyPage.

Digi. 2017b. "Instagram Prop DataViz: Interactions, Likes and Profile Stats for 28 Removed Accounts." Tableau, November 7. https://public.tableau.com/profile/digi#!/vizhome/InstagramPropDataViz/TopInstagramPostsbyLikesComments OverTime.

Dabbous, Y., and K. Nasser. 2009. "A Waste of Public Diplomacy? The Performance of Al-Hurra TV among Lebanon's University Students." *Middle East Journal of Culture and Communication* 2 (1): 100–114.

Daily Beast. 2016. "Pentagon Paid for Fake 'Al Qaeda' Videos." January 10. https://www.thedailybeast.com/pentagon-paid-for-fake-al-qaeda-videos.

Daily Star. 2017. "Syrian Hackers Take Down Lebanese State Television Website." July 4. https://www.dailystar.com.lb/News/Lebanon-News/2017/Jul-04/411606-syrian-hackers-take-down-lebanese-state-television-website.ashx.

Daniels, J. 2009. "Cloaked Websites: Propaganda, Cyber-Racism and Epistemology in the Digital Era. *New Media and Society* 11 (5): 659–683.

Darwish, K., D. Alexandrov, P. Nakov, and Y. Mejova. 2017. "Seminar Users in the Arabic Twitter Sphere." In *International Conference on Social Informatics*. New York: Springer.

Deans, J., J. Plunkett, and J. Halliday. 2013. "BBC Weather Twitter Account Taken Over by Syrian Regime Supporters." *Guardian*, March 21. http://www.theguardian.com/media/2013/mar/21/bbc-weather-twitter-syrian-regime.

Dearden, L. 2015. "British Isis Jihadists 'Had Phones Hacked by GCHQ' Before They Were Killed by Drone Strikes." *Independent*, September 16. https://www.independent.co.uk/news/uk/home-news/british-isis-jihadists-had-phones-hacked-by-gchq-before-they-were-killed-by-drone-strikes-10503076.html.

Deeby, D. 2017. "State-Sponsored Cyberattacks on Canada Successful About Once a Week." CBC, October 30. http://www.cbc.ca/news/politics/cyber-attacks-canada-cse-1.4378711.

Deibert, R. 2016. "How Foreign Governments Spy Using PowerPoint and Twitter." *Washington Post*, August 2. https://www.washingtonpost.com/posteverything/wp/2016/08/02/how-foreign-governments-spy-using-email-and-powerpoint/?utm_term=.b8d7e13004c9.

Democracy Now. 2006. "I Was a Propaganda Intern in Iraq." August 21. http://www.democracynow.org/2006/8/21/i_was_a_propaganda_intern_in.

Denning, D. E. 1999. *Information Warfare and Security*, Vol. 4. Reading, MA: Addison-Wesley.

Denning, D. E. 2001. "Activism, Hacktivism, and Cyberterrorism: The Internet as a Tool for Influencing Foreign Policy." In *Networks and Netwars: The Future of Terror, Crime, and Militancy*, edited by J. Arquilla and D. Ronfeldt, 239–289. Santa Monica, CA: RAND.

Derville, T. 2005. "Radical Activist Tactics: Overturning Public Relations Conceptu-alizations." *Public Relations Review* 31 (4): 527–533.

Dervin, B., and L. Foreman-Wernet. 2012. "Sense-Making Methodology as an Approach to Understanding and Designing for Campaign Audiences: A Turn to Communicating Communicatively." In *Public Communication Campaigns*, edited by R. Rice and C. Atkin, 147–162. Thousand Oaks, CA: SAGE.

Dery, M. 1993. *Culture Jamming. Hacking, Slashing, and Sniping in the Empire of Signs*, Vol. 25. Westfield, NJ: Open Media.

Dewey, C. 2013. "The State Department's Arabic Outreach Team Spoofed an al-Qaeda Video." *Washington Post*, July 9. https://www.washingtonpost.com/news /worldviews/wp/2013/07/09/the-state-departments-arabic-outreach-team-spoofed -an-al-qaeda-video/.

Dewey, C. 2016. "98 Personal Data Points that Facebook Uses to Target Ads to You." *Washington Post*, August 19. https://www.washingtonpost.com/news/the-intersect /wp/2016/08/19/98-personal-data-points-that-facebook-uses-to-target-ads-to-you/.

DeYoung, K., and E. Nakashima. 2017. "UAE Orchestrated Hacking of Qatari Government Sites, Sparking Regional Upheaval, According to U.S. Intelligence Officials." *Washington Post*, July 16. https://www.washingtonpost.com/world /national-security/uae-hacked-qatari-government-sites-sparking-regional-upheaval -according-to-us-intelligence-officials/2017/07/16/00c46e54-698f-11e7-8eb5 -cbccc2e7bfbf_story.html.

Digital Outreach Team (DOT). 2007. "What You Don't Know about 9/11 Attacks." November 29. https://www.youtube.com/watch?v=S01RaG9mGLc.

Digital Outreach Team (DOT). 2014. November 25. https://vine.co/v /O1D3dEFrgWK.

Digital Outreach Team (DOT). n.d. YouTube channel. Accessed January 12, 2021. https://www.youtube.com/user/StateDepartment/about.

Dizard, W. P. 2004. *Inventing Public Diplomacy: The Story of the US Information Agency*. New York: Lynne Rienner.

Dobrokhotov, R. 2017. "Russia's Soft Warfare." Al Jazeera, February 27. https://www .aljazeera.com/indepth/opinion/2017/02/russia-soft-warfare-cyberwar-hackers -fake-news-170227070148722.html.

Druckman, J. N. 2004. "Political Preference Formation: Competition, Deliberation, and the (Ir)relevance of Framing Effects." *American Political Science Review* 98 (4): 671–686.

Dunn, B. 2018. "Don't Call It a Comeback: Anonghost Hacking Everything in Site to Start December." Rouge Media, December 10. https://roguemedia.co/2018/12/10 /dont-call-it-a-comeback-anonghost-hacking-everything-in-site-to-start-december/.

Dutta-Bergman, M. J. 2006. "US Public Diplomacy in the Middle East: A Critical Cultural Approach." *Journal of Communication Inquiry* 30 (2): 102–124.

DW. 2015. "Saudi Arabia Rebuffs Iran's Accusations over Hajj Stampede." September 27. https://www.dw.com/en/saudi-arabia-rebuffs-irans-accusations-over-hajj -stampede/a-18743994.

Egypt Today. 2018. "Mauritania Official Accuses Doha of Funding MB in Nouak-chott." September 8. https://www.egypttoday.com/Article/2/57272/Mauritania -official-accuses-Doha-of-funding-MB-in-Nouakchott.

El-Bar, K. 2016. "Billboards Bearing Khamenei's Words on Hajj Dispute Seen in Baghdad." Middle East Eye, September 7. https://www.middleeasteye.net/news /billboards-bearing-khameneis-words-hajj-dispute-seen-baghdad.

El-Nawawy, M. 2006. "US Public Diplomacy in the Arab World: The News Credibility of Radio Sawa and Television Alhurra in Five Countries." *Global Media and Communication* 2 (2): 183–203.

El-Nawawy, M., and A. Iskandar. 2008. *Al-jazeera: The Story of the Network That Is Rattling Governments and Redefining Modern Journalism.* New York: Basic Books.

Elswah, M., P. Howard, and V. Narayanan. 2019. *Iranian Digital Interference in the Arab World. The Computational Propaganda Project: Algorithms, Automation, and Digital Politics.* Oxford Internet Institute. https://comprop.oii.ox.ac.uk/research /working-papers/iranian-digital-interference-in-the-arab-world/.

El-Taaey, N. 2017. "Famous Hacker Hussein Mahdy Retires and Reveals What Was Not Anticipated." Lebanon Today, June 26. http://tiny.cc/o2c3ez.

Elver, H. 2012. "Racializing Islam Before and After 9/11: From Melting Pot to Islamophobia." *Transnational Law and Contemporary Problems* 2 (11): 119–174.

Emmons, A. 2018. "Saudi Arabia Planned to Invade Qatar Last Summer: Rex Tillerson's Efforts to Stop It May Have Cost Him His Job." The Intercept, August 1. https://theintercept.com/2018/08/01/rex-tillerson-qatar-saudi-uae/.

Entman, R. 1991. "Symposium Framing US Coverage of International News: Contrasts in Narratives of the KAL and Iran Air Incidents." *Journal of Communication* 41 (4): 6–27.

Entman, R. M. 1993. "Framing: Toward Clarification of a Fractured Paradigm." *Journal of Communication* 43 (4): 51–58.

Entman, R. 2010. "Framing Media Power." In *Doing News Framing Analysis: Empirical and Theoretical Perspectives,* edited by P. D'Angelo and J. Kuypers, 331–355. London: Routledge.

Entman, R., and S. Stonbely. 2018. "Political Scandals as a Democratic Challenge: Blunders, Scandals, and Strategic Communication in US Foreign Policy: Benghazi vs. 9/11." *International Journal of Communication* 12.

Erdbrink, T. 2012. "Iran Confirms Attack by Virus that Collects Information." *New York Times,* May 29. http://www.nytimes.com/2012/05/30/world/middleeast/iran -confirms-cyber-attack-by-new-virus-called-flame.html.

Esposito, J. L., and D. Mogahed. 2007. *Who Speaks for Islam?* New York: Gallup.

Estes, A. C. 2013. "Anonymous Hits Israel with a Massive Cyber Attack, Israel Attacks Back." The Wire, April 7. http://www.thewire.com/global/2013/04/anonymous -hits-israel-massive-cyber-attack-israel-attacks-back/63969/.

European Commission. 2018. *A Multi-Dimensional Approach to Disinformation: Report of the Independent High Level Group on Fake News and Online Disinformation.* Luxembourg: Publications Office of the European Union.

Ezell, D. 2012. *Beyond Cairo: US Engagement with the Muslim World.* Hampshire, UK: Palgrave Macmillan.

Facebook Newsroom. 2018a. "Removing Bad Actors on Facebook." July 31. https:// newsroom.fb.com/news/2018/07/removing-bad-actors-on-facebook/.

Facebook Newsroom. 2018b. "Taking Down More Coordinated Inauthentic Behavior." August 21. https://about.fb.com/news/2018/08/more-coordinated-inauthentic -behavior/.

Farkas, J., J. Schou, and C. Neumayer. 2017. "Cloaked Facebook Pages: Exploring Fake Islamist Propaganda in Social Media." *New Media and Society* 20 (1): 146144481770775.

Farwell, J. P. 2010. "Jihadi Video in the 'War of Ideas.'" *Survival* 52 (6): 127–150.

FBI. 2016. "Syrian Cyber Hackers Charged." March 22. https://www.fbi.gov/news /stories/two-from-syrian-electronic-army-added-to-cybers-most-wanted.

Fernandez, A. 2015. "'Contesting the Space': Adversarial Online Engagement as a Tool for Combating Violent Extremism." *Soundings: An Interdisciplinary Journal* 98 (4): 488–500.

Ferran, L. 2012. "MiniFlame: Researchers Say 'Extremely Targeted' Cyber Attack Hit Lebanon, Iran." ABC News, October 15. http://abcnews.go.com/blogs/headlines /2012/10/miniflame-researchers-say-extremely-targeted-cyber-attack-hit-lebanon -iran/.

Fielding, N., and I. Cobain. 2011. "Military's 'Sock Puppet' Software Creates Fake Online Identities to Spread Pro-American Propaganda." *Guardian*, March 17. https://www.theguardian.com/technology/2011/mar/17/us-spy-operation-social -networks.

FireEye Intelligence. 2013. "Syrian Electronic Army Hacks Major Communications Websites." July 30. http://www.fireeye.com/blog/technical/cyber-exploits/2013/07 /syrian-electronic-army-hacks-major-communications-websites.html.

FireEye Intelligence. 2018a. "M-Trends 2018." https://www.fireeye.com/content/dam /collateral/en/mtrends-2018.pdf.

FireEye Intelligence. 2018b. "Suspected Iranian Influence Operation Leverages Network of Inauthentic News Sites and Social Media Targeting Audiences in U.S., UK, Latin America, Middle East." https://www.fireeye.com/blog/threat-research /2018/08/suspected-iranian-influence-operation.html.

Fisher, A. 2015. "How Jihadist Networks Maintain a Persistent Online Presence." *Perspectives on Terrorism* 9 (3).

Fisher, M. 2015. "Did a Congressman Just Acknowledge the US Took Down North Korea's Internet in December?" Vox News, March 17. https://www.vox.com/2015/3 /17/8235831/north-korea-internet-hack.

Flangan, B. 2012. "Sophisticated Flame Computer Virus Detected in UAE." The National, June 5. http://www.thenational.ae/business/industry-insights /technology/sophisticated-flame-computer-virus-detected-in-uae.

Fontenelle, I., and M. Pozzebon. 2017. "Jamming the Jamming: Brazilian Protests as an Illustration of a New Politics of Consumption." *Culture and Organization* 25 (5): 353–367.

Forest, J. J. 2009. *Influence Warfare: How Terrorists and Governments Fight to Shape Perceptions in a War of Ideas.* New York: ABC-CLIO.

Fowler, E., M. Franz, and T. Ridout. 2018. *Political Advertising in the United States.* London: Routledge.

Franceschi-Bicchierai, L. 2014. *Egyptian Cyber Army: The Hacker Group Attacking ISIS Propaganda Online.* Mashable, November 23. http://mashable.com/2014/11/23 /egyptian-cyber-army-isis-baghdadi-hack/#ofmmKQ.7Faqo.

Franceschi-Bicchierai, L. 2016. "The 'Million Dollar Dissident' Is a Magnet for Government Spyware." Motherboard, August 26. https://motherboard.vice.com /en_us/article/mg7pjy/ahmed-mansoor-million-dollar-dissident-government -spyware.

Franceschi-Bicchierai, L. 2018. "How 'Mr. Hashtag' Helped Saudi Arabia Spy on Dissidents." Motherboard, October 29. https://motherboard.vice.com/en_us /article/kzjmze/saud-al-qahtani-saudi-arabia-hacking-team.

Free Iraq Radio. 2015. "About us." http://www.iraqhurr.org/.

Freer, C. 2017. "Social Effects of the Qatar Crisis." IndraStra Global, October 10. http://www.indrastra.com/2017/10/Social-Effects-of-Qatar-Crisis-003-10-2017 -0013.html.

Freeze, C. 2017. "China Hack Cost Ottawa 'Hundreds of Millions,' Documents Show." *Globe and Mail*, March 30. https://www.theglobeandmail.com/news /national/federal-documents-say-2014-china-hack-cost-hundreds-of-millions-of -dollars/article34485219/.

Freitang, A. R., and A. Q. Stokes. 2009. *Global Public Relations: Spanning Borders, Spanning Cultures*. London: Routledge.

Frenkel, S. 2015. "Meet the Mysterious New Hacker Army Freaking Out the Middle East." BuzzFeed, June 24. https://www.buzzfeednews.com/article/sheerafrenkel /who-is-the-yemen-cyber-army.

Fung, B. 2020. "Hacking Attempts Originating in Iran Nearly Triple Following Soleimani Strike, Researchers Say." CNN Business, January 8. https://www.cnn .com/2020/01/08/tech/iran-hackers-soleimani/index.html.

Future of Iraq. 2007. "Iraq Civil Wars Campaign." http://www.youtube.com/watch?v =AWOQG2OkG3k.

Future of Iraq. 2009a. "New Baby." Accessed on December, 20, 2012. http://www .youtube.com/watch?v=eZHUE32IRQs.

Future of Iraq. 2009b. "US Withdrawal." Accessed on December 24, 2012. http:// www.youtube.com/watch?v=3UZNxzyTBlc.

Gaouette, N., and E. Labott. 2016. "John Kerry Goes to Hollywood for Help Countering ISIS." CNN, February 19. http://www.cnn.com/2016/02/19/politics /hollywood-john-kerry-isis-propaganda/.

Gapper, J. 2010. "Keep the Spies from Our Computers." *Financial Times*, August 4. https://www.ft.com/content/bfe23646-9ff6-11df-8cc5-00144feabdco.

GCHQ. 2000. "Full-Spectrum Cyber Effects." https://edwardsnowden.com/docs/doc /full-spectrum-cyber-effects-final.pdf.

GCHQ. 2014. "The Art of Deception: Training for a New Generation of Online Covert Operations." https://edwardsnowden.com/2014/02/25/the-art-of-deception -training-for-a-new-generation-of-online-covert-operations/.

Gellman, B., and E. Nakashima. 2013. "U.S. Spy Agencies Mounted 231 Offensive Cyber-operations in 2011, Documents Show." *Washington Post*, August 31. https://www.washingtonpost.com/world/national-security/us-spy-agencies -mounted-231-offensive-cyber-operations-in-2011-documents-show/2013/08/30 /d090a6ae-119e-11e3-b4cb-fd7ce041d814_story.html.

Gellman, B., and A. Soltani. 2014. "NSA Surveillance Program Reaches 'into the Past' to Retrieve, Replay Phone Calls." *Washington Post*, March 18. https://www .washingtonpost.com/world/national-security/nsa-surveillance-program-reaches -into-the-past-to-retrieve-replay-phone-calls/2014/03/18/226d2646-ade9-11e3-a49e -76adc9210f19_story.html.

Geltzer, J. 2017. "What Trump's Qatar Tweets Revealed." *The Atlantic*, June 7. https://www.theatlantic.com/international/archive/2017/06/trump-qatar-saudi -arabia-terrorism-corker/529479/.

Georgy, M., M. El Dahan, and K. Abdelaziz. 2019. "Special Report: Abandoned by the UAE, Sudan's Bashir Was Destined to Fall." Reuters, July 3. https://www.reuters .com/article/us-sudan-bashir-fall-specialreport/special-report-abandoned-by-the -uae-sudans-bashir-was-destined-to-fall-idUSKCN1TY0MV.

Gilbert, D. 2017. "Cyber Arms Race." Vice News, March 26. https://news.vice.com /story/the-u-s-government-is-stockpiling-lists-of-zero-day-software-bugs-that-let-it -hack-into-iphones.

Gilbert, D. 2019. A Senior Twitter Exec Has Been Moonlighting in the British Army's Information Warfare Unit." Vice News, September 30. https://www.vice.com/en _us/article/ywa5m7/a-senior-twitter-exec-has-been-moonlighting-in-the-british -armys-information-warfare unit.

Giles, K. 2016. *Handbook of Russian Information Warfare*. NATO Defense College. http://www.ndc.nato.int/news/news.php?icode=995.

Gleicher, N. 2018. "Taking Down Coordinated Inauthentic Behavior from Iran." Facebook Newsroom, October 26. https://newsroom.fb.com/news/2018/10 /coordinated-inauthentic-behavior-takedown/.

Gleicher, N. 2019a. "Removing Coordinated Inauthentic Behavior from Iran." Facebook Newsroom, January 31. https://newsroom.fb.com/news/2019/01 /removing-cib-iran/.

Gleicher, N. 2019b. "Removing More Coordinated Inauthentic Behavior from Iran." Facebook Newsroom, May 28. https://newsroom.fb.com/news/2019/05/removing -more-cib-from-iran/.

Gleicher, N. 2019c. "Removing Coordinated Inauthentic Behavior in UAE, Egypt and Saudi Arabia." Facebook Newsroom, August 1. https://newsroom.fb.com/news /2019/08/cib-uae-egypt-saudi-arabia/.

Gleicher, N. 2019d. "Removing More Coordinated Inauthentic Behavior from Iran and Russia." Facebook, October 21. https://about.fb.com/news/2019/10/removing -more-coordinated-inauthentic-behavior-from-iran-and-russia/.

Global Coalition. 2016. "Countering Daesh's Propaganda." http://theglobalcoalition .org/mission/countering-daeshs-propaganda/.

Global Engagement Center. 2014. "Welcome to the 'Islamic State' Land." August 22. https://www.youtube.com/watch?v=-wmdEFvsYoE.

Global Engagement Center. 2016. YouTube. https://www.youtube.com/channel /UCUjopo5TdYn5qGC5QmbkpcQ.

Gobran, A. 2011. "Morocco's Hackers Block an Algerian Hacker and Promise More." Hespress, December 26. https://www.hespress.com/tendances/44013.html.

Goldman, D. 2012. "The Real Iranian Threat: Cyberattacks." CNN Money, November 5. http://money.cnn.com/2012/11/05/technology/security/iran-cyberattack/index.html.

Goodman, D. 2012. "Major Banks Hit with Biggest Cyberattacks in History." CNN Money, September 28. http://money.cnn.com/2012/09/27/technology/bank -cyberattacks/index.html.

Gray, C. H., and Á. J. Gordo. 2014. "Social Media in Conflict: Comparing Military and Social-Movement Technocultures. *Cultural Politics* 10 (3): 251–261.

Greenberg, A. 2012. "Anonymous Hackers Ramp Up Israeli Web Attacks and Data Breaches as Gaza Conflict Rages." *Forbes*, November 19. http://www.forbes.com /sites/andygreenberg/2012/11/19/anonymous-hackers-ramp-up-israeli-web-attacks -and-databreaches-as-gaza-conflict-rages-2/.

Greenberg, A. 2017. "New Group of Iranian Hackers Linked to Destructive Malware." Wired, September 20. https://www.wired.com/story/iran-hackers-apt33/.

Grim, R. 2017. "Gulf Government Gave Secret $20 Million Gift to D.C. Think Tank." The Intercept, August 10. https://theintercept.com/2017/08/09/gulf-government -gave-secret-20-million-gift-to-d-c-think-tank/.

Grim, R., and B. Walsh. 2017. "Leaked Documents Expose Stunning Plan to Wage Financial War on Qatar—and Steal the World Cup." The Intercept, November 9. https://theintercept.com/2017/11/09/uae-qatar-oitaba-rowland-banque-havilland -world-cup/.

Grimes, R. 2011. "Stuxnet Marks the Start of the Next Security Arms Race." Info-World, January 25. http://www.infoworld.com/d/security-central/stuxnet -marksthe-start-the-next-security-arms-race-282.

Groll, E. 2016. "The UAE Spends Big on Israeli Spyware to Listen in on a Dissident." Foreign Policy, August 25. https://foreignpolicy.com/2016/08/25/the-uae-spends -big-on-israeli-spyware-to-listen-in-on-a-dissident/.

Guardian. 2013. "Former U.S. General James Cartwright Named in Stuxnet Leak Inquiry." June 28. http://www.theguardian.com/world/2013/jun/28/general -cartwright-investigated-stuxnet-leak.

Guardian. 2019. "US Launched Cyber Attack on Iranian Rockets and Missiles." June 23. https://www.theguardian.com/world/2019/jun/23/us-launched-cyber -attack-on-iranian-rockets-and-missiles-reports.

Guardian. 2020. "US Government Agency Website Hacked by Group Claiming to Be from Iran." January 5. https://www.theguardian.com/world/2020/jan/05/us -government-agency-website-hacked-by-group-claiming-to-be-from-iran.

Gulf News. 2017a. "Global Campaign against Qatar's Financing of Terrorism Launched." June 30. http://gulfnews.com/news/gulf/qatar/global-campaign -against-qatar-s-financing-of-terrorism-launched-1.2051324.

Gulf News. 2017b. "Saudi Arabia Targeted in Cyber Spying Campaign." November 21. http://gulfnews.com/news/gulf/saudi-arabia/saudi-arabia-targeted-in-cyber-spying -campaign-1.2127967.

Hack Webs. 2016. Facebook page. March 8. http://tiny.cc/eir7ez.

Haeri, S. 1989. Law of Desire: Temporary Marriage in Shi'i Iran. New York: Syracuse University Press.

Handelman, J. 1999. "Culture Jamming: Expanding the Application of the Critical Research Project." In Advances in Consumer Research, Vol. 26, edited by E. J. Arnould and L. M. Scott, 399–404. Provo, UT: Association for Consumer Research.

Harris, S. 2009. "The Cyberwar Plan." National Journal Magazine, November 14. http://www.nationaljournal.com/member/magazine/the-cyberwar-plan-20091114.

Hart, P. T. 1998. Saudi Arabia and the United States: Birth of a Security Partnership. Bloomington: Indiana University Press.

Harwood, A. 2017. "The Qatari Hack Cements the Middle East as the Worst Region in the World for Fake News." The Independent, July 18. http://www.independent .co.uk/voices/qatar-uae-saudi-arabia-fake-news-middle-easy-worst-in-world -a7846571.html.

Hedges, M., and G. Cafiero. 2017. "The GCC and the Muslim Brotherhood: What Does the Future Hold?" Middle East Policy 24 (1): 129–153.

Hegghammer, T. 2006. "Terrorist Recruitment and Radicalization in Saudi Arabia." Middle East Policy 8 (4): 39–60.

Hern, A. 2015. "Hacking Team Hacked: Firm Sold Spying Tools to Repressive Regimes, Documents Claim." Guardian, July 6. https://www.theguardian.com /technology/2015/jul/06/hacking-team-hacked-firm-sold-spying-tools-to -repressive-regimes-documents-claim.

Hern, A. 2017. "Google Accused of Spreading Fake News." Guardian, March 6. https://www.theguardian.com/technology/2017/mar/06/google-accused-spreading -fake-news.

Herrera, L. 2014. *Revolution in the Age of Social Media: The Egyptian Popular Insurrection and the Internet.* New York: Verso Trade.

Hersh, E. D. 2015. *Hacking the Electorate: How Campaigns Perceive Voters.* Cambridge: Cambridge University Press.

Heussner, K. 2010. "Hacker Posts Video Claiming 'Here You Have' Worm." ABC News, September 13. http://abcnews.go.com/Technology/anti-us-hacker-claims -worm/story?id=11624252.

Hillygus, D. S., and T. G. Shields. 2014. *The Persuadable Voter: Wedge Issues in Presidential Campaigns.* Princeton, NJ: Princeton University Press.

Hirst, M., J. Harrison, and P. Mazepa. 2014. *Communication and New Media: From Broadcast to Narrowcast.* Don Mills, Ontario: Oxford University Press.

Hoewe, J., and B. J. Bowe. 2018. "Magic Words or Talking Point? The Framing of 'Radical Islam' in News Coverage and Its Effects. *Journalism*, 1–19. doi:10.1177/1464884918805577.

Holtmann, P. 2013. "Countering al-Qaeda's Single Narrative." *Perspectives on Terrorism* 7 (2): 141–145.

Howard, A. 2017. "The Qatari Hack Cements the Middle East as the Worst Region in the World for Fake News." The Independent, July 18. http://www.independent.co .uk/voices/qatar-uae-saudi-arabia-fake-news-middle-easy-worst-in-world-a7846571 .html.

Howard, P. N., B. Ganesh, D. Liotsiou, J. Kelly, and C. François. 2018. "The IRA, Social Media and Political Polarization in the United States, 2012–2018." University of Oxford.

Howard, P. N., and Kollanyi, B. 2016. *Bots, #StrongerIn, and #Brexit: Computational Propaganda during the UK-EU Referendum.* Oxford: Project on Computational Propaganda.

Huey, L. 2015. "This Is Not Your Mother's Terrorism: Social Media, Online Radicalization and the Practice of Political Jamming." *Journal of Terrorism Research* 6 (2).

HuffPost Arabi. 2017a. "Shamoon Hits Again: This Is How Saudi Companies Avoid Iranian Attacks." January 24. http://www.huffpostarabi.com/2017/01/24/story_n _14355710.html.

HuffPost Arabi. 2017b. "Shamoon Hits Again: This Is How Saudi Companies Avoid Iranian Attacks." February 27. http://www.huffpostarabi.com/2017/02/27/story_n _15041630.html.

HuffPost Arabi. 2017c. "The Saudi Information Minister: Qatar Employs 23,000 Twitter Users to Sow Division." June 6. http://www.huffpostarabi.com/2017/07 /06/story_n_17408562.html.

HuffPost Arabi. 2017d. "Qatar Files a Lawsuit against SkyNews Arabia and Al Arabiya in London." June 19. http://www.huffpostarabi.com/2017/06/19/story_n _17210874.html.

HuffPost Arabi. 2017e. "An iPhone with a European Number Was Used in the Hacking." July 20. http://www.huffpostarabi.com/2017/07/20/story_n_17541988.html.

HuffPost Arabi. 2017f. "Lifting the Ban on Qatar Websites in Saudi Arabia." July 24. http://www.huffpostarabi.com/2017/07/24/story_n_17568516.html.

HuffPost Arabi. 2017g. "The Accused Live in Arab Countries Including Saudi Arabia and Egypt." August 28. http://www.huffpostarabi.com/2017/08/28/story_n _17851342.html.

Huffpost Arabi. 2017h. "They Targeted Embassies and Diplomats: The Gaza Hacking Team Returns Targeting Arab Countries." October 31. http://www.huffpostarabi .com/2017/10/31/story_n_18419850.html.

HuffPost Arabi. 2017i. "The UAE Gives El-Sisi a French Espionage System." November 9. http://www.huffpostarabi.com/2017/11/09/story_n_18513146.html.

HuffPost Arabi. 2017j. "Jordan Counters 70 Million Cyber Attacks in One Year." November 11. http://www.huffpostarabi.com/2017/11/20/story_n_18601654.html.

Hughes, D. 2012. "Hillary Clinton: U.S. Hacked Yemen al-Qaida Sites. ABC News, May 23. http://abcnews.go.com/blogs/headlines/2012/05/secretary-clinton-we -hacked-yemen-al-qaeda-sites/.

Human Rights Watch. 2016. "140 Characters." https://features.hrw.org/features /HRW_2016_reports/140_Characters/index.html.

hussein adriano. 2014. "Excerpt on the Egyptian Cyber Army on Cairo 360 Show." September 14. https://www.youtube.com/watch?v=lxjF5YBH-6U.

hussein adrinao. n.d. YouTube channel. https://www.youtube.com/user/husseinadriano /videos.

Iannelli, L. 2016. *Hybrid Politics: Media and Participation.* Thousand Oaks, CA: SAGE.

IIP Digital. 2016. http://iipdigital.usembassy.gov/iipdigital-ar/index .html#axzz3czDWEK22.

International Telecommunication Union. 2012. *Connect Arab Summit 2012: Connecting the Unconnected by 2015: ICT Adoption and Prospects in the Arab Region.* CH-1211 Geneva, Switzerland.

Iraqi Sumer. 2009. "Iraqi Advertisements." http://www.youtube.com/playlist?list =PLFA2ACoC77B49A5D9.

Iraq Liberation Act. 1998. *Iraq Liberation Act of 1998.* Public Law 105–338. 105th Congress. https://www.gpo.gov/fdsys/pkg/PLAW-105publ338/html/PLAW-105publ338 .html.

Jaber, N. 2017. "Did Assad Dispense with the Syrian Electronic Army?" Alaraby, August 19. https://goo.gl/m7mxjy.

Jackson, D. 2017. "Issue Brief: Distinguishing Disinformation from Propaganda, Misinformation, and 'Fake News.'" National Endowment for Democracy, October 17. https://www.ned.org/issue-brief-distinguishing-disinformation-from -propaganda-misinformation-and-fake-news/.

Jameson, F. 1992. *Postmodernism, or the Culture of Late Capital.* Durham, NC: Duke University Press.

Jenkins, T. 2016. *The CIA in Hollywood: How the Agency Shapes Film and Television.* Austin: University of Texas Press.

Jilani, Z., and A. Emmons. 2017. "Hacked Emails Show UAE Building Close Relationship with D.C. Think Tanks that Push Its Agenda." The Intercept, July 30. https://theintercept.com/2017/07/30/uae-yousef-otaiba-cnas-american-progress -michele-flournoy-drone/.

Johnson, A. 2006. "TV Ad Aimed at Would-Be Bombers." *Toronto Star*, October 12. https://www.pressreader.com/canada/toronto-star/20061012/281616710859367.

Johnson, D. W. 2016. *Campaigning in the Twenty-First Century: Activism, Big Data, and Dark Money.* London: Routledge.

Jordan, T. 2008. *Hacking: Digital Media and Technological Determinism.* Oxford: Polity.

Kani, A. 2016. Facebook page. https://www.facebook.com/Amreekani.

Kareem, F. 2017. "Hackers Post Nazi Insults, Pro-Turkey Messages on Hundreds of Twitter Accounts." *Washington Post*, March 15. https://www.washingtonpost.com /world/hackers-open-new-front-in-turkeys-escalating-feud-with-europe/2017/03/15 /e8d27f84-097b-11e7-8884-96e6a6713f4b_story.html.

Kareem, F., and M. Ryan. 2017. "The UAE's Hunt for Its Enemies Is Challenging Its Alliance with the United States." *Washington Post*, August 3. https://www .washingtonpost.com/world/middle_east/uaes-drive-for-regional-influence-tests -its-military-alliance-with-the-united-states/2017/08/03/448683ee-6bd2-11e7-abbc -a53480672286_story.html.

Karp, P. 2019. "Russian Twitter Trolls Stoking Anti-Islamic Sentiment in Australia, Experts Warn." *Guardian*, November 20. https://www.theguardian.com/australia -news/2018/nov/20/russian-twitter-trolls-stoking-anti-islamic-sentiment-in -australia-experts-warn.

Kaspersky. 2017. "A Notorious Gaza Team Cybergang Upgrades Its Malicious Toolset with Exploits and Possibly with Android Spyware." October 30. https://www .kaspersky.com/about/press-releases/2017_a-notorious-gaza-team-cybergang -upgrades-its-malicious-toolset.

Katz, R. 2014. "The State Department's Twitter War with ISIS Is Embarrassing." *Time*, September 14. http://time.com/3387065/isis-twitter-war-state-department/.

Kavanaugh, A. L., E. A. Fox, S. D. Sheetz, S. Yang, L. T. Li, D. J. Shoemaker, and L. Xie. 2012. "Social Media Use by Government: From the Routine to the Critical." *Government Information Quarterly* 29 (4): 480–491.

Kavanaugh, S., and G. Shiloach. 2015. "ISIS Hackers Sharpen Skills Used for Cyber Terror in Secret Forum." Vocativ, December 28. http://www.vocativ.com/264640 /isis-hackers-sharpen-skills-used-for-cyber-terror-in-secret-forum/.

Kenski, K., B. W. Hardy, and K. H. Jamieson. 2010. *The Obama Victory: How Media, Money, and Message Shaped the 2008 Election*. Oxford: Oxford University Press.

Kerr, S., A. Raval, and A. England. 2018. "Saudi 'Prince of Darkness' Lingers in the Shadows." *Financial Times*, November 18. https://www.ft.com/content/e9940fc8 -e9a3-11e8-a34c-663b3f553b35.

Khamis, S. 2011. "The Transformative Egyptian Media Landscape: Changes, Challenges and Comparative Perspectives." *International Journal of Communication* 5 (19).

Khan, S. O. 2012. "2012 Cyberwatch Year in Review: Middle East and North Africa, Southeast Asia, Latin America and the Caribbean." Citizen Lab. https://citizenlab .ca/2012/12/2012-year-in-review-cyberwatch/.

Khashoggi, J. 2018. "Who Is Saud al-Qahtani, the Fired Saudi Royal Court Adviser?" Al Jazeera, October 20. https://www.aljazeera.com/news/2018/10/saud-al-qahtani -fired-saudi-royal-court-adviser-181020125449478.html.

Khatib, L., W. Dutton, and M. Thelwall. 2011. "Public Diplomacy 2.0: An Exploratory Case Study of the US Digital Outreach Team." *Public Diplomacy* 2.

Kianpour, S. 2018. "Emails Show UAE-Linked Effort against Tillerson." BBC News, March 5. https://www.bbc.com/news/world-us-canada-43281519.

King, E. 2013. "Snowden Spyware Revelations: We Need to Unmask the Five-Eyed Monster." *Guardian*, November 26. https://www.theguardian.com/commentisfree /2013/nov/26/snowden-spyware-five-eyed-monster-50000-networks-five-eyes -privacy.

Kirchgaessner, S. 2020. "Revealed: The Saudi Heir and the Alleged Plot to Undermine Jeff Bezos." *Guardian*, January 21. https://www.theguardian.com/world/2020/jan /21/revealed-the-saudi-heir-and-the-alleged-plot-to-undermine-jeff-bezos.

Kirchgaessner, S., and N. Hopkins. 2019. "Saudi Arabia Accused of Hacking London-Based Dissident." *Guardian*, May 28. https://www.theguardian.com/world/2019 /may/28/saudi-arabia-accused-of-hacking-london-based-dissident-ghanem -almasarir.

Kirkpatrick, D. 2017. "Journalist Joins His Jailer's Side in a Bizarre Persian Gulf Feud." *New York Times*, July 1. https://www.nytimes.com/2017/07/01/world/middleeast /qatar-egypt-united-arab-emirates-mohamed-fahmy.html.

Kirkpatrick, D., and A. Ahmed. 2018. "Hacking a Prince, an Emir and a Journalist to Impress a Client. *New York Times*, August 31. https://www.nytimes.com/2018/08 /31/world/middleeast/hacking-united-arab-emirates-nso-group.html.

Kirkpatrick, D., and S. Frenkel. 2017. "Hacking in Qatar Highlights a Shift Toward Espionage for Hire." *New York Times*, June 8. https://nyti.ms/2s1Ux1x.

Klimburg, A. 2011. "Mobilising Cyber Power." *Survival* 53 (1): 41–60.

Klobucher, D. 2013. "Cyber-Attacks against Banks Continue: Wall Street, We Have a Problemo, Bro." *Forbes*, January 18. https://www.forbes.com/sites/sap/2013/01/18 /cyber-attacks-against-banks-continue-wall-street-we-have-a-problemo-bro/.

Klotz, R. J. 2007. "Internet Campaigning for Grassroots and Astroturf Support." *Social Science Computer Review* 25 (1): 3–12.

Knell, Y. 2012. "New Cyber Attack Hits Israeli Stock Exchange and Airline." BBC, January 16. https://www.bbc.com/news/world-16577184.

Kosoff, M. 2017. "The Russian Troll Farm that Weaponized Facebook Had American Boots on the Ground." *Vanity Fair*, October 18. https://www.vanityfair.com/news /2017/10/the-russian-troll-farm-that-weaponized-facebook-had-american-boots-on -the-ground.

Kovacs, E. 2014a. "Egyptian Military and Government Websites Defaced by Hacktivist." Softpedia, April 3. https://news.softpedia.com/news/Egyptian-Military-and -Government-Websites-Defaced-by-Hacktivist-435687.shtml.

Kovacs, E. 2014b. "Kali Linux Mailing List Hacked by Libyan Group." Softpedia, May 1. https://news.softpedia.com/news/Kali-Linux-Mailing-List-Hacked-by -Libyan-Group-440128.shtml.

Kraidy, M. M. 2008. *Arab Media and US Policy: A Public Diplomacy Reset.* Stanley Foundation. http://repository.upenn.edu/asc_papers/182.

Kreiss, D., and S. C. McGregor. 2017. "Technology Firms Shape Political Communication: The Work of Microsoft, Facebook, Twitter, and Google with Campaigns during the 2016 US Presidential Cycle." *Political Communication*, 1–23.

Kreiss, D., and G. Welch. 2015. "Strategic Communication in a Networked Age." In *Controlling the Message: New Media in American Political Campaigns*, edited by V. Farrar-Myers and J. Vaughn, 13–31. New York: New York University Press.

Kruckeberg, D., and M. Vujnovic. 2005. "Public Relations, Not Propaganda, for US Public Diplomacy in a Post-9/11 World: Challenges and Opportunities." *Journal of Communication Management* 9 (4): 296–304.

Kumar, M. 2012. "Al Jazeera News Network Website Hacked by Pro-Assad Hackers." Hacker News, September 4. https://thehackernews.com/2012/09/al-jazeera-news -network-website-hacked.html.

Kundnani, A. 2014. *The Muslims Are Coming! Islamophobia, Extremism, and the Domestic War on Terror.* New York: Verso Books.

Kurdistan 24. 2019. "Iraq Government Websites Hacked in 'Largest Operation' Yet." September 27. https://www.kurdistan24.net/en/news/018ebfb3-1c36-4f5a-81d8 -798da19ed435.

Lahlali, E. M. 2011. *Contemporary Arab Broadcast Media.* Edinburgh: Edinburgh University Press.

Lee, N. 2013. *Counterterrorism and Cybersecurity.* New York: Springer Science.

Lenderking, T., P. Cammack, A. Shihabi, and D. Des Roches. 2017. "The GCC Rift: Regional and Global Implications." *Middle East Policy* 24 (4): 5–28.

Levin, S. 2017. "Pay to Sway: Report Reveals How Easy It Is to Manipulate Elections with Fake News." *Guardian*, June 13. https://www.theguardian.com/media/2017/jun/13/fake-news-manipulate-elections-paid-propaganda.

Levy, S. 1984. *Hackers: Heroes of the Computer Revolution*, Vol. 14. Garden City, NY: Anchor Press/Doubleday.

Lewandowsky, S., W. G. Stritzke, A. M. Freund, K. Oberauer, and J. I. Krueger. 2013. "Misinformation, Disinformation, and Violent Conflict: From Iraq and the 'War on Terror' to Future Threats to Peace." *American Psychologist* 68 (7): 487–501.

Ling, J. 2017. "Canada's Cyber Spy Agency Is About to Get a Major Upgrade." Vice News, June 21. https://news.vice.com/en_ca/article/9kdmvz/cse-is-getting-a-major-upgrade.

Londoño, E. 2009. "A High-Priced Media Campaign that Iraqis Aren't Buying." *Washington Post*, June 7. https://www.pressreader.com/usa/the-washington-post-sunday/20090607/281612416371100.

Long, D. E. 1985. *The United States and Saudi Arabia: Ambivalent Allies*, No. 3. Boulder, CO: Westview.

Lord, C. 2006. *Losing Hearts and Minds? Public Diplomacy and Strategic Influence in the Age of Terror*. New York: Greenwood.

Lucas, G. 2017. *Ethics and Cyber Warfare: The Quest for Responsible Security in the Age of Digital Warfare*. Oxford: Oxford University Press.

Lundry, A. 2012. "Making It Personal: The Rise of Microtargeting." In *Margin of Victory: How Technologists Help Politicians Win Elections*, edited by N. G. Pearlman, 161–174. New York: Praeger.

MacAskill, E. 2017. "Iran to Blame for Cyber-Attack on MPs' Emails—British Intelligence." *Guardian*, October 14. https://www.theguardian.com/world/2017/oct/14/iran-to-blame-for-cyber-attack-on-mps-emails-british-intelligence.

MacKinnon, R. 2011. "Networked Authoritarianism in China and Beyond: Implications for Global Internet Freedom. *Journal of Democracy* 22, 32–46. doi:10.1353/jod.2011.0033.

Magleby, D., and K. Patterson. 2006. "Stepping Out of the Shadows? Ground-War Activity in 2004." In *The Election after Reform: Money, Politics, and the Bipartisan Campaign Reform Act*, edited by Michael J. Malbin, 161–189. New York: Rowman & Littlefield.

Manjoo, F. 2017. "How Twitter Is Being Gamed to Feed Misinformation." *New York Times*, May 31. https://www.nytimes.com/2017/05/31/technology/how-twitter-is-being-gamed-to-feed-misinformation.html.

Marczak, B., J. Scott-Railton, A. Senft, B. Abdul Razzak, and R. Deibert. 2018. "The Kingdom Came to Canada: How Saudi-Linked Digital Espionage Reached Canadian Soil." Citizen Lab. https://citizenlab.ca/2018/10/the-kingdom-came-to-canada-how-saudi-linked-digital-espionage-reached-canadian-soil/.

Mark, D. 2009. *Going Dirty: The Art of Negative Campaigning*. New York: Rowman & Littlefield.

Markoff, J. 2009. "Old Trick Threatens the Newest Weapons." *New York Times*, October 26. http://www.nytimes.com/2009/10/27/science/27trojan.html.

Marquis-Boire, M. 2012. "Backdoors Are Forever: Hacking Team and the Targeting of Dissent." Citizen Lab. October 10. https://citizenlab.ca/2012/10/backdoors-are-forever-hacking-team-and-the-targeting-of-dissent/.

Matthes, J., and M. Kohring. 2008. "The Content Analysis of Media Frames: Toward Improving Reliability and Validity." *Journal of Communication* 58 (2): 258–279.

Maza, C. 2017. "Saudi Arabia's Government Might Be Getting Help from Social Media Giants to Shut Down Dissent." *Newsweek*, December 22. http://www .newsweek.com/saudi-arabia-crack-down-social-media-dissent-754257.

Mazzetti, M., A. Goldman, R. Bergman, and N. Perlroth. 2019. "A New Age of Warfare: How Internet Mercenaries Do Battle for Authoritarian Governments." *New York Times*, March 21. https://www.nytimes.com/2019/03/21/us/politics /government-hackers-nso-darkmatter.html.

Mazzetti, M., D. Kirkpatrick, and M. Haberman. 2018. "Mueller's Focus on Adviser to Emirates Suggests Broader Investigation." *New York Times*, March 3. https://nyti .ms/2F86rdF.

Mazzetti, M., N. Perlroth, and R. Bergman. 2019. "It Seemed Like a Popular Chat App. It's Secretly a Spy Tool." *New York Times*, December 22. https://www.nytimes .com/2019/12/22/us/politics/totok-app-uae.html.

McInnis, K. 2016. *Coalition Contributions to Countering the Islamic State*. Congressional Research Service. https://www.fas.org/sgp/crs/natsec/R44135.pdf.

McKernan, B. 2017. "Al Jazeera Hack: Publisher under Cyber Attack on All Websites, Facebook and Twitter Pages." The Independent, June 8. http://www.independent .co.uk/News/world/al-jazeera-attack-hack-qatar-cyber-facebook-twitter-website -news-a7779826.html.

McLaughlin, J. 2016. "Spies for Hire: How the UAE Is Recruiting Hackers to Create the Perfect Surveillance State." The Intercept, October 24. https://theintercept .com/2016/10/24/darkmatter-united-arab-emirates-spies-for-hire/.

McQuade, S. 2009. *Encyclopedia of Cybercrime*. New York: Greenwood.

Mejias, U. A., and N. E. Vokuev. 2017. "Disinformation and the Media: The Case of Russia and Ukraine." *Media, Culture and Society* 39 (7): 1027–1042.

Memmot, M. 2013. "NPR.org Hacked; 'Syrian Electronic Army' Takes Responsibility." NPR, April 16. http://www.npr.org/blogs/thetwo-way/2013/04/16/177421655 /npr-org-hacked-syrian-electronic-army-takes-credit.

Menn, J. 2016. "Apple Fixes Security Flaw after UAE Dissident's iPhone Targeted." Reuters, August 25. https://www.reuters.com/article/us-apple-iphone-cyber/apple -fixes-security-flaw-after-uae-dissidents-iphone-targeted-idUSKCN1102B1.

Meyer, A. H. 2003. *Quiet Diplomacy: From Cairo to Tokyo in the Twilight of Imperialism*. Bloomington, IN: iUniverse.

Michel, C. 2017a. "Russian Propaganda Promoting Texas Secession Moves to Instagram." Think Progress, October 10. https://thinkprogress.org/instagram -russia-texas-secession-b766b2df9e65/.

Michel, C. 2017b. "Russia-Linked Pro-Confederate Propaganda Still Available on Instagram." Think Progress, December 22. https://thinkprogress.org/russian -confederate-material-instagram-3e3d3894bd70/.

Middle East Eye. 2017a. "UK Arms Firm Sold Spyware to Repressive Middle East States." June 15. http://www.middleeasteye.net/news/bae-systems-sold-surveillance -software-used-repression-across-middle-east-report-1614150131.

Middle East Eye. 2017b. "Steve Bannon Says Trump's Saudi Visit Started Qatar Crisis." October 23. http://www.middleeasteye.net/news/steve-bannon-says -trumps-visit-saudi-sparked-qatar-blockade-1719031821.

Middle East Monitor. 2017. "Qatar Complaints against Al-Arabiya and Sky News Arabia." June 20. https://www.middleeastmonitor.com/20170620-qatar -complaints-against-al-arabiya-and-sky-news-arabia/.

Milan, S. 2015. "Hacktivism as a Radical Media Practice." In *The Routledge Companion to Alternative and Community Media*, edited by C. Atton, 550–560. London: Routledge.

Miller, G., and S. Higham. 2015. "In a Propaganda War against ISIS, the U.S. Tried to Play by the Enemy's Rules." *Washington Post*, May 8. https://www.washingtonpost.com/world/national-security/in-a-propaganda-war-us-tried-to-play-by-the-enemys-rules/2015/05/08/6eb6b732-e52f-11e4-81ea-0649268f729e_story.html.

Miller, M. 1997. "Frame Mapping and Analysis of News Coverage of Contentious Issues." *Social Science Computer Review* 15 (4): 367–378.

Miller, M., and B. Riechert. 2001. "Frame Mapping: A Quantitative Method for Investigating Issues in the Public Sphere." *Progress in Communication Sciences*, 16:61–76.

Mitre. 2019. *Groups*. https://attack.mitre.org/groups/.

Mobtada. 2013. "Algerian Hacker Hacks Saudi Arabian Ministry of Media Website and Posts Algeria's Flag." May 25. https://www.mobtada.com/details/65494.

Moore, J. 2016. "Pro-Palestinian Hackers Suspected of Disrupting Israeli Television with Muslim Holy Sites." *Newsweek*, November 30. http://www.newsweek.com/pro-palestinian-hackers-suspected-disrupting-israeli-television-muslim-holy-526799.

Morgan, G. 2016. *Global Islamophobia: Muslims and Moral Panic in the West*. London: Routledge.

Murphy, L. 2013. "Anonymous Isn't Ready to Publish the Identities of the Syrian Electronic Army—Yet." Daily Dot, September 4. http://www.dailydot.com/news/anonymous-syrian-electronic-army-names/.

Murphy, L. 2015. "The Curious Case of the Jihadist Who Started Out as a Hacktivist." *Vanity Fair*, December 15. https://www.vanityfair.com/news/2015/12/isis-hacker-junaid-hussain.

Naimi, A. 2017. "Iraqi Cyber Army: A Tool for Embassies and Religious Clerics." Al Araby, July 12. https://goo.gl/4bEVj2.

Nakashima, E., and J. Warrick. 2012. "Stuxnet Was Work of U.S. and Israeli Experts, Officials Say. *Washington Post*, June 2. https://www.washingtonpost.com/world/national-security/stuxnet-was-work-of-us-and-israeli-experts-officials-say/2012/06/01/gJQAInEy6U_story.html.

Nassif, D. 2008. "We Do Not Spread Propaganda for the United States." *Middle East Quarterly* 15 (2): 63–69. http://www.meforum.org/1880/daniel-nassif-we-do-not-spread-propaganda-for.

National Security Agency. 2012. (U) *SIGNINT Strategy: 2012–2016*. February 23. https://edwardsnowden.com/2013/11/23/sigint-strategy-2012-2016/.

National Security Archive. 2004. Baghdad Operations Center. U.S. Department of Justice, May 13. http://nsarchive.gwu.edu/NSAEBB/NSAEBB279/23.pdf.

National Strategy for Counterterrorism. 2011. The White House. https://obamawhitehouse.archives.gov/sites/default/files/counterterrorism_strategy.pdf.

NBC News. 2014. "Snowden Docs Show British Spies Used Sex and 'Dirty Tricks.'" February 7. https://www.nbcnews.com/news/investigations/snowden-docs-british-spies-used-sex-dirty-tricks-n23091.

NBC News. 2018. "'ISIS Hackers' Threats Against U.S. Military Wives Actually Came from Russian Trolls." May 8. https://www.nbcnews.com/storyline/isis-terror/u-s-military-wives-threatened-russian-hackers-posing-isis-n872251.

Neuman, W., M. Just, and A. Crigler. 1992. *Common Knowledge: News and the Construction of Political Meaning*. Chicago: University of Chicago Press.

Newton, C. 2017. "Saudi Lobby Pays $138,000 for Anti-Qatar Ads in the US." Al Jazeera, July 25. http://www.aljazeera.com/news/2017/07/saudi-lobby-pays-138000-anti-qatar-ads-170725041529752.html.

O'Donnell, V., and G. S. Jowett. 2012. *Propaganda and Persuasion.* Thousand Oaks, CA: SAGE.

Office of Inspector General. 2008. *Alhurra's Programming Policies and Procedures. ISP-IB-08-45, May 2008.* United States Department of State and the Broadcasting Board of Governors. https://www.stateoig.gov/system/files/106057.pdf.

O'Loughlin, B. 2015. "The Permanent Campaign." *Media, War and Conflict* 8 (2): 169–171.

One Iraq News. 2017. "Details Published for the First Time. Hussein Mahdy Reveals to (One News) about the 'Crack' that Led to His Arrest." July 2. http://tiny.cc/dpd3ez.

OpenNet Initiative. 2009. "Internet Filtering in the Middle East and North Africa." http://opennet.net/sites/opennet.net/files/ONI_MENA_2009.pdf.

Orient News. 2016. "Al-Arabya Net Website Hacked." January 5. https://orient-news.net/ar/news_show/98958/0/%D8%A7%D8%AE%D8%AA%D8%B1%D8%A7%D9%82-%D9%85%D9%88%D9%82%D8%B9-%D8%A7%D9%84%D8%B9%D8%B1%D8%A8%D9%8A%D8%A9-%D9%86%D8%AA.

Osgood, K. 2006. *Total Cold War: Eisenhower's Secret Cold War Battle at Home and Abroad.* Lawrence: University of Kansas.

Pagliery, J. 2017. "WikiLeaks Claims to Reveal How CIA Hacks TVs and Phones All Over the World." CNN Tech, March 7. http://money.cnn.com/2017/03/07/technology/wikileaks-cia-hacking/index.html.

Pamment, J. 2012. *New Public Diplomacy in the 21st Century: A Comparative Study of Policy and Practice.* London: Routledge.

Park, S. J., Y. S. Lim, S. Sams, S. M. Nam, and H. W. Park. 2011. "Networked Politics on Cyworld: The Text and Sentiment of Korean Political Profiles." *Social Science Computer Review* 29 (3): 288–299.

Parkin, S. 2013. "The Video-Game Invasion of Iraq." *New Yorker*, November 13. https://www.newyorker.com/tech/annals-of-technology/the-video-game-invasion-of-iraq.

Payne, J. 2012. "Feminist Media as Alternative Media? Theorising Feminist Media from the Perspective of Alternative Media Studies. In *Feminist Media: Participatory Spaces, Networks and Cultural Citizenship*, edited by E. Zobl and R. Drüeke, 55–72. Berlin: Transcript-Verlag.

Pearce, K. E., and S. Kendzior. 2012. "Networked Authoritarianism and Social Media in Azerbaijan." *Journal of Communication* 62 (2): 283–298.

Perlroth, N. 2016. "Governments Turn to Commercial Spyware to Intimidate Dissidents." *New York Times*, May 29. https://www.nytimes.com/2016/05/30/technology/governments-turn-to-commercial-spyware-to-intimidate-dissidents.html.

Perlroth, N. 2018. "Lebanese Intelligence Turned Targets' Android Phones into Spy Devices, Researchers Say." *New York Times*, January 18. https://nyti.ms/2FRlAB7.

Perlroth, N., and C. Krauss. 2018. "A Cyberattack in Saudi Arabia Had a Deadly Goal. Experts Fear Another Try." *New York Times*, March 15. https://www.nytimes.com/2018/03/15/technology/saudi-arabia-hacks-cyberattacks.html.

Pew Research Center. 2017. "Americans Express Increasingly Warm Feelings toward Religious Groups." http://www.pewforum.org/2017/02/15/americans-express-increasingly-warm-feelings-toward-religious-groups/.

Pollack, J. 2002. "Saudi Arabia and the United States, 1931–2002." *Middle East Review of International Affairs* 6 (3): 77–102.

Popken, B. 2017a. "Russian Trolls Pushed Graphic, Racist Tweets to American Voters." NBC News, November 30. https://www.nbcnews.com/tech/social-media/russian-trolls-pushed-graphic-racist-tweets-american-voters-n823001.

Popken, B. 2017b. "Russian Trolls Went on Attack during Key Election Moments." NBC News, December 20. https://www.nbcnews.com/tech/social-media/russian-trolls-went-attack-during-key-election-moments-n827176.

Powers, S., and M. Jablonski. 2015. *The Real Cyber War: The Political Economy of Internet Freedom*. Champaign: University of Illinois Press.

Pressman, J. 2009. "Power without Influence: The Bush Administration's Foreign Policy Failure in the Middle East." *International Security* 33 (4): 149–179.

Proctor, P. 2012. "War without Violence: Leveraging the Arab Spring to Win the War on Terrorism." *Journal of Strategic Security* 5 (2): 47–64.

Rackaway, C. 2014. *Communicating Politics Online*. London: Springer.

Radio Sawa. 2016. "About us." https://www.radiosawa.com/2020/02/27/%D9%86%D8%AD%D9%86.

Raincoaster. 2015. "'I Attacked #Joomla.' An Interview with Dr.AFNDENA of AnonCoders." The Cryptosphere, June 11. https://thecryptosphere.com/2015/06/11/i-attacked-joomla-an-interview-with-dr-afndena-of-anoncoders/.

Rampton, S. 2007. "Shared Values Revisited." PR Watch, October 17. http://www.prwatch.org/node/6465/print.

Rapoza, K. 2012. "Iran Facing 'Stuxnet on Steroids' Attack." *Forbes*, May 29. https://www.forbes.com/sites/kenrapoza/2012/05/29/iran-facing-stuxnet-on-steroids-attack/#e72bc5133aed.

Rawnsley, G. 2011. "The Media and Information Environments Ten Years after 9/11." *Journal of Media and Information Warfare* 4, 19–35.

Reporters without Borders. 2013. *Enemies of the Internet: 2013 Report*. http://surveillance.rsf.org/en/wp-content/uploads/sites/2/2013/03/enemies-of-the-internet_2013.pdf.

Reporters without Borders. 2014. *Enemies of the Internet 2014*. https://rsf.org/sites/default/files/2014-rsf-rapport-enemies-of-the-internet.pdf.

Reuters. 2017. "Mauritania Breaks Diplomatic Ties with Qatar, Gabon Voices Condemnation." June 6. https://www.reuters.com/article/us-gulf-qatar-mauritania/mauritania-breaks-diplomatic-ties-with-qatar-gabon-voices-condemnation-idUSKBN18X2ZH.

Reuters. 2018. "How the Man Behind Khashoggi Murder Ran the Killing via Skype." October 22. https://www.reuters.com/article/us-saudi-khashoggi-adviser-insight/how-the-man-behind-khashoggi-murder-ran-the-killing-via-skype-idUSKCN1MW2HA.

Revise, N. 2014. "The US Has Launched a Social Media Offensive against ISIS." Business Insider, August 31. http://www.businessinsider.com/afp-us-cyber-warriors-battling-islamic-state-on-twitter-2014-8.

Richards, J. 2014. *Cyber-War: The Anatomy of the Global Security Threat*. New York: Springer.

Richelson, J. T. 2013. *National Security Agency Tasked with Targeting Adversaries' Computers for Attack Since Early 1997*. National Security Archive Electronic Briefing Book No. 424. http://www2.gwu.edu/~nsarchiv/NSAEBB/NSAEBB424/.

Riley, M. 2016. "Saudi Central Bank Systems Said to Be Struck by Iran Malware." Bloomberg, December 2. https://www.bloomberg.com/news/articles/2016-12-02/saudi-central-bank-computers-said-to-be-damaged-by-iran-malware.

Ritter, S., and S. M. Hersh. 2005. *Iraq Confidential: The Untold Story of America's Intelligence Conspiracy.* London: IB Tauris.

Robb, D. L. 2004. *Operation Hollywood: How the Pentagon Shapes and Censors the Movies.* New York: Prometheus.

Robbins, J. W., and N. Magee. 2008. *The Sleeping Giant Has Awoken: The New Politics of Religion in the United States.* New York: Continuum.

Rocha, R., and J. Yates. 2019. "Twitter Trolls Stoked Debates about Immigrants and Pipelines in Canada, Data Show." CBC, February 12. https://www.cbc.ca/news/canada/twitter-troll-pipeline-immigrant-russia-iran-1.5014750.

Rojas, P. 2003. "The Paranoia that Paid Off." *Guardian*, April 24. https://www.theguardian.com/technology/2003/apr/24/security.newmedia.

Rosenberg, E. 2017. "Alex Jones Apologizes for Promoting 'Pizzagate' Hoax." *New York Times*, March 25. https://nyti.ms/2ohIWpD.

RSLF (Royal Saudi Land Forces). n.d. *Managing Cyber War.* https://rslf.gov.sa/Arabic/LFDepartments/ElectronicWarfareDept/Pages/default.aspx.

RT. 2013. "Anonymous Launches Massive Cyber Assault on Israel." April 6. https://www.rt.com/news/opisrael-anonymous-final-warning-448/.

RT Arabic. 2017. "Moscow Establishes a Unit to Counter Cyberattacks." February 22. https://goo.gl/FFgrLa.

RT Arabic. 2019. "Iraq . . . Hackers Penetrate the Anti-Terrorism Agency and Call for a Coup." November 25. https://arabic.rt.com/middle_east/1062835--بعد-ي/إختراقه-حسابات-جهاز-مكافحة-الإرهاب-العراق-هكر-يدعو-لإنقلاب-عسكر.

Rugh, W. A. 2004a. *Arab Mass Media: Newspapers, Radio, and Television in Arab Politics.* New York: Greenwood.

Rugh, W. 2004b. "Comments on Radio Sawa and al Hurra Television." Information Warfare, April 29. http://www.iwar.org.uk/psyops/resources/middle-east/RughTestimony040429.pdf.

Rugh, W. 2006. *American Encounters with Arabs: The "Soft Power" of US Public Diplomacy in the Middle East.* New York: Greenwood.

Rugh, W. 2014. *Front Line Public Diplomacy: How US Embassies Communicate with Foreign Publics.* Hampshire, UK: Palgrave Macmillan.

Russell, A. 2004. "CIA Plot Led to Huge Blast in Siberian Gas Pipeline. *Telegraph*, February 28. http://www.telegraph.co.uk/news/worldnews/northamerica/usa/1455559/CIA-plot-led-to-huge-blast-in-Siberian-gas-pipeline.html.

Russell, J. 2013. "Perspectives: The Quilliam Foundation—Fighting Extremism." BBC, October 29. http://www.bbc.co.uk/religion/0/24706419.

Sakr, N. 2008. "Diversity and Diaspora Arab Communities and Satellite Communication in Europe." *Global Media and Communication* 4 (3): 277–300.

Sanger, D. E. 2012. "Obama Order Sped Up Wave of Cyberattacks Against Iran." *New York Times*, June 1. http://www.nytimes.com/2012/06/01/world/middleeast/obama-ordered-wave-of-cyberattacks-against-iran.html.

Sanger, D., and N. Perlroth. 2015. "Iranian Hackers Attack State Dept. via Social Media Accounts." *New York Times*, November 24. http://nyti.ms/1YrGM3z.

Sankin, A., and W. Turton. 2015. "How to Destroy an American Family." Daily Dot, November 24. https://www.dailydot.com/layer8/how-to-destroy-an-american-family/.

Sardarizzadeh, S. 2016. "Iran-Saudi Tensions Erupt in 'Cyberwar.'" BBC, June 3. https://www.bbc.com/news/world-middle-east-36438333

Sauter, M. 2014. *The Coming Swarm: DDOS Actions, Hacktivism, and Civil Disobedience on the Internet.* New York: Bloomsbury.

Say No to Terror. 2009. Facebook page. https://www.facebook.com/saynototerror.

Say No to Terror. 2010a. "No Life Where Terrorism Resides." August 5. http://www.youtube.com/watch?v=ZfaL21xi5ccandlist.

Say No to Terror. 2010b. YouTube channel. Accessed January 12, 2021. http://www.youtube.com/user/saynototerror.

Say No to Terror. 2010c. "A Watchful Eye Is Better than a Crying One." December 2. http://www.youtube.com/watch?v=MTwz-jLxAh4andlist.

Say No to Terror. n.d. Twitter profile. Accessed January 11, 2021. http://twitter.com/saynototerror.

Scharr, J. 2013. "What Is the Syrian Electronic Army?" Live Science, September 1. http://news.yahoo.com/syrian-electronic-army-123906820.html.

Schmid, A. P. 2014. "Al-Qaeda's 'Single Narrative' and Attempts to Develop Counter-Narratives: The State of Knowledge." The Hague: ICCT.

Schmitt, E. 2015. "U.S. Intensifies Effort to Blunt ISIS' Message." *New York Times*, February 16. http://www.nytimes.com/2015/02/17/world/middleeast/us-intensifies-effort-to-blunt-isis-message.html.

Schmitt, M. N., ed. 2013. *Tallinn Manual on the International Law Applicable to Cyber Warfare.* Cambridge: Cambridge University Press.

Schneider, M. C. 2007. "Gender Bending: Candidate Strategy and Voter Response in a Marketing Age." Ph.D. diss., University of Minnesota.

Sciutto, J., and J. Herb. 2017. "Exclusive: The Secret Documents that Help Explain the Qatar Crisis." CNN, July 11. http://www.cnn.com/2017/07/10/politics/secret-documents-qatar-crisis-gulf-saudi/index.html.

Scott, P. D. 2007. *The Road to 9/11: Wealth, Empire, and the Future of America.* Berkeley: University of California Press.

Scott-Railton, J., B. Abdul Razzak, A. Hulcoop, M. Brooks, and K. Kleemola. 2016. "Syria and the Iranian Connection." Citizen Lab, August 2. https://citizenlab.ca/2016/08/group5-syria/.

SEAOfficialChannel. 2013a. YouTube channel. http://www.youtube.com/user/SEAOfficialChannel/about.

SEAOfficialChannel. 2013b. "Al-Mayadeen—on the Ground—SEA." September 23. http://www.youtube.com/watch?v=gBRZRnzIi3w.

Shaban, M. 2018. "The Oppositional Figure Omar Abdul Aziz Narrates His Last Conversation with Jamal Khashoggi Before His Trip." EuroNews, October 23. https://arabic.euronews.com/2018/10/19/saudi-opponent-omar-abdel-aziz-tells-euronews-what-happened-in-last-contact-with-khashoggi.

Shachtman, N. 2009. "27,000 Work in Pentagon PR and Recruiting." Wired, May 2. https://www.wired.com/2009/02/27000-work-in-p/.

Shachtman, N. 2012. "Bank Hackers Deny They're Agents of Iran." Wired, November 27. https://www.wired.com/2012/11/bank-hackers-deny-theyre-agents-of-iran/.

Shapiro, L. 2017. "Anatomy of a Russian Facebook Ad." *Washington Post*, November 1. https://www.washingtonpost.com/graphics/2017/business/russian-ads-facebook-anatomy/?utm_term=.e404de7888a5.

Sheret Hacker Iraq. 2019. "Episode One of How to Become a Professional Hacker." June 25. https://www.youtube.com/watch?v=94ByGJYxDYI.

Shiaa Hacker Boys. 2012. "Hacking American Devices." November 8. https://www.youtube.com/watch?v=F4I4QQTXıDI.

Shiloach, G. 2016a. "Iran and Saudi Senior Clerics Swap Barbs over Upcoming Hajj." Vocativ, September 8. http://www.vocativ.com/357418/iranandsaudiseniorclericssw apbarbsoverupcominghajj/.

Shiloach, G. 2016b. "Pro-ISIS Hackers Got a Raqqa Activist Group Blocked on Telegram." Vocativ, November 2. http://www.vocativ.com/372672/proisishackersg otaraqqaactivistgroupblockedontelegram.

Shugerman, E. 2017. "Jared Kushner 'Tried and Failed to Get a $500m Loan from Qatar Before Pushing Trump to Take Hard Line Against Country.'" *The Independent*, July 10. http://www.independent.co.uk/news/world/americas/us-politics /jared-kushner-qatar-loan-trump-saudi-arabia-hard-line-a7834536.html.

Siapera, E. 2012. *Understanding New Media*. Thousand Oaks, CA: SAGE.

Siapera, E., M. Boudourides, S. Lenis, and J. Suiter. 2018. "Refugees and Network Publics on Twitter: Networked Framing, Affect, and Capture." *Social Media + Society* 4 (1). https://doi.org/10.1177/2056305118764437.

Silva, M. 2019. "Algeria protests: How Disinformation Spread on Social Media." BBC Trending, September 17. https://www.bbc.com/news/blogs-trending-49679634.

Silverman, J. 2014. "The State Department's Twitter Jihad: Can a Bureaucracy Out-tweet the Terrorists?" Politico Magazine, July 22. https://www.politico.com /magazine/story/2014/07/the-state-departments-twitter-jihad-109234_full.html# .VYA1dflVhHw.

Sly, L. 2015. "Iraqis Think the U.S. Is in Cahoots with the Islamic State, and It Is Hurting the War. *Washington Post*, December 1. https://www.washingtonpost .com/world/middle_east/iraqis-think-the-us-is-in-cahoots-with-isis-and-it-is -hurting-the-war/2015/12/01/d00968ec-9243-11e5-befa-99ceebcbb272_story.html.

Smith, A., C. Black, and J. Thomas. 2016. "Soap Operas and Fakery: Selling Peace in Iraq." *Sunday Times*, October 2.

Snow, G. M. 2011. "Statement before the Senate Judiciary Committee, Subcommittee on Crime and Terrorism," Washington, D.C., April 12. http://www.fbi.gov/news /testimony/cybersecurity-responding-to-the-threat-of-cyber-crime-and-terrorism.

Snowden, E. 2014. "JTRIG Tools and Techniques." https://edwardsnowden.com/wp -content/uploads/2014/07/jtrigall.pdf.

Solomon, E. 2017. "The $1bn Hostage Deal that Enraged Qatar's Gulf Rivals." *Financial Times*, June 5. https://www.ft.com/content/dd033082-49e9-11e7-a3f4 -c742b9791d43.

Solon, O. 2017. "How Syria's White Helmets Became Victims of an Online Propaganda Machine." *Guardian*, December 18. https://www.theguardian.com/world /2017/dec/18/syria-white-helmets-conspiracy-theories.

Soules, M. 2015. *Media, Persuasion and Propaganda*. Edinburgh: Edinburgh University Press.

Spillius, A. 2009. "Iraq Insurgents Hacked Predator Drone Video Feed. *Telegraph*, December 17. http://www.telegraph.co.uk/news/worldnews/middleeast/iraq /6834884/Iraq-insurgents-hacked-Predator-drone-video-feed.html.

SPOC. 2011. *End of Mission Report: October 2005 to November 2011*. Strategic Programs Operations Center. United States Forces—Iraq. Contract: W52P J—11— D 0008.

Spraks, R. 2014. "How Hackers Took Over CBC, Other Media Websites." *Toronto Star*, November 27. https://www.thestar.com/news/canada/2014/11/27/syrian _electronic_army_claims_cbc_other_media_website_hacks.html.

Springer, P. J., ed. 2017. *Encyclopedia of Cyber Warfare*. New York: ABC-CLIO.

Spy Files. 2014. WikiLeaks. https://wikileaks.org/spyfiles/.

Stacey, E. 2017. *Combating Internet-Enabled Terrorism: Emerging Research and Opportunities: Emerging Research and Opportunities*. Hershey, PA: IGI Global.

Stein, G. J. 1998. "Information War—Cyberwar—Netwar." In *Battlefield of the Future: 21st Century Warfare Issues*, edited by B. R. Schneider and L. E. Grinter. Air War College, Maxwell Air Force Base, Montgomery, AL (No. AWC-3).

Stevenson, R. L. 1974. *Audience Segmentation: An Approach to International Communications*. 57th Annual Meeting of the Association for Education in Journalism, San Diego, August 18–21.

Stohl, M. 2008. "Old Myths, New Fantasies and the Enduring Realities of Terrorism." *Critical Studies on Terrorism* 1 (1): 5–16.

Strauss, A. 2012. "Acting Intelligently: A Brief History of Political Analytics." In *Margin of Victory: How Technologists Help Politicians Win Elections*, edited by N. G. Pearlman, 175–188. New York: Praeger.

Stubbs, J., and C. Bing. 2018. "Special Report: How Iran Spreads Disinformation Around the World." Reuters, November 30. https://www.reuters.com/article/us -cyber-iran-specialreport/special-report-how-iran-spreads-disinformation-around -the-world-idUSKCN1NZ1FT.

Suebsaeng, A. 2014. "The State Department Is Actively Trolling Terrorists on Twitter." *Mother Jones*, March 5. http://www.motherjones.com/politics/2014/02 /state-department-cscc-troll-terrorists-twitter-think-again-turn-away.

Sussman, G. 2010. *Branding Democracy: US Regime Change in Post-Soviet Eastern Europe*, Vol. 17. Bern, CH: Peter Lang.

Sutter, J. 2012. "Anonymous Declares 'Cyberwar' on Israel." CNN, November 20. http://www.cnn.com/2012/11/19/tech/web/cyber-attack-israel-anonymous/index .html.

SWI. 2017. "Nine Years Imprisonment Sentence to a Palestinian Who Hacked the Israeli Unmanned Drone System." February 3. http://www.swissinfo.ch/ara/ اخترق-نظام-طائرات-اسرائيلية-بدون-طيار/42933152-السجن-تسع-سنوات-لفلسطيني-

Swisher, C., and R. Grim. 2018. "Jared Kushner's Real-Estate Firm Sought Money Directly from Qatar Government Weeks Before Blockade." The Intercept, March 2. https://theintercept.com/2018/03/02/jared-kushner-real-estate-qatar -blockade/.

Syrian Electronic Army. 2013a. "Our Facebook Page Number 260." December 5. http://sea.sy/article/id/2023/ar.

Syrian Electronic Army. 2013b. Facebook page. https://www.facebook.com/SEA.P .260.

Syrian Electronic Army. n.d.(a). About. http://sea.sy/index/ar.

Syrian Electronic Army. n.d.(b). Twitter profile. Accessed January 12, 2021. https:// twitter.com/Official_SEA16.

Syrianeso. 2011. YouTube channel. http://www.youtube.com/user/syrianeso/about.

Syrianeso. 2012a. "Anonymous Website Hacked and Defaced by SEA." July 18. http://www.youtube.com/watch?v=_EGqCjHm5jE.

Syrianeso. 2012b. "The Video that Made Everyone Who Saw It Cry—The Syrian Arab Army." August 10. http://www.youtube.com/watch?v=LnwfKBFdFxc.

Syrianes1. 2011. YouTube channel. May 11. http://www.youtube.com/user/syrianes1
/about.

Syrian Observatory for Human Rights (SOHR). 2016. "About 450 Thousand Were
Killed and More Than Two Millions Were Injured in 69 Months of the Start of the
Syrian Revolution." December 13. https://www.syriahr.com/en/56923/.

Syrianoo Hacker. 2012. "Hacking Important Russian Government Website. Syrian
Revolution Hackers." February 5. https://www.youtube.com/watch?v=tg-bZfT
_m2sandt=1s.

Tafoya, W. L. 2011. *Cyber Terror.* Federal Bureau of Investigation. http://www.fbi.gov
/stats-services/publications/law-enforcement-bulletin/november-2011/cyber-terror.

Taylor, P. 2002. *Global Communications, International Affairs and the Media since
1945.* London: Routledge.

Terror Has No Religion. 2006. Accessed on December 20, 2012, via Wayback
Machine Internet Archive. http://www.noterror.info/, https://archive.org/web/.

Terror Has No Religion. 2007a. "Suicidal Terror." http://www.youtube.com/watch?v
=4JbdbYlr3kkandfeature=related.

Terror Has No Religion. 2007b. "Intrusion." http://www.youtube.com/watch?v
=jt6z75SeyLg.

Terror Has No Religion. 2007c. "Know Your Enemy. http://www.youtube.com/watch
?v=cCLy6KvKBrY.

Terror Has No Religion. 2007d. "The Match." http://www.youtube.com/watch?v
=604-jOx-Z3Yandfeature=relmfu.

Terror Has No Religion. 2007e. "Iraqi Football Team." http://www.youtube.com
/watch?v=cunw1MWwN90.

Terror Has No Religion. 2007f. "Kidnapping." http://www.youtube.com/watch?v
=0OhiXIpPQnw.

Thelwall, M. 2009. *Introduction to Webometrics: Quantitative Web Research for the
Social Sciences.* San Rafael, CA: Morgan and Claypool.

TIB, N. 2004. "Supervisory Control and Data Acquisition (SCADA) Systems."
http://www.librarie.co.ke/books/SCADA%20Basics%20-%20NCS%20
TIB%2004-1.pdf

Tilouine, J., and G. Kadiri. 2018. "A Addis-Abeba, le siège de l'Union africaine
espionné par Pékin." *Le Monde,* January 26. https://www.lemonde.fr/afrique
/article/2018/01/26/a-addis-abeba-le-siege-de-l-union-africaine-espionne-par-les
-chinois_5247521_3212.html.

Tolz, V. 2017. "From a Threatening 'Muslim Migrant' Back to the Conspiring 'West':
Race, Religion, and Nationhood on Russian Television during Putin's Third
Presidency." *Nationalities Papers* 45 (5): 742–757.

Tolz, V., and Y. Teper. 2018. "Broadcasting Agitainment: A New Media Strategy of
Putin's Third Presidency." *Post-Soviet Affairs* 34 (4): 213–227.

Turner, S. 2003. The Dilemma of Double Standards in US Human Rights Policy."
Peace and Change 28 (4): 524–554.

Turow, J., M. X. Delli Carpini, N. Draper, and H. Howard-Williams. 2012. *Americans
Roundly Reject Tailored Political Advertising at a Time When Political Campaigns
Are Embracing It.* Philadelphia: University of Pennsylvania, Annenberg School of
Communication.

Tv4teen. 2011. "See How Sectarian Terrorists Are: Are You Sunni or Shiite?"
http://www.youtube.com/watch?v=kd15vbLo8-Q.

Twitter. 2019. "New Disclosures to Our Archive of State-Backed Information Operations." December 20. https://blog.twitter.com/en_us/topics/company/2019/new-disclosures-to-our-archive-of-state-backed-information-operations.html.

Twitter. n.d.(a). "Elections Integrity: Twitter's Focus Is on a Healthy Public Conversation." Accessed January 12, 2021. https://about.twitter.com/en_us/values/elections-integrity.html#data.

Twitter. n.d.(b). "Spam and Fake Accounts." Accessed January 12, 2021. https://help.twitter.com/en/safety-and-security#spam-and-fake-accounts.

Ulrichsen, K. 2017. "The GCC Crisis: Regional Realignment or Paralysis?" *Turkish Policy Quarterly* 16 (3): 71–79.

United States Agency for Global Media (USAGM). n.d.(a). "Who We Are." https://www.usagm.gov/who-we-are/.

United States Agency for Global Media (USAGM). n.d.(b). "Middle East Broadcasting Networks." https://www.bbg.gov/networks/mbn/.

United States Information Agency. 1998. *United States Information Agency.* Washington, D.C.

USA in Arabic. 2016. Facebook page. https://www.facebook.com/USAbilAraby/.

U.S. Central Intelligence Agency. 1950. "National Intelligence Survey- Iraq, Section 43, Religion, Education, and Public Information," FOIA Electronic Reading Room. https://www.cia.gov/readingroom/docs/DOC_0001252339.pdf.

U.S. Department of State. 2011. Center for Strategic Counterterrorism Communications. http://www.state.gov/documents/organization/116709.pdf

U.S. Department of State. 2015a. "(SBU) Paris Visit. Sensitive but Unclassified. Note for the Secretary." June 9. https://assets.documentcloud.org/documents/2101556/diplo.pdf.

U.S. Department of State. 2015b. "Launch of the Sawab Center." Office of the Spokesperson, Washington D.C. July 8. http://www.state.gov/r/pa/prs/ps/2015/07/244709.htm.

U.S. House of Representatives Permanent Select Committee on Intelligence. 2018a. "Exposing Russia's Effort to Sow Discord Online: The Internet Research Agency and Advertisements." https://democrats-intelligence.house.gov/social-media-content/.

U.S. House of Representatives Permanent Select Committee on Intelligence. 2018b. "Social Media Advertisements." https://democrats-intelligence.house.gov/social-media-content/social-media-advertisements.htm.

U.S. House of Representatives Permanent Select Committee on Intelligence. 2018c. "Metadata." https://democrats-intelligence.house.gov/uploadedfiles/ai_metadata.pdf.

Valantin, J. M. 2005. *Hollywood, the Pentagon and Washington.* New York: Anthem.

Valentino-DeVries, J., and D. Yadron. 2015. "Cataloging the World's Cyberforces." *Wall Street Journal*, October 11. https://www.wsj.com/articles/cataloging-the-worlds-cyberforces-1444610710.

Valeriano, B., and R. Maness. 2012. "The Fog of Cyberwar: Why the Threat Doesn't Live Up to the Hype. *Foreign Affairs*, November 21. http://www.foreignaffairs.com/articles/138443/brandon-valeriano-and-ryan-maness/the-fog-of-cyberwar.

Valeriano, B., and R. Maness. 2015. *Cyber War versus Cyber Realities: Cyber Conflict in the International System.* New York: Oxford University Press.

Vaughan, J. R. 2005. *The Failure of American and British Propaganda in the Arab Middle East, 1945–57.* New York: Palgrave Macmillan.

Vegh, S. 2002. "Hacktivists or Cyberterrorists? The Changing Media Discourse on Hacking." *First Monday* 7 (10).

Ventre, D. 2011. *Cyberware and Information Warfare.* London: Wiley.

Vine. 2014, November 25. Digital Outreach Team, November 25. https://vine.co/v /O1D3dEFrgWK.

Vitalis, R. 2000. "American Ambassador in Technicolor and Cinemascope: Hollywood and Revolution on the Nile." In *Mass Mediations: New Approaches to Popular Culture in the Middle East and Beyond*, edited by W. Armbrust. Berkeley: University of California Press.

Vosoughi, S., D. Roy, and S. Aral. 2018. "The Spread of True and False News Online." *Science* 359 (6380): 1146–1151.

Walker, P. 2014. "North Korea Internet Service Resumes After Shutdown." *Guardian*, December 23. https://www.theguardian.com/world/2014/dec/23/north-korea -internet-shutdown.

Waltz, K. N. 2010. *Theory of International Politics.* Long Grove, IL: Waveland.

Wang, J. 2007. "Telling the American Story to the World: The Purpose of US Public Diplomacy in Historical Perspective." *Public Relations Review* 33 (1): 21–30.

Warrick, J. 2018. "Hacked Messages Show Qatar Appearing to Pay Hundreds of Millions to Free Hostages." *Washington Post*, April 28. https://www .washingtonpost.com/world/national-security/hacked-messages-show-qatar -appearing-to-pay-hundreds-of-millions-to-free-hostages/2018/04/27/46759ce2 -3f41-11e8-974f-aacd97698cef_story.html.

Wei, W. 2013. "Google Oman Domain Hijacked by Moroccan Hackers. Hacker News, April 21. https://thehackernews.com/2013/04/google-oman-domain-hijacked-by -moroccan.html.

Weimann, G. 2005. "Cyberterrorism: The Sum of All Fears?" *Studies in Conflict and Terrorism* 28 (2): 129–149.

Welch, M. 2006. *Scapegoats of September 11th: Hate Crimes and State Crimes in the War on Terror.* New Brunswick, NJ: Rutgers University Press.

Weller, T. 2012. "The Information State: An Historical Perspective on Surveillance." In *Routledge Handbook of Surveillance Studies*, edited by D. Lyon, K. Ball, and K. Haggerty, 57–63. London: Routledge.

White, J. 2005. "Military Planting Articles in Iraq Papers." *Washington Post*, December 1. http://www.washingtonpost.com/wp-dyn/content/article/2005/11/30 /AR2005113001876.html.

White House. 2013. "Liberty and Security in a Changing World: Report and Recommendations of the President's Review Group on Intelligence and Communications Technologies." December 12. https://obamawhitehouse.archives.gov/blog/2013/12 /18/liberty-and-security-changing-world.

WikiLeaks. 2004. "Indo-US Cyber Security Forum Preparatory Consultations in New Delhi." E.O. 12958. U.S. Embassy New Delhi. http://wikileaks.org/cable /2004/11/04NEWDELHI7026.html.

WikiLeaks. 2005. "Favorable Views of U.S. Surge Upward in Arab/Muslim Morocco. What Went Right?" From Rabat, Morocco. September 23. https://wikileaks.org /plusd/cables/05RABAT2004_a.html.

WikiLeaks. 2006a. "Beywatch: Are You Really American? Tunisians Want to Know!" E.O. 12958. August 21. https://wikileaks.org/plusd/cables/06TUNIS2170_a.html.

WikiLeaks. 2006b. "Turkey: Contesting Terrorist Use of the Internet." From Ankara, Turkey, to Secretary of State. December 7. https://wikileaks.org/plusd/cables /06ANKARA6612_a.html.

WikiLeaks. 2006c. "Digital Outreach to Oman." From Muscat, Oman, to Secretary of State. December 13. http://wikileaks.cabledrum.net/cable/2006/12 /06MUSCAT1684.html.

WikiLeaks. 2007. "East Africa Regional Strategic Initiative (RSI), March 16–17." From Djibouti. April 10. https://wikileaks.org/plusd/cables/07DJIBOUTI425_a.html.

WikiLeaks. 2008a. "PRT Wasit Gets a Laugh." From Baghdad Embassy to Secretary of State. May 9. http://wikileaks.redfoxcenter.org/cable/2008/05 /08BAGHDAD1444.html.

WikiLeaks. 2008b. "Baghdad Requests Participation in the Rhythm Road American Music Abroad Program's New Season." From Baghdad Embassy to Secretary of State. September 22. http://wikileaks.zilog.es/cable/2008/09/08BAGHDAD3051 .html.

WikiLeaks. 2009a. "Oman—Building on the President's Cairo Speech." E.O. 12958. July. https://wikileaks.org/plusd/cables/09MUSCAT799_a.html.

WikiLeaks. 2009b. "SECNAV, GOJ Officials Discuss 'Unshakeable' Alliance, China Concerns." U.S. Embassy Tokyo. E.O. 12958. August 27. http://wikileaks.org/cable /2009/08/09TOKYO2002.html.

WikiLeaks. 2010. Doc#120315. https://wikileaks.org/saudi-cables/doc120315.html.

WikiLeaks. 2014a. "R: New Opportunity—Bahrain." April 14. https://wikileaks.org /hackingteam/emails/emailid/12802.

WikiLeaks. 2014b. "FinFisher." September 15. https://wikileaks.org/spyfiles4 /customers.html.

WikiLeaks. 2015. "R: Hackers Training." July 8. https://wikileaks.org/hackingteam /emails/emailid/12534.

WikiLeaks. n.d. "licenses_32." https://wikileaks.org/spyfiles/document/finfisher /customers/#licenses_32.

Wilke, J. 2008. "Propaganda." In *The International Encyclopedia of Communication*, edited by Wolfgang Donsbach, 1–5. New York: Wiley.

Wintour, P. 2017. "Qatar: FBI Says Russian Hackers 'Planted Fake News Story' that Led to Crisis." *Guardian*, July 6. https://www.theguardian.com/world/2017/jun/07 /qatar-fbi-says-russian-hackers-planted-fake-news-story-that-led-to-crisis-report.

Woolley, S. C., and D. Guilbeault. 2017. "Computational Propaganda in the United States of America: Manufacturing Consensus Online." *Computational Propaganda Research Project Working Paper*.

Xenos, M. 2008. "New Mediated Deliberation: Blog and Press Coverage of the Alito Nomination." *Journal of Computer-Mediated Communication* 13 (2): 485–503.

Yahoo! News. 2012. "Al Jazeera Says Hackers Sent False Mobile Texts." September 9. http://news.yahoo.com/al-jazeera-says-hackers-sent-false-mobile-texts-154921087 .html.

Yahoo! News. 2013. "Hackers Call Iraqi PM 'Oppressor' on His Website." February 12 http://news.yahoo.com/hackers-call-iraqi-pm-oppressor-website-111725197.html.

Yon, R. 2016. "The Use of Propaganda and Social Media." In *The New Islamic State: Ideology, Religion and Violent Extremism in the 21st Century*, edited by J. Covarrubias and T. Lansford, 55–72. London: Routledge.

YouTube. 2007. "Terrorism . . . Iraq. December 30. http://www.youtube.com/watch?v =7iFYPifTqwk.

YouTube. 2008a. "Dirty Wahhabism . . . Know Your Enemy." March 19. http://www .youtube.com/watch?v=MhfgRTuuOkM.

YouTube. 2008b. "Terrorism Has No Religion—4." May 7. http://www.youtube.com /watch?v=DwRCH6ylXy4.

YouTube. 2011a. "See How Sectarian Terrorists Are: Are You Sunni or Shiite?" May 4. http://www.youtube.com/watch?v=kd15vbLo8-Q.

YouTube. 2011b. "The Good Morning Program on Dunya TV . . . Thank you." May 23. http://www.youtube.com/watch?v=yZzmMmTb6wQ.

YouTube. 2011c. "Jihad, I'm a Muslim; I'm with It." July 12. http://www.youtube.com /watch?v=D-ebD_Dgf8U.

YouTube. 2011d. "Jihad, I'm a Muslim; I'm with it." July 20. http://www.youtube.com /watch?v=FybRZ4T6WXI.

YouTube. 2012a. "Jihad Campaign, I'm a Muslim; I'm with It." March 7. http://www .youtube.com/watch?v=oL-F—Bm9dM.

YouTube. 2012b. "Assalah Nasri Mocks the Anthem of Her Home Country and Tonny Scolds Her." July 28. http://www.youtube.com/watch?v=InmbgpaFGcQ.

YouTube. 2013a. SEAOfficialChannel. Retrieved from http://www.youtube.com/user /SEAOfficialChannel/about.

YouTube. 2013b. "Hacking Qatar Foundation—SEA." March 1. http://www.youtube .com/watch?v=BCBWkNgBTZc.

Index

About the Author

AHMED AL-RAWI is an assistant professor of news, social media, and public communication at the School of Communication at Simon Fraser University, Canada. He is the director of the Disinformation Project, which empirically examines fake news discourses in Canada on social media and news media. Al-Rawi previously worked as a communication officer for the International Committee of the Red Cross in Iraq and served as an assistant professor at Erasmus University Rotterdam in the Netherlands and at Concordia University in Montreal, Canada. His research expertise is related to social media, global communication, news, and disinformation. He has authored four books and more than seventy peer-reviewed book chapters and articles published in a variety of journals, including *Online Information Review*, *Social Science Computer Review*, and *Information, Communication & Society*.

Printed and bound by CPI Group (UK) Ltd, Croydon, CR0 4YY

16/04/2025

14658332-0001